AUTHOR	CLASS
CHANDLER, D	940.27

TITLE

Waterloo

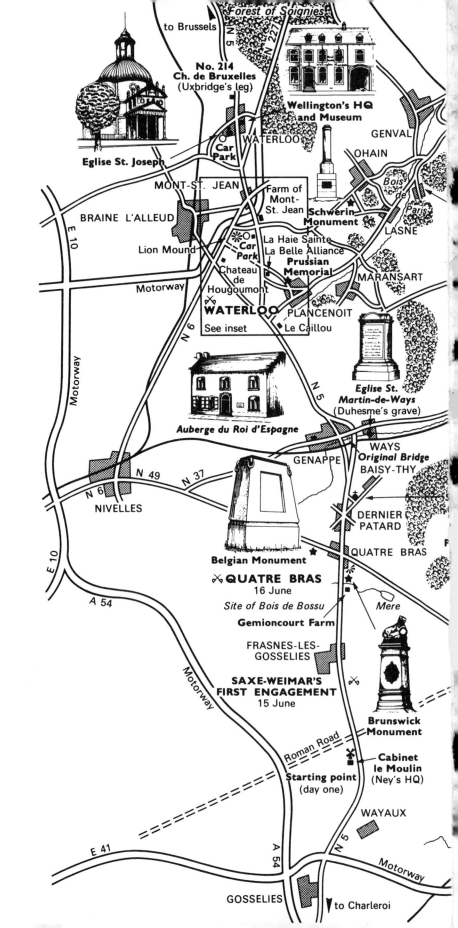

to Brussels

Forest of Soignies

No. 214
Ch. de Bruxelles
(Uxbridge's leg)

Wellington's HQ
and Museum

GENVAL

OHAIN

WATERLOO

Car
Park

Eglise St. Joseph

MONT-ST. JEAN

Farm of
Mont-
St. Jean

*Bois
de
Paris*

Schwerin
Monument

BRAINE L'ALLEUD

LASNE

Lion Mound

La Haie Sainte
La Belle Alliance

Prussian
Memorial

Car
Park

Chateau
de
Hougoumont

MARANSART

Motorway

WATERLOO

PLANCENOIT

See inset

Le Caillou

Motorway

Eglise St.
Martin-de-Ways
(Duhesme's grave)

Auberge du Roi d'Espagne

WAYS

Original Bridge

GENAPPE

BAISY-THY

DERNIER
PATARD

N 49   N 37

QUATRE BRAS

N 6

NIVELLES

Belgian Monument

QUATRE BRAS
16 June

Mere

Site of Bois de Bossu

Gemioncourt Farm

FRASNES-LES-
GOSSELIES

SAXE-WEIMAR'S
FIRST ENGAGEMENT
15 June

A 54

Brunswick
Monument

Roman Road

Cabinet
le Moulin
(Ney's HQ)

Starting point
(day one)

WAYAUX

E 41

A 54

Motorway

GOSSELIES   to Charleroi

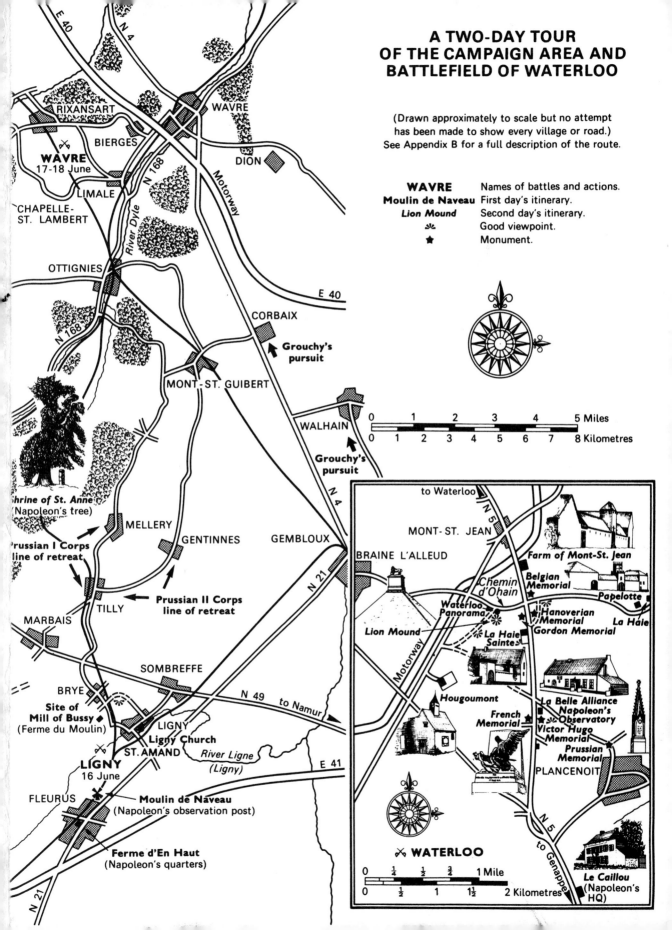

A TWO-DAY TOUR OF THE CAMPAIGN AREA AND BATTLEFIELD OF WATERLOO

(Drawn approximately to scale but no attempt
has been made to show every village or road.)
See Appendix B for a full description of the route.

WAVRE	Names of battles and actions.
Moulin de Naveau	First day's itinerary.
Lion Mound	Second day's itinerary.
⚔	Good viewpoint.
★	Monument.

Main map labels

E 40
N 4
RIXANSART
WAVRE
BIERGES
WAVRE
17-18 June
DION
Motorway
LIMALE
N 168
CHAPELLE-
ST. LAMBERT
River Dyle
OTTIGNIES
N 168
E 40
CORBAIX
**Grouchy's
pursuit**
MONT-ST. GUIBERT
WALHAIN
**Grouchy's
pursuit**
N 4
Shrine of St. Anne
(Napoleon's tree)
**Prussian I Corps
line of retreat**
MELLERY
GENTINNES
GEMBLOUX
N 21
**Prussian II Corps
line of retreat**
TILLY
MARBAIS
SOMBREFFE
BRYE
N 49   to Namur
**Site of
Mill of Bussy**
(Ferme du Moulin)
LIGNY
**Ligny
Church**
ST. AMAND
*River Ligne
(Ligny)*
E 41
LIGNY
16 June
Moulin de Naveau
(Napoleon's observation post)
FLEURUS
N 21
Ferme d'En Haut
(Napoleon's quarters)

Inset map (Waterloo battlefield)

to Waterloo
N 5
MONT-ST. JEAN
BRAINE L'ALLEUD
Farm of Mont-St. Jean
*Chemin
d'Ohain*
**Belgian
Memorial**
Papelotte
*Waterloo
Panorama*
**Hanoverian
Memorial**
Lion Mound
La Haie
*La Haie
Sainte*
Gordon Memorial
Motorway
Hougoumont
**La Belle Alliance
Napoleon's
Observatory**
**French
Memorial**
**Victor Hugo
Memorial**
**Prussian
Memorial**
PLANCENOIT
N 5
to Genappe
⚔ **WATERLOO**

0	¼	½	¾	1 Mile
0	½	1	1½	2 Kilometres

Le Caillou
(Napoleon's HQ)

Scale (main map)

0	1	2	3	4	5 Miles
0	1 2	3 4 5	6 7		8 Kilometres

Waterloo
THE HUNDRED DAYS

Waterloo
THE HUNDRED DAYS

David Chandler

GEORGE PHILIP

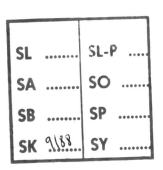

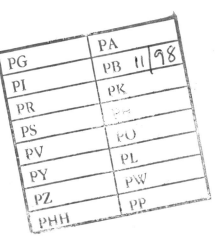

First published in 1980 by
Osprey Publishing Limited,
12–14 Long Acre, London WC2E 9LP

Reprinted 1987

British Library Cataloguing in Publication Data
Chandler, David
    Waterloo: hundred days
    i. Waterloo (Belgium), Battle of, 1815
    I. Title
    940.2′7   DC242

ISBN 0540 01170 3

Maps and diagrams drawn by Richard and
Hazel Watson from sketches prepared by
the author.

Printed in Great Britain by BAS Printers Limited,
Over Wallop, Hampshire.

Contents

List of Maps and Diagrams

The map for a two-day tour of the campaign area and the battlefield of Waterloo can be found on the endpapers.

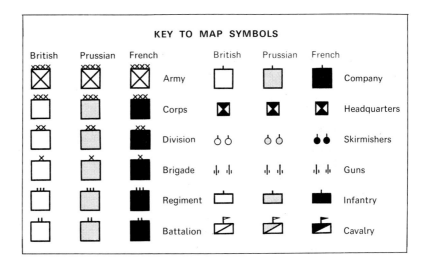

Acknowledgements

The author would like to record his gratitude to those who helped him in the preparation of this book, including Gabriel Pantucci, Jeremy Harwood and Sarah Snape, together with the Librarians and staff of the MOD Library (Central and Army) in Whitehall and of the Central Library, RMA Sandhurst. He would also like to thank Mrs. Janet Donaldson for typing the manuscript, his wife, Gill, for undertaking the thankless task of preparing the index, and his son John for successfully deciphering a line of Napoleon's handwriting.

RMAS   D.G.G.
September 1979

For
Brigadier (Retd) Peter Young, DSO, MC, MA

Soldier, Scholar, Friend

and sometime Reader in Military History
at the Royal Military Academy, Sandhurst

Introduction

No battle has received more attention from soldiers and historians, or evoked greater popular interest and recognition, than Waterloo. In the long history of Western civilization, probably only Zama (202 B.C.) and Tours (A.D. 732) have proved of equal importance, and only Gettysburg has been written about as often.

The perennial appeal of Waterloo is probably due to a number of interrelated factors. It was a struggle between military giants of differing military gifts and attainments—the strategic genius and charisma of Napoleon pitted against the tactical skill and staying power of Wellington, and the loyal simplicity and tough fighting qualities of Blücher. The battle also marks the end of an era of European history in a very real sense, and hence has an added fascination. Sir Winston Churchill once described battles as 'punctuation marks on the pages of secular History', and few great actions have led to more significant results: the emergence of Great Britain and Prussia as the most prestigious military leaders of Europe, the military eclipse of France and the temporary stay in the progress of liberalism throughout the Continent, and a serious (although ultimately unsuccessful, alas) international search through the Congress system for a way to avoid future recourse to wars as a means of settling international problems—these trends and their effects would dominate European history for half a century. The subject, moreover, is remarkable for its compactness; the essential parts of the story were all concentrated into four short days, 15 to 18 June, 1815, and yet how rich, varied and terrible were the events crowded into that short period of time— no less than four major engagements, five great errors of judgement, two 'chance decisions' that greatly affected the ultimate outcome, several violent fluctuations in martial fortune, and a grisly total of 115,000 casualties over the four-day span. The climax was dramatic by any standards—the total defeat of an Empire, the complete eclipse of the greatest soldier of modern history—and all in the space of one single Sunday afternoon.

And yet few historical subjects have been the subject of so much controversy and differing interpretation. The inevitable conflict between fact and fiction, reality and myth, has persisted ever since, and the fact that the subject has been viewed from three quite different national viewpoints has often added to the general obscurity. To the French, Napoleon's defeat has usually been a subject for grief-stricken incredulity—and the modern visitor to the Belgian battlefield south of Brussels may well come away in some doubt as to the ultimate outcome of the great battle, so strong is the prevalent Napoleonic mystique. As Napoleon himself remarked on a later occasion, 'Everything failed me just when everything had succeeded.' To the French, then, his cataclysmic defeat is often put down as an historical fluke, an undeserved fate. In Great Britain, many a history book vastly exaggerates the British role in the campaign and battle; Belgians, Dutch and Hanoverians—who accounted for almost two-thirds of the Allied manpower—often go unmentioned, and the Prussian intervention is played down in importance. Germans, on the other hand, sometimes represent the whole campaign as having been borne on the backs of the Prussian army, Wellington being accused of failing to come to Blücher's aid at Ligny on the 16th in direct contrast with Prussian loyalty to the common cause two days later. True objectivity is difficult, indeed almost impossible, to achieve, but a generally balanced picture—ignoring all the extreme points of view—needs to be sought out if even a reasonably accurate portrayal is to be painted.

Of course the would-be historian of so complex an event as a major battle faces daunting difficulties. As Wellington himself wrote to one would-be chronicler, John Croker, on 8 August, 1815 '... The object which you propose to yourself is very difficult of attainment, and, if really attained, is not a little invidious. The history of a battle is not unlike the history of a ball. Some individuals may recollect all the little events of which the great result is the battle won or lost; but no individual can recollect the order in which, or the exact moments at which, they occurred, which makes all the difference to their value and importance.' Perhaps this was one reason for the Duke's disinclination, unlike Napoleon, to write down his own version of events. Perhaps, again unlike Napoleon during his weary years of exile, he just could not find the time. Certainly he had little respect for the would-be historians of his own day. As he remarked to Sir John Sinclair in 1816, 'I am really disgusted with and ashamed of all I have seen of the battle. The number of writings upon it would lead the world to believe that the British Army had never fought a battle before.' To add a further volume to the hundreds already available may therefore cause an author some little hesitation.

However, a personal acquaintance with the actual ground—acquired on some half-dozen battlefield tours with British officers and officer-cadets during recent years—together with a considerable period of studying and writing about Napoleon and his wars, brought me to submit a new account, one which would include several maps to give, simultaneously with the text, a clear visual representation of the whole affair. These maps, together with some of the very fine works of art inspired by this great subject, provided any necessary justification for the undertaking of this volume.

No campaign can be properly understood unless it is placed in its proper historical context. Therefore three chapters—the first and the last two—are devoted to an analysis of the events leading up to, and stemming from, the great events of mid-June 1815. As von Clausewitz would describe it in the 1830s, a battle is '. . . the bloody solution of the crisis', and so the prelude leading to the crisis of Waterloo, and both its immediate and longer-term after-effects, deserve some attention.

Misunderstandings can also arise unless some space is devoted to the examination of both the leaders and the led—the strategic concepts, tactical formations, organizations and weapon capacities of the armies involved in the conflicts. It is rarely possible to cover everything, but chapters on the com-manders-in-chief and their respective armies have been included so as to elucidate these subjects to some degree.

Finally, it needs to be appreciated that a 'whole is a sum of its parts'. It would have been an error to devote all the remaining space solely to the events of 18 June, 1815. This campaign is in fact a pair of double-battles: namely Ligny and Quatre Bras on the 16th, and Waterloo and Wavre two days later, and accordingly all four engagements find a place in our narrative and analysis. Similarly, it has been deemed advisable to develop this campaign from the point of view of the side which took the military initiative at the outset, in order to keep the complex moves in some form of perspective. Our starting point, therefore, is generally the view of the French high command. 'Never did I see such a pounding match', reminisced Wellington of Waterloo. The attritional nature of this great struggle will become clear in the pages that follow.

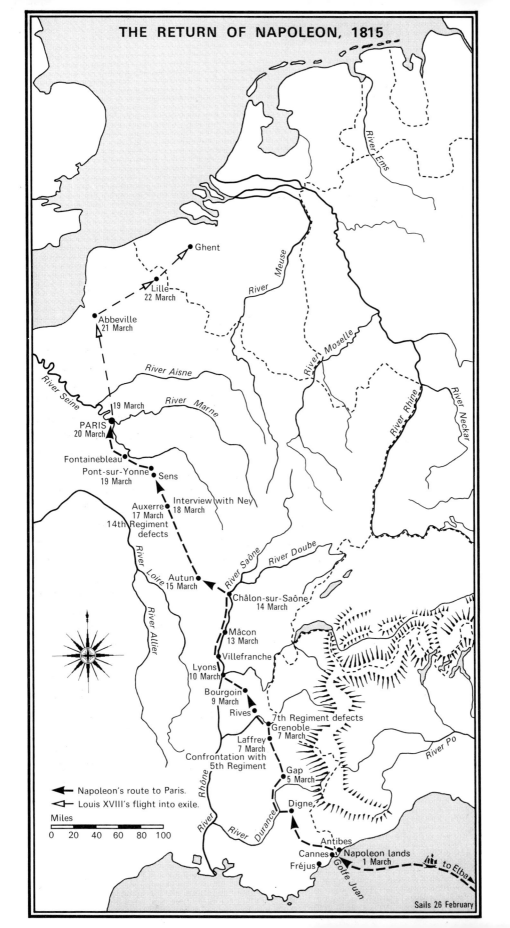

THE RETURN OF NAPOLEON, 1815

Ghent

Lille
22 March

Abbeville
21 March

River Ems

River Meuse

River Moselle

River Rhine

River Neckar

River Aisne

River Marne

River Seine

19 March

PARIS
20 March

Fontainebleau
Pont-sur-Yonne ● Sens
19 March

Interview with Ney
18 March

Auxerre
17 March
14th Regiment
defects

River Saône

River Doube

River Loire

Autun
15 March

Châlon-sur-Saône
14 March

River Allier

Mâcon
13 March

Villefranche

Lyons
10 March

Bourgoin
9 March

Rives

7th Regiment defects

Grenoble
7 March

Laffrey
7 March

Confrontation with
5th Regiment

Gap
5 March

River Po

River Durance

Digne

◀— Napoleon's route to Paris.

◁— Louis XVIII's flight into exile.

Miles

0   20   40   60   80   100

Rhône
River

Antibes

Cannes ● Napoleon lands
1 March

Fréjus

Golfe Juan

to Elba

Sails 26 February

Chapter One

A European Crisis

On 26 February, 1815, a small vessel slipped away from Porto Ferrajo on the island of Elba. Its illustrious passenger was Napoleon Bonaparte—known as 'General Bonaparte' to many of his foes, but to most Frenchmen as '*l'Empereur*'. The flotilla of small craft that accompanied him on his secret voyage carried a handful of officers and the 1,050 soldiers of his escort, who had shared his ten-month exile on the tiny Mediterranean principality. Three days later the ships discharged their passengers between Cannes and Antibes on the south coast of France. What was to prove Napoleon's last great gamble had begun.

As he left Fontainebleau the previous April, Napoleon had been heard to mutter, half to himself, that he would be back in France in time to see the violets bloom the following year. Few had heeded the prophecy at the time—but now it appeared he had kept his promise. Faced by his sudden return, most Frenchmen accorded the newcomer a cautious welcome, being unsure of what it might portend. Amazement, rather than acclaim, greeted his arrival. At Marseilles, Marshal Massena treated the news with caution. It is true he made no attempt to intercept his former Emperor with the troops under his command, but neither did he hasten to assist him. Rather, men watched and waited. Meanwhile, with typical resolution and energy, Napoleon plunged inland towards Grenoble, following hill tracks through the notoriously Bourbonist areas of Provence. Ahead of him lay all the traditional elements of Greek tragedy—great achievement matched by even greater disaster—for one of the shortest yet most decisive campaigns in military history was in the making, which would culminate in possibly the most famous battle of modern history. But during those early March days that saw the launching of his adventure, the dramatic climax still lay four months away.

'The devil is unchained.' News of Napoleon's disappearance from Elba was first relayed by the British Commissioner, Sir Neil Campbell, as early as 28 February through agencies in Genoa and Florence. But Campbell expected his erstwhile charge to head for Italy, so the initial hunt headed away in the wrong direction. This circumstance provided Napoleon with his opportunity of evading interception by the Royal Navy.

It is said that bad news travels fast. Nevertheless, it took all of four days for the tidings to reach the corpulent and ailing Louis XVIII in Paris, despite the existence of an efficient visual telegraph service linking the capital with the great naval base of Toulon. News of Napoleon's landing reached Vienna on 7 March, causing the Duke of Wellington, since February Lord Castlereagh's replacement as senior British representative at the Congress of Vienna, to cancel a hunting engagement. Graver matters now demanded his full attention. As Tsar Alexander I of Russia remarked to the famous victor of the Peninsular War, 'It is for you to save the world again.'

London learnt of the development a short while later—the news causing some anxiety on the Stock Exchange, already a notorious barometer of international as well as domestic climate. However, throughout the capitals of Europe the consensus of opinion was that the new intrusion by 'the Corsican Ogre' would be a short-lived affair. The restrained popular reaction within France itself was reassuring; the Bourbon court betrayed few signs of overt alarm, and the commander-in-chief of its army, Michel Ney, 'the bravest of the brave' and former Napoleonic marshal and favourite, left Paris for the south, declaring that he would return bringing the Corsican upstart 'in an iron cage'. This touch of Alsatian bravado would prove a singularly idle boast.

Whilst the Allied leaders conferred in desultory and indecisive fashion and the world speculated, Napoleon acted. As he well knew, his immediate fortunes did not lie in the reactions of statesmen in Vienna or London, or even in Paris, but in those of the French populace and soldiery as a whole. If they rejected him, he was doomed; if they accepted him—well, he had better than an even chance of regaining the throne of France. For months now he had known—thanks to the reports smuggled into Elba by genuine friends or devious politicians, determined to assure their personal positions no matter what might befall by keeping at least a tenuous link with their former master—of the mounting tide of grievances and anxieties within France. The honeymoon period of the restored Bourbons had been short indeed. The acquisitive and suspicious peasantry—royal guarantees not withstanding—feared for the broad acres they had acquired at knock-down prices at the expense of the clergy and the nobility during the upheaval of the French Revolution. The bourgeoisie feared for their profits and for their savings, as high bread prices and financial uncertainty swept the country. The old soldiers, particularly the officers, rotting on half pay or summarily dismissed following the restoration of the Bourbons, were another source of widespread disaffection as they eyed, half-contemptuously and half-enviously, those of their former comrades who had agreed to take service under the restored regime. The 'new' aristocracy and meritocracy of imperial civil servants loathed the returned émigrés, who, clamorous for restitution and redress, flocked about the Bourbon court. As for the heir of St. Louis, he was little more than a mere name or cipher to the vast majority of his supposedly devoted subjects. Twenty-five years of exile as a British pensioner, dependent on alien hospitality, was hardly a sound basis for a successful and prosperous reign, and Louis XVIII's brief popularity of April 1814, when he had represented the return of peace and stability and above all the ending of the hated 'blood-tax' of conscription, soon evaporated.

All this Napoleon knew. He was equally informed about the cracks in the façade of Allied unity at the Congress of Vienna. As the powers sought to set back the clock and re-establish the frontiers of 1791, Britain, Austria and Bourbon France found themselves at considerable variance with Prussia and Russia—above all Russia—over the shape of the 'brave old world' they were attempting to restore. On all sides, therefore, the former Emperor received tidings of division and discontent. As early as December 1814 the exile was credibly reported by allied agents to have declared that it would soon be necessary for him '. . . to take the field again', but the remark was ignored as just another piece of vindictive wishful thinking by 'Napoleon the Little', now reduced to being the ruler of the tiny island of Elba. They would have been wiser to have heeded his *obiter dicta* more carefully, for who but fools would have supposed that such an open and advantageously placed cage as Elba would for long contain the eagle? Now Napoleon was back in France, playing upon his adopted countrymen's various aspirations and fears as his small column wound its way northwards.

But Frenchmen still hesitated to reveal their innermost

OVERLEAF *The Campaign of France, 1814* by Meissonier. Between January and April Napoleon fought one of his most brilliant campaigns at the head of a scratch army of pensioners, invalids and schoolboys. In the end a combination of massive Allied forces, national war exhaustion and a mutiny by some of his marshals forced the Emperor to abdicate at Fontainebleau. After his return from Elba, he was determined to avoid a war fought on French soil— hence the decision to invade Belgium in June 1815

feelings. Colonel Girod de l'Ain, travelling from Switzerland to rejoin General Curial in Paris, took the precaution of carrying two cockades for his hat—one the Bourbon white, the other the imperial *tricolor*—and switched them diplomatically according to the type of flags he saw flying in each town along his route. But already the balance had begun to swing. After a rebuff at Antibes and a perilous crossing of snow-clad mountains to Digue, Napoleon had suddenly faced the crisis of his home-coming. At the Laffrey Defile, not far from Grenoble, the narrow way was found blocked on 7 March by the 5th Regiment of the Line, drawn up in battle order. It was a tense moment, but as each side looked to their muskets' priming, Napoleon strode forward and in a superb if theatrical gesture threw open the breast of his grey overcoat and invited the Bourbon troops '. . . to fire upon your Emperor'. Heedless of their officers, the rank and file flung down their muskets and flocked forward with repeated cheers to mingle with Napoleon's supporters. Next day, the 7th Regiment behaved in the same way, and for Napoleon the great crisis was over. 'Before Grenoble I was only an adventurer,' Napoleon later mused upon St. Helena, 'after Grenoble, I was a Prince.'

Soon a battalion formed by 700 veteran officers was protecting his person, and more and more troops rallied to his cause; even Ney, at the head of 6,000 men, could not resist the old magnetic attraction of the Emperor, but changed sides, following the example of the 14th of the Line, near Auxerre on the 18th. The omens were now unmistakable. The Bourbon hold on the country—or at the very least on the army—was a thing of the past. On 9 March the troops at Lyons had raised the *tricolor* and shouted '*Vive l'Empereur!*' until they were hoarse in the very face of the Duc d'Artois, Louis XVIII's brother. A week later and the Emperor's bandwaggon was rolling in earnest, and his march towards Paris became a triumphal progress along roads and streets lined with cheering crowds.

The royal government received news of these unanticipated events with growing dismay. In a last attempt to rally popular sentiment, the Bourbon ministers promised wholesale conces-sions, but even the public appearance of the King adorned with the sash of the *Légion d'Honneur* was greeted with derision. The Paris mob, ever sensitive to the swing of the political pendulum, began to chant disconcerting slogans dating from the grim days of 1792.

'Down with the priests! Down with the nobles!

Death to the Royalists! Bourbons to the scaffold!'

As news of mounting military desertions reached Paris, a wit displayed a letter supposed to have been sent from Napoleon to Louis XVIII. 'My Good Brother,' this missive ran, 'there is no need to send any more troops; I already have enough.' Faced by these growing signs of popular disaffection, the Bourbon ministers decided that the King must leave his capital with no further delay. At dead of night on 19 March, therefore, Louis XVIII set out from Paris with his court to seek renewed exile over the Belgian frontier. Just twenty-one hours later, Napoleon was swept into the Tuileries Palace amidst an ecstatic crowd of ex-soldiers and servants: the reins of power were again within his grasp. These events caused the greatest excitement in Paris, not least in the schoolrooms. The fourteen-year-old Hippolyte Carnot, son of 'the Organiser of Victory', who had served both the revolutionary and Napoleonic regimes as Minister of War, recorded how he and his fellows '. . . jumped over the benches, threw open the doors, cheered, embraced one another—we were wild with excitement', when they noticed that the Bourbon flag had just been replaced by the *tricolor* atop the Vendôme Column.

A Paris broadsheet, hawked about the streets, summarizes the drama of Napoleon's progress from Elba to Paris, and makes clear his developing popularity:
'The Tiger has broken out of his den
The Ogre has been three days at sea
The Wretch has landed at Fréjus
The Buzzard has reached Antibes
The Invader has arrived in Grenoble
The General has entered Lyons
Napoleon slept at Fontainebleau last night
The Emperor will proceed to the Tuileries today
His Imperial Majesty will address his loyal subjects tomorrow.'
Twenty-three days had swept him back to his throne. The use he would make of his new opportunity had still to be revealed.

A great deal depended on his gaining a semblance of recognition from the European powers. The people of France, for all their disenchantment with the Bourbons, desired the continuation of peace and progress towards prosperity before everything else. Aware of this deep-rooted sentiment, Napoleon promised all types of reforms, and hesitated to reimpose the hated 'blood-tax' of conscription. For several weeks, therefore, he extended peace feelers towards Vienna and London, hoping for a miracle —namely recognition of his position as *de facto*, if not *de jure*, ruler of France. In this he was speedily disillusioned. If he had correctly judged the underlying mood of the French people, he now entirely misread the state of international sentiment. Later, on St. Helena, he criticized himself for returning as early as March: a few more months, and Allied disunity might well have caused the complete breakdown of the great Congress. As it now transpired, however, the sudden and unexpected re-appearance of 'the sheep-worrier of Europe' to threaten the flock caused them to forget their differences and band together in self-defence. After a single week of hesitation, the statesmen hastened to take determinant action. On 13 March, seven days before he even reached Paris, the Congress of Vienna formally declared Napoleon an outlaw. Five days after his triumphant arrival in the Tuileries, the Seventh Coalition formally came into existence. By the respective treaties, Austria, Prussia and Russia undertook to provide over 700,000 men between them as soon as they could be mobilized under the overall command of Prince Schwarzenberg. Great Britain, with many of its most experienced regiments over the Atlantic fighting the United States, provided immediate subsidies to the tune of five million pounds (the great banking house of Rothschild supplying much of the specie), promised that as many troops as possible would be transferred to Belgium, and undertook to send Wellington to the area forthwith. The Duke was to assume command over all British and Belgo–Dutch forces in the Flanders region, where between them he and the Prussian Blücher were to collect 150,000 men as soon as possible and more thereafter. Finally, the powers in concert agreed that there were to be no individual agreements with Napoleon, befall what might. The adventurer was to be extirpated, and the menace of French militarism that he represented extinguished for ever. As Wellington wrote to Lord Castlereagh, Foreign Secretary, on 26 March: 'Bonaparte and the French nation will not allow them [the Allies] to remain at peace, and they must be prepared either to give up all their conquests to the Rhine, or for active hostilities to resume. It is the desire for war, particularly in the army, which has brought Bonaparte back, and has formed for him any party, and has given him any success.' In this assessment he was not strictly correct: France *did* desire peace in fact, but not at the price of a Bourbon restoration. Nevertheless, the powers clearly recognized the choice before them, and determined to tackle the menace once and for all. Consequently, Napoleon's tentative feelers for peace were ignored, and preparations for a renewed armed struggle put in hand.

Any hopes that his overtures might have been well received

Joachim Murat, King of Naples (1767–1815) by Matania. Napoleon's brother-in-law was the most dashing cavalry commander in the Europe of his day. His political flair, however, was fatally undermined by his vanity. In 1815 his premature and ill-considered actions on Napoleon's behalf led to his disownment by the Emperor and, ultimately, to the firing-squad. 'Save the head—fire at the heart!' was his final request

were considerably compromised by the rash actions of the Emperor's brother-in-law, the disgraced Joachim Murat, King of Naples. The ruthless steps Murat had taken in the hope of securing his own position in Naples the previous year had earned him Napoleon's bitter denunciation, and yet the plans of the Sicilian house of Bourbon, egged on by the implacable British, made him well aware that his future was at best anomalous despite the promises of the Emperor Francis. Learning of Napoleon's return to France, the hot-headed Gascon dashed off an offer of his services to Napoleon, and without any consideration of the likely outcome of his action (and without any consultation with the Emperor) he issued a manifesto on 15 March and declared war on Austria with no more ado. Advancing on Rome with 40,000 men and fifty-six guns, the self-styled 'Liberator of Italy' at first faced little opposition. The Pope fled to Genoa at his approach, and the Neapolitan advance proceeded in two columns, one deep into Tuscany, the other towards Bologna by way of Ancona. However, if there was no active resistance to his progress there was equally no sign of popular support, and the occupation of Bologna proved a barren success. News from Naples, where he had left Queen Caroline as Regent, that an Anglo–Sicilian expeditionary force was about to invade the south of Italy, caused him to reconsider —but the forces of Austrian retribution were at last on the move. The Neapolitans took possession of Florence, but pressures from the north could not be withstood for long, and on 2 May the battle of Tolentino ended Murat's chances of retaining his kingdom. Deserted by many of his troops, he fled for the coast, and escaped by sea to France, where he landed near Toulon.

His repeated offer of his sabre to his brother-in-law met only an icy silence. He was formally forbidden to travel to Paris, and kicked his heels around Lyons in despairing inactivity, learning that Naples had welcomed the return of its former Bourbon rulers. The end of the road was not far distant for the former *beau sabreur* of the *Grande Armée*. After Waterloo he would flee to Corsica, and from there mount a last despairing venture, landing at Pizzo in Calabria at the head of only thirty followers in a bid to regain his throne by inciting a popular insurrection. Within days he had been rounded up and defeated in a brief skirmish, and on 13 October he met his fate with customary panache before a firing squad. But all this lay ahead in the spring of 1815. At that time Murat represented an unforeseen complication to Napoleon's peace offensive, nothing more.

By early April Napoleon was clearly aware that he would have

Many of Napoleon's personal effects, including the imperial toothbrush, were taken from his travelling coach which was captured near Genappe after Waterloo

From the same coach came the Emperor's court sword and two scabbards. Presumably their owner had intended to wear them during state receptions and other ceremonies after his triumphal entry into Brussels. Fate ordained otherwise

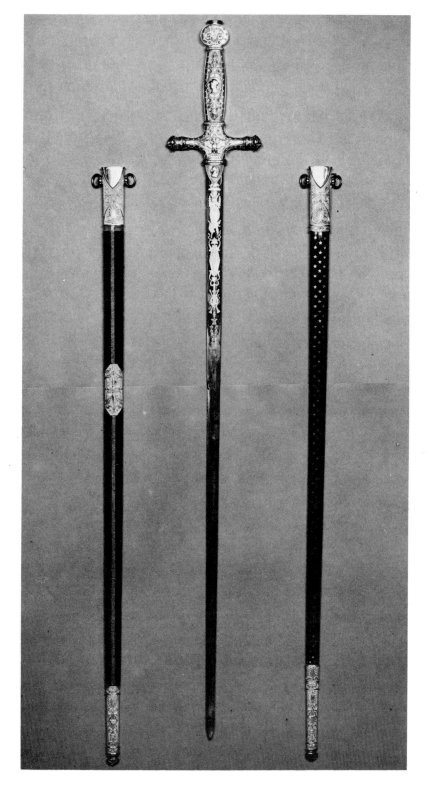

Napoleon's gold-mounted pistols were also part of the spoils of war that fell into Allied hands after Waterloo. The coach itself ended up in Madame Tussaud's in London, where it was later destroyed by a fire

to fight to survive. In all probability he had never expected anything else, but he was understandably eager to appear as the aggrieved party for reasons of French internal propaganda. At best, he had hoped for a breathing space which would enable him to rearm and prepare. In this he was to be largely disappointed, given the speed of the Allied reaction. In late April, therefore, he ordered the reimposition of conscription, but it would be some months before the newly raised or recalled levies could be formed into an effective army. Indeed, the military omens were anything but propitious for France, once it was clear that the Allies were taking the field. Napoleon had taken over practically the whole 200,000 strong Bourbon army, and perhaps half as many more old 'grumblers' and a leavening of genuine new volunteers would quietly rally to the *tricolor*, but this still left a large deficiency in the ranks if they were to be called upon to face over half a million Allies by late July. Not until the end of the year could the Emperor hope to field anything approaching an equivalent force, and long before that the enemy armies would be deep into France.

Napoleon, therefore, was on the horns of a strategic dilemma. Should he wait defensively around Paris, allowing his strength to grow, and invite the foe to attack—as in 1814? Or should he strike at once with such power as might be available by early June against the only enemies that could be in position by then— namely the Allied and Prussian forces facing the north-east frontiers of France? The choice was thus between a desperate and probably long-drawn struggle of attrition on the one hand and a lightning rapier-stroke, risking all to gain all in one great effort, on the other. Were the latter to succeed, such a prestigious victory, even if only over a sixth part of the Allied military potential, would rally French support behind Napoleon, and conceivably dissuade the Austrians and Russians from pressing conclusions. Such a defeat of Wellington might well bring down the Tory administration of Lord Liverpool in London, and any Whig-complexioned government, in the traditions of the great Charles James Fox, might be half-prepared to seek a compromise peace. Further, Napoleon clearly saw the disadvantages of subjecting his people to a new destructive struggle fought over much the same regions as had seen the campaign of the previous year. To fight and win abroad—that is to say over the French frontiers—had much to recommend it on political, social and economic grounds. But it required a neat calculation of the odds to reach a decision. Nevertheless, Napoleon had always favoured *blitzkrieg*, so the

Napoleon's monogrammed drinking glass (and leather container), together with his collapsible 'monocular' spy-glass that would easily slip into a pocket of his famous *redingote grise* on campaign

choice was made, and plans and preparations would soon begin.

At some unspecified date in early May the decision was taken in great secrecy. All the organs of state publicity and propaganda were brought into play to rally the people behind their Emperor. The spirit of 1792, when France had faced massive invasion, was freely reinvoked. The sad necessity to reimpose conscription was attributed to the bellicosity and intransigence of the powers of Europe. Vast programmes of rearmament were prescribed and emergency measures announced in an attempt to find and refurbish sufficient weaponry and equipment. Behind this façade of national activity and sense of purpose, Marshal Davout, newly appointed Minister of War and Military Governor of Paris, was secretly ordered on 13 May to submit reports on the state of canals and rivers in the Mons and Charleroi areas of the frontier region, and to report on the availability of bridging equipment. Clearly by that date the Emperor had decided on a blow against Wellington and Blücher.

Meanwhile Napoleon busied himself with the deployment of the meagre military resources immediately available to his hand. For the *Armée du Nord*, the force selected to carry out the great stroke he was secretly preparing, a total of 128,000 troops (to include local garrison forces in the fortresses near the Franco–Belgian frontier) was envisaged. These troops were to assemble around Beaumont during the first weeks of June, and we shall return later to give a more detailed description of the composition of this force. Even though this army was but a shadow of the great French armies Napoleon had led into the field in earlier years, and was inferior in numbers to the Allied and Prussian forces already assembled over the Meuse, it was a giant compared with the forces that could be paraded to hold other sectors of the long French frontiers. To block the anticipated invasion route of some 210,000 Austrians, who would be backed in due course by all of a further 200,000 Russians, commanded respectively by the Prince of Schwarzenberg and the Russian Barclay de Tolly, Napoleon placed his trusted aide, General Rapp, at the head of a pathetic 23,000 men, with orders to watch the central reaches of the Rhine from the vicinity of Strasbourg. Further south, General Lecourbe, with just 8,400 troops, was to garrison the French Jura against a possible threat posed by 37,000 Swiss under Bachmann, although the cantons were still neutral at this juncture. Based in Lyons, Marshal Suchet, one of the most brilliant soldiers the long wars had produced, was given command of the *Armée des Alpes*, 23,500 strong, which was associated with Marshal Brune's skeleton force of 5,500 men holding the Riviera. Between them, they were to stave off the anticipated onslaught by at least 50,000 Austrian troops of General Frimont's Army of Upper Italy and General Onasco's 23,000 men of the Army of Naples, newly disaffected from its allegiance to Napoleon's brother-in-law.

Such were the measures taken to protect the 600 miles of France's eastern frontiers. To guard the Pyrenees against any Spanish or Portuguese incursion, Generals Clausel and Decaen commanded 6,800 and 7,600 men based upon Bordeaux and Toulouse respectively. Finally to check and ultimately repress the pro-Bourbon revolts which had already sprung into life in parts of Brittany and the Cevennes region, traditional royalist strongholds both, General Lamarque was given 10,000 men for internal security operations centred around the Loire valley. Perhaps as many as 50,000 more troops were scattered in garrisons, including 20,000 retained in the Paris region under Davout, charged with the double role of guarding the fortresses and of training up the anticipated flood of new and recalled conscripts of the Class of 1815 now beginning to report to the regimental depots. Of course the full weight of the Allied attack upon France would not be felt until the autumn, by which time many conscripts should be available for service, but for all that Napoleon's resources were stretched pathetically thinly. Over half of his total manpower of 232,000 men was allocated for his gamble in the north. Its significance to his chances of survival is therefore clear. What would come to be called the 'Campaign of Waterloo' would indeed be a gamble on the grand scale.

Returning our attention to 'the other side of the hill', we must examine certain of the Allied preparations and plans in rather more detail. Not fully appreciating France's numerical weakness, the Allied leaders were not unduly optimistic about their immediate prospects were Napoleon to attack without delay. Many of the Allied troops were either recently demobilized or far distant from the scenes of impending action. Most of Wellington's veterans of the Peninsular War, for example, were in Canada or the eastern United States. At the moment when news arrived in Brussels (9 March) of Napoleon's return to France, only some 64,000 Allied troops were immediately available, namely 20,000 under the youthful and inexperienced Prince of Orange, some 30,000 Prussians under Kleist von Nollendorf, and 14,000 'turbulent and dissatisfied Saxons'. Not a few of these troops had until recently been subjects or allies of the French Empire and their loyalty was suspect. Initially,

Field-Marshal Gebhard Leberecht von Blücher, Prince of Wahlstadt (1742–1819) by Schadow. The septuagenarian warrior proved the soul of Prussian resistance to Napoleon, against whom he conducted a personal vendetta. Although his orders for his cavalry to bring Napoleon in 'dead or alive' were not fulfilled, he was only narrowly prevented from blowing up the Pont de Jéna in Paris during the Allied occupation. A fiery commander of great determination, who behaved more like a subaltern than a general, he relied heavily on Gneisenau for advice on strategy and logistics. He was much loved by his young Prussian conscripts, who dubbed him 'Old Forwards' and 'Papa Blücher'

therefore, their commanders decided to revictual key fortresses and, in the event of an alarm, to unite their forces two marches from the Meuse near Tirlemont.

Although no attack developed during March or early April, the handful of British formations already in Flanders were vastly relieved when Wellington arrived to assume command on 4 April. 'Glorious news! Nosey has got command!' exulted Sgt. Wheeler of the 51st Regiment. 'Won't we give them a drubbing now!' In fact the first two months of his command were ostensibly peaceful, although the problems of coalition warfare soon asserted themselves. King William I of the Netherlands promised much by way of reinforcements and supplies, but produced next to nothing. His son, 'the Young Frog' (as the Prince of Orange was nicknamed), did not prove the easiest of subordinates after relinquishing command to Wellington, and continually threatened to take the bit between his teeth and mount an ill-considered offensive against France on his own initiative. Nor was the attitude of the exiled Bourbons at Ghent exactly helpful; their military contribution to the cause was minimal, but their demands proved both strident and continuous. Even worse from the Duke's point of view, many of his officers and men of British origin were of unknown capacity and mettle. Much had to be done, therefore, to create a viable army and lick it into some shape, but no man was more capable of such a task than the Duke.

Nevertheless, the Prussian high command looked at their Allies with some doubt in April and May. Their reappointed commander-in-chief, the veteran Prince Blücher von Wahlstadt, already in his seventy-third year, had little direct personal knowledge of Wellington and his redcoats, whilst his chief-of-staff, the brilliant Count von Gneisenau, was already known for his anglophobic leanings. Fortunately his Quartermaster-General, Baron von Müffling, was an admirer of the Duke, and his eventual role as principal liaison officer between the two armies would prove of the greatest significance at several critical moments. His chief's first concern, however, was to place the Prussian army on a war footing. Blücher lost no time in ordering the disaffected Saxon troops back over the Rhine, and then proceeded to build up his Prussian army to a strength of 128,000 troops and almost 300 guns. As we shall see, this was nearly accomplished by mid-May. But the vast majority of his soldiers were raw conscripts with scant or no experience of the realities of warfare, although most of their senior leaders were veterans of proven merit. Such, then, were the Allied forces collecting in Belgium in preparation for the great battle.

The broad placings of the various Allied armies—both actual and intended—have already been described in the passages dealing with the French deployment. The overall strategic concept of the leaders of the Seventh Coalition called for a massive concentration of power along the whole of France's eastern frontier, followed by two major offensives under the general command of Prince Schwarzenberg over the Meuse and the Rhine towards Paris, and a smaller advance heading for Lyons—which would crush the French forces between them. To mass the requisite troops, however, would take several more months, and in the meantime it behoved Wellington and Blücher, as commanders of the only armies already assembled,

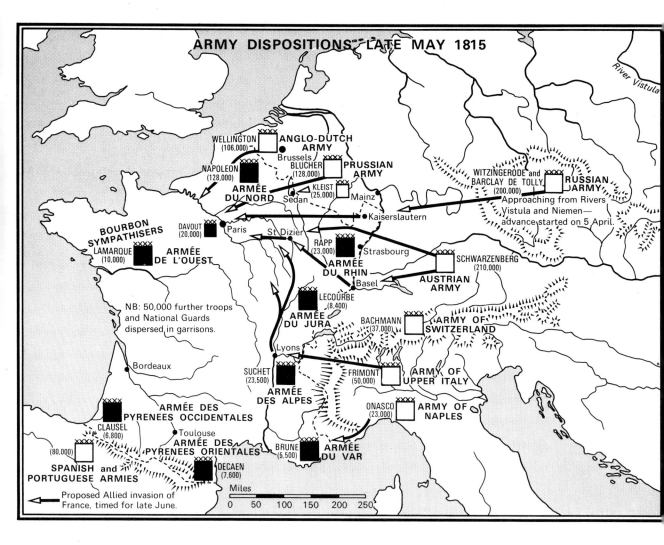

ARMY DISPOSITIONS LATE MAY 1815

River Vistula

WELLINGTON (106,000)
ANGLO-DUTCH ARMY
Brussels
NAPOLEON (128,000)
BLUCHER (128,000)
PRUSSIAN ARMY
WITZINGERODE and BARCLAY DE TOLLY (200,000)
RUSSIAN ARMY
KLEIST (25,000)
ARMÉE DU NORD
Sedan
Mainz
Approaching from Rivers Vistula and Niemen—advance started on 5 April.
Kaiserslautern
BOURBON SYMPATHISERS
DAVOUT (20,000)
Paris
St Dizier
RAPP (23,000)
LAMARQUE (10,000)
ARMÉE DE L'OUEST
Strasbourg
SCHWARZENBERG (210,000)
ARMÉE DU RHIN
AUSTRIAN ARMY
Basel
NB: 50,000 further troops and National Guards dispersed in garrisons.
LECOURBE (8,400)
ARMÉE DU JURA
BACHMANN (37,000)
ARMY OF SWITZERLAND
Bordeaux
Lyons
SUCHET (23,500)
FRIMONT (50,000)
ARMY OF UPPER ITALY
ARMÉE DES ALPES
ONASCO (23,000)
ARMY OF NAPLES
ARMÉE DES PYRENEES OCCIDENTALES
CLAUSEL (6,800)
Toulouse
ARMÉE DES PYRENEES ORIENTALES
BRUNE (5,500)
ARMÉE DU VAR
(80,000)
SPANISH and PORTUGUESE ARMIES
DECAEN (7,600)
Miles
0 50 100 150 200 250

Proposed Allied invasion of France, timed for late June.

to draw up contingency plans for concerted action in the immediate future. On 3 May, accordingly, the two leaders held a
joint-staff conference at Tirlemont. Blücher, ever the fire-eater,
pressed for an advance into France early in June, but was
persuaded by the more cautious Wellington to await the arrival
of the Austrians and Russians at their appointed stations before
undertaking a major aggressive action. Müffling recorded that
it was the failure of the Dutch to honour their promises, together
with the general slowness of the other Allies in taking the field,
that persuaded Blücher to make wholehearted co-operation
with the Duke his first priority. Initially, he had planned to
operate with the Austrians and Russians, but they could not
appear for some time as we have seen. As a result, it was agreed
that in the event of a French attack, both armies would be
careful to draw together rather than operate as two separate
entities. Furthermore, to placate Blücher's urge for offensive
action, both armies would commence an advance over the
Meuse towards Maubeuge in France on 12 July, if circumstances
permitted. As we shall see, however, the French would get their
blow in first.

Such, then, were the background circumstances and respective plans of the major contestants in the spring of 1815. Next
we must turn to consider the three senior commanders in rather
more detail, for a struggle of military giants was in the making.

Chapter Two

A Trio of Great Generals

Of the three commanders-in-chief about to enter the lists on the Franco–Belgian frontier, the Emperor Napoleon indubitably entered the campaign with the greatest reputation. 'I used to say of him', Wellington freely recalled in later years, 'that his presence in the field was worth 40,000 men.'

Napoleon, indeed, was a military phenomenon, the greatest soldier of modern history and possibly the greatest of all time, his only serious rivals for the title being Alexander the Great of Macedon and the Mongol Emperor Genghis Khan. Since 1796 Napoleon had dominated Europe, and, in fact, the world, with a dazzling display of military virtuosity; and if the discerning could detect signs of decline in his powers as early as 1806, the slope to failure had only become steep by late 1812, and his reputation as a leader of genius was still without equal in 1815, in spite of his recent period of eclipse. Nor should the constructive talents he displayed be overlooked. His reconstruction of revolutionary France from a faction-torn and near-ruined country into a highly developed nation state, capable of withstanding a dozen years of almost incessant major wars under his firm yet turbulent rule, was little short of miraculous. His name will inevitably conjure up the figure of a conqueror and warlord, for such proved to be his destiny, but the great codes of civil and economic law which bear his name and the myriad other administrative reforms he inspired from 1800 demand equal recognition. More than any other man, Napoleon refashioned continental Europe into the form it was to retain until the present day, abolishing the outdated Holy Roman Empire and helping to create concepts of national identity, and legal systems, that still survive. Here was a mortal of no common clay.

Napoleon I, Emperor, King of Italy (1769–1821) portrayed in his study (1810) by Jacques-Louis David in the heyday of the First Empire. Napoleon began to put on weight in 1807, and had already developed his well-known stance. Less well known is the fact that he needed spectacles for reading. He wears his favourite uniform, the green undress uniform of a colonel of the *Chasseurs-à-cheval* of the Imperial Guard. (David also painted an otherwise identical portrait showing him wearing a colonel of Grenadiers uniform, and the clock points to twelve minutes past four.) Intended for propaganda purposes, the sword is carefully balanced against the pen, and great stress is laid on the *Code Civil*—part of Napoleon's lasting legal achievement

His origins were humble enough. Born at Ajaccio on 15 April, 1769, into an obscure Corsican family with aristocratic pretensions, Napoleon was educated in France and eventually emerged as a junior artillery officer in 1785. The French Revolution created opportunities both in Corsica and France that he was not slow to seize. Chance placed him in command, as a mere captain, of the guns taking part in the siege of Toulon in 1793, and his conduct earned him whirlwind promotion to *général de brigade* within three months. Closely associated with the fortunes of the Jacobin faction, he almost shared in Robespierre's fall the next year, but survived. Caught up in the uncertain eddies of revolutionary politics, he was alternately employed and unemployed until, on 5 October, 1795, he was in the right place at the right time to rescue the Directory from a revolt, and the 'whiff of grapeshot' in Paris established his fortune once and for all. Promoted *général de division*, he was appointed to command the Army of Italy the following February, but before his departure for Nice he found time to marry Josephine de Beauharnais, the widow of a general and the cast-off mistress of Director Barras. At this juncture he was in his twenty-seventh year.

The long years of adventure and success that followed need but the briefest summary here—for they are well known. Two campaigns in Italy, divided by an excursion to Egypt and Syria in 1798–99, saw his military talents burgeon. Battles such as Arcola, Rivoli, the Pyramids and Marengo established his reputation as a great general once and for all. These years also saw his rapid political climb. The mere general commanding an army emerged, by dint of adroit manoeuvre and no little good fortune, as one of three Consuls after the *coup d'état de Brumaire* in October 1799, and a few more months sufficed to make him First Consul and effectively ruler of France. After Marengo and Hohenlinden in 1800, he brought a grateful France a brief period of peace, and launched into his great schemes of reform. Peace proved short-lived, and soon the perennial rivalry with Great Britain in the commercial and colonial fields brought a limited renewal of conflict in 1803, and a spate of plots against his life by Bourbon agents. To confirm his position, Napoleon won plebiscites from the French people and became Consul-for-Life, and then, in May 1804, took the final step to the throne by being proclaimed Emperor of France and King of Italy. 'If only our father could see us now,' he murmured to elder brother Joseph at his coronation in Notre Dame on 2 December. It was all a far cry from the genteel poverty of Ajaccio and from the strict revolutionary ideals of the intervening years. Since 1800 he had reconciled free-thinking France with the Papacy, inspired massive codes of law, created a new nobility, instituted the *Légion d'Honneur* to reward both soldiers and civilians of talent (in pursuit of his conviction that 'it is with baubels that men are led'), and, perhaps most significantly of all, fashioned a superb war machine in what would soon be known as *la grande armée*. All this he had achieved by the time he was thirty-six.

Soon, however, this marvellous career came to be dominated by the needs of war. British hostility remained both inveterate and secure behind the barrier of the English Channel and the protective screen of the Royal Navy. Furthermore, British diplomacy and wealth were instrumental—aided by such massive errors as the summary execution of the Duc d'Enghien and too-obvious French territorial ambitions along the Rhine—in creating new international coalitions on the Continent. Learning of Austrian and Russian intentions, Napoleon gave up all ideas of invading Great Britain and rushed his troops from the camp of Boulogne to the Rhine, and thence to the Danube. Two great successes—at Ulm and Austerlitz—laid the Third Coalition in ruins by December 1805. But Britain remained in the war, and, since Trafalgar had made her virtually impregnable against direct attack, continued to stir up trouble for Napoleon. Tactless handling of Prussian aspirations soon embroiled France in the War of the Fourth Coalition. A *blitzkrieg* campaign culminating in the double victory of Jena–Auerstädt (October 1806) led to the physical conquest of three-quarters of Prussian soil, but did not bring peace, for Russia was again involved. It took two more campaigns (one in the depths of winter), the French near-defeat of Eylau and the great triumph of Friedland, to bring Tsar Alexander and the hapless Frederick William III of Prussia to terms. The celebrated Congress of Tilsit, July 1807, brought Napoleon to the apparent *apogée* of his power. All of continental Europe west of the Niemen was in greater or lesser degree subject to the Emperor's will, and the Tsar was now both friend and ally.

But Britain remained unquelled. In an attempt to ruin the sources of her prosperity and power, Napoleon had already, in December 1806, declared an all-out embargo on trade with the British Isles. The Continental System, as this became called, proved Napoleon's greatest error of grand strategy, and the turning point in his fortunes. In the first place it was unsuccessful; secondly it was highly unpopular, particularly in Holland, Italy and the Scandinavian countries; thirdly it led directly to

OVERLEAF *The Battle of Marengo, 14th June 1800* by Baron Lejeune. This success in North Italy was Napoleon's first victory as First Consul and head of state. In fact he was fortunate to emerge the winner: only the opportune arrival of General Desaix at the head of Boudet's division swung the fortunes of the day. However, the battle holds a special place in the mythology of the First Empire, and to this day countless diners pay unconscious homage to Napoleon's success when they order the Emperor's favourite dish, *poulet à la Marengo*

further wars which hopelessly overextended France's resources and ultimately led to the Empire's collapse. To begin with, in December 1807, the enforcement of the policy involved the invasion of Portugal, and this in turn led to a deep embroilment with the corrupt Bourbon regime in Spain. When Napoleon conspired to replace their king with his own brother Joseph in April 1808, the Spanish people revolted, and their appeals for aid brought Britain's small but effective and well-led army on to the Continent. There then began the seven-year Peninsular War, which tied down some 200,000–300,000 French troops each year, and cost one hundred casualties a day, in the prosecution of an endless struggle against the Spanish guerrillas backed by the Anglo–Portuguese army. In an attempt to smash the trouble without delay and avenge the defeats of Vimeiro and Bailen, Napoleon led his best troops to Spain in late 1808. Victory attended his arms as usual, but his absence in the Peninsula induced Austria to prepare a new war, and this, together with plots in Paris, compelled Napoleon to leave Spain before its conquest was complete. A running sore was thus created, for his marshals never proved capable of solving the problem, and the Emperor never chose to return to Spain. A sharp campaign served to bring Austria back to heel, but there were already signs in France of growing unrest caused by the high taxes and the ceaseless demands for men and more men to fill the ranks of the army. The French Empire's decline had begun.

Irritation with the effects of the Continental System proved an important factor in the erosion and ultimate disappearance of the special relationship with Tsarist Russia. Another factor was Napoleon's marriage to the Archduchess Marie Louise of Austria, following his divorce from the childless Josephine. This mounting tension in turn led Napoleon to his second great strategic error of judgement—the declaration of war against Russia in June 1812 at a time when, over 1,000 miles away, the great Spanish struggle was approaching its climax as Wellington at last assumed the offensive. Napoleon probably intended no more than to bully Alexander into compliance with his requirements by a major demonstration of force along his frontiers, but the Tsar called his bluff, and left the French with no option but to invade. By the new year of 1813, half a million French and Allied soldiers had died in Russia and Poland.

The consequences of this cataclysmic defeat grew inexorably. First Prussia, and then Austria, deserted the French alliance and joined the Sixth Alliance. Step by step, Napoleon was

Countess Marie Walewska (1789–1817), the most beautiful and most loyal of Napoleon's mistresses. She entered his life in Poland, 1807, bore him a son in 1810 —Alexandre Florian Joseph (who later became a Foreign Minister of France)—and visited him for the last time during the exile on Elba in 1814. The soldiers nicknamed her 'the Emperor's Polish wife', and a deep affection marked their relationship

forced back through central Europe. He could still win victories —as at Lützen, Bautzen and Dresden—but he could not exploit them, and by now his foes were becoming aware of the counters to his strategic systems. The great defeat of Leipzig, October 1813, deprived France of control of all territory east of the Rhine, and the year had cost another half-million casualties. In Spain, meanwhile, Joseph's rule had effectively come to an end after Wellington's success at Vitoria. The Empire was crumbling fast, as the states of Germany and of the Confederation of the Rhine deserted one by one, followed by Murat's Naples. The end was now in sight, but it took the three-month campaign of 1814, the capture of Paris and the revolt of his marshals to convince Napoleon of the need to abdicate and go into exile. The Empire seemed to be over—until the dramatic events of March 1815 threw this back into doubt.

In the years of his greatness, Napoleon's achievement had rested on two groups of attributes. First was his sheer mastery of the military profession. From his first commissioning, he spared no pains to increase his knowledge of soldiering, reading avidly the campaigns of earlier commanders and seizing every opportunity that came his way. Many of his strategic ideas were formulated by 1788—the envelopment of the opponent's army and the manoeuvre based upon the central position. These were by no means new concepts—Napoleon was a great borrower of other men's ideas—but the ruthless energy with which they were put into operation from 1796 onwards was unique. His armies marched faster, fought with greater spirit, and were led by abler men than those of most of his opponents, with their hidebound eighteenth-century concepts. As has been well said, 'Napoleon contributed little to the armies of France—except victory'. He saw how to make the most out of the martial qualities of his adopted people, and employed the enthusiasm and sense of purpose generated by the Revolution to provide the momentum.

Secondly there were the facets of his personality. He knew how 'to speak to the soul' of his officers and men. Partly he used material rewards and incentives—titles, medals, awards; partly he resorted to deliberate theatrical measures to bend men to his will; but above all there was the sheer power of personality or charisma that emanated from his large, grey eyes which so many of his contemporaries described. He was a master of man-management. The least word of praise was treasured unto death by the recipient; the slightest rebuke could reduce a hardened grenadier to tears. Ministers and marshals wondered at the

breadth of his intellect; ordinary citizens and soldiery became willing propagators of his legend. All feared his rages; all admired his abilities and application, for no subject seemed beyond his powers. His memory appeared limitless, as did his capacity for applied hard work. This combination of qualities set him apart from other men, and accounts in large measure for their willingness to accept his will, and even die in execution of his orders. 'So it is', recalled the war-hardened General Vandamme, 'that I, who fear neither God nor devil, tremble like a child at his approach.'

Of course there was a reverse to the coin. Long before 1815 many of the old qualities were producing monstrous distortions or perversions. As a commander, Napoleon was becoming predictable, and his foes were beginning to appreciate the counter-measures and use them against him. Increasingly he refused to face up to reality, believing what he chose to, and not what the facts warranted. He had become a tyrant and the repressor of many of the qualities he had once represented. A

A personal field kit presented to one of Napoleon's marshals. The Emperor was lavish with awards, titles and marks of favour for those he deemed to have served him well. Besides medals, social advancement and large cash-grants, these included more personal gifts, ranging from inscribed sabres and ceremonial swords to sets of campaigning equipment

supreme egotist, he ruthlessly suppressed all traces of criticism, and made ever greater demands on his people and allies. Nevertheless, when all was said and done, he remained a giant surrounded by pygmies; his reputation survived his fall, for his basic greatness was inviolable.

In one respect, however, he committed a cardinal error in 1815; he evinced scant respect for his opponents, and in this his self-confidence was wholly excessive. He believed that he had got Blücher's measure in 1806—an officer dominated by a brainless hussar-complex that would cause him to rush to his doom. As for Wellington, his scorn for the 'sepoy general', as he dubbed him, was in no way mitigated by the treatment the Duke had meted out to his ablest marshals in Spain. On 18 June he would round on Soult, when he suggested the immediate recall of Grouchy's forces, with some revealing words. 'Because you have been beaten by Wellington you consider him a good general, but *I* tell you that Wellington is a *bad* general and that the English are *bad* troops. The whole affair will not be more serious than swallowing one's breakfast.' In point of fact, he was to find Wellington, his redcoats and allies, singularly indigestible on that particular fateful day.

The 'Iron Duke', as history has dubbed the Duke of Wellington, shared one basic attribute with the Emperor Napoleon in 1815—both were aged forty-six. Arthur was the third son of Garret Wesley, first Earl Mornington (in 1798 the family changed the spelling to Wellesley, an earlier form), a prominent if somewhat impecunious Anglo–Irish peer with a strong interest in musical composition, who sired all of five sons and a single daughter. Arthur shared his natal year with a large number of contemporaries destined to become almost as prominent as himself in their later lives, including General Sir John Moore, and, of his other foes besides Napoleon, Marshals Ney, Lannes and Soult—all were born during 1769. At first there was little to single out the boy from the rest. A rather delicate child who delighted in playing the violin, he made no real mark at either Eton or the French Royal Academy of Equitation at Angers.

Drifting into, rather than specifically choosing, a military career, in 1787 he was gazetted as Ensign into the 73rd Highland Regiment, from which he transferred—as a lieutenant—one year later into the 41st, becoming at the same time an *aide-de-camp* to the Viceroy of Ireland. This proved but the first of a whole series of rapid transfers from regiment to regiment, and, thanks to patronage and purchase, the young officer, aged only

twenty-five, emerged with the rank of Lieut.-Colonel of the 33rd of Foot (later the Duke of Wellington's Regiment) after only seven years of commissioned service. Nor did his advancement pause even there. The involvement of Great Britain in the War of the First Coalition against France from 1793 ensured that he soon saw active service, and in 1794 he was placed in temporary

Field-Marshal Sir Arthur Wellesley, first Duke of Wellington (1769–1852) as sketched by Goya. Wellington clinched a brilliant military career—begun in India, continued in Spain, Portugal and the South of France through the long Peninsular War (1807–1814)—by defeating with Blücher's aid the Emperor Napoleon in person in one of the truly decisive battles of modern history. A fine strategist and military logistician, his greatest skills were as a battlefield commander. His attitude towards both officers and men was stern and patrician, and he once referred to the latter disparagingly as 'the scum of the earth, enlisted for drink'. Nevertheless, his officers respected him, calling him 'the Peer', whilst his rank and file would do anything for 'Old Hookey' or, more prosaically, 'that bugger that beats the French'

command of a brigade during the ill-fated Flanders campaign under 'the Grand Old Duke of York'. This experience, as he afterwards noted, at least taught him 'what one ought not to do, and that is always something'. Next, on 3 May, 1796, one month after Napoleon had assumed command over the Army of Italy, Arthur Wellesley was awarded the army rank of colonel, and a month later sailed for India in command of the 33rd of Foot.

The eight years he spent in India (1797–1805) proved the vital formative period of his military career, and indeed of his life. During this time he rose to the rank of Major-General (being appointed to this rank in April 1802). This rapid preferment owed little to the fact that his brilliant elder brother Richard had been appointed Governor-General in 1798, but a great deal to the burgeoning of his latent talents as soldier, administrator and diplomat. By hard experience—and not a few early mistakes—he learnt much about campaigning under monsoon conditions, the crossing of rivers in the face of the enemy, the handling of subtle opponents and shifty native allies amongst the Princes of the sub-continent, and, perhaps most important of all, the realities of military administration and the significance of personal reconnaissance. He won considerable reputation for his conduct at Seringapatam (1799), and later emerged as the victor of the Maharatta War with the successes of Assaye and Argaum (both 1803) to his credit. The three Wellesley brothers, Richard, Henry and Arthur, did much to extend and consolidate the British hold on India, and the rule they imposed proved just, as well as firm.

Arthur Wellesley emerged from India a mature man and leader. Hard service and simple living had strengthened his constitution and general health. His total opposition to corruption in a land where, and at a time when, vast fortunes could be made by the less scrupulous, allied to his considerable diplomatic and administrative skills developed under the need to organize and run captured territories, laid the foundations for both his years as a commander in the Peninsula and for his later role as a politician and Prime Minister of Great Britain.

His character was stern and aristocratic. He would not countenance misconduct or tyrannous conduct, but demanded an integrity in his subordinates that would match his own. Outwardly he was often very hard on his officers, ruthlessly criticizing their efforts and pointing out their shortcomings and failings. He was equally critical of his allies, and made no secret of his occasional disdain for his own troops. But his sheer professional competence and brilliance caused his contemporaries to overlook or tolerate his aloofness, and all recognized that he was harder on himself than on any other man. Thus the 'Sepoy General', who at length returned to England in 1805, was ready to command against the French conquerors of Europe, and ultimately to beard the Emperor Napoleon himself.

But before he was called to major command, three more years of important domestic development and further military experience awaited him. Following a brief and quite fortuitous meeting with Admiral Nelson shortly before the latter set out

for Trafalgar, he was sent on a brief excursion to the River Elbe area in command of a brigade from December 1805 to the following February. In April 1806 he entered Parliament, and also married Kitty Pakenham, daughter of Lord Longford. Unfortunately the marriage was not to prove very happy, but a son and heir was born to the union. But soon military preoccupations demanded all his attention. First came the command of part of south-east England's coast against the threat of French invasion, and then, in 1807, a role in the expedition to Copenhagen. This period also saw him appointed Chief Secretary for Ireland in the Tory ministry of the Duke of Portland.

From 1808 commenced the most significant period of his military career to date. Promoted Lieutenant-General in April, within three months he was on his way to Portugal in temporary command of the British expeditionary force. Victor of Vimeiro, he narrowly avoided censure over the subsequent Convention of Cintra which followed his supercession in command by more senior generals newly arrived in the theatre of war. Next year, however, following the death of Sir John Moore at Corunna and the evacuation of the British army, Wellesley was reappointed to the full command of the force that returned to Portugal in April 1809. The outline of the six years of campaigns that ensued can only be briefly summarized here. Suffice it to say that Sir Arthur proved highly adept at defending Portugal during the Douro operations of that year, and by his use of the Lines of Torres Vedras to confound Marshal Massena in 1810. He proved equally capable of co-operating with Spanish guerrilla forces, did his best to sustain the remnants of the Spanish regular army (as during the Talavera campaign of 1809), and succeeded in tying down Marshal Soult's forces in the south of Spain throughout 1811. Then, in 1812, as Napoleon drew many of his best forces out of the Peninsula to mount the attack on Russia, Wellington (the title he had assumed on being made a viscount after Talavera) passed over on to the strategic offensive, undertaking the reconquest of Spain after capturing the frontier fortresses of Ciudad Rodrigo and Badajoz. A string of great victories followed—Salamanca in 1812, Vitoria and Sorauen the following year, and then, after a long struggle amidst the Pyrenees, the culminating success at Toulouse in the south of France, fought before news of Napoleon's abdication at Fontainebleau some days earlier could reach him. During these halcyon years, marshal after marshal of Napoleon's Empire had met defeat at his hands, either singly or in combination. His reputation as a battle commander was firmly established.

Wellington's medical chest. Generals went to war in the early nineteenth century with many 'little comforts' and personal possessions designed to ease the discomforts of campaigning. Wellington was less well-equipped than most in this respect, but this medical chest provided him with the pills and potions needed to ward off the ailments likely to attack even as fit a man as he, who schooled himself by hard riding every day in all weathers. In general terms he enjoyed excellent health

Vitoria in 1813 had earned him the baton of Field-Marshal, and on his return to England in the early summer of 1814 he was received into the House of Lords as, simultaneously on the same day, Viscount, Earl, Marquess and Duke—honours successively earned since Talavera in 1809 but for which he had never found time to return to England to receive. From August 1814 to March 1815 he served as British Ambassador to the Bourbon Court in Paris, but this gave way, as we have seen, to his transfer to first Vienna and then to the command in Flanders.

Wellington demonstrated his mastery of the art and science of warfare at every level. True, his view of war was largely conditioned by eighteenth-century preconceptions rather than by new ideas, but nobody had ever made the former work more effectively, not even the great Frederick. At the level of grand strategy he was a realist: he was aware that he commanded Britain's only army, and that it had to be cared for despite the demands of allies who could not always be relied upon to fulfil their undertakings. This he had learnt as early as the Talavera campaign of 1809—and from that date he never again relied on Spanish promises of supply or transport, but set about evolving the famous logistical 'triple system' (the use of rivercraft, ox-waggon convoys and mule trains to move up the supplies from his secure base of Lisbon—and later Santander—to the front by way of intermediary depots). At the level of strategy, he realized from the first the importance of operating in conjunction with the Spanish and Portuguese guerrilla forces. The French could not both hold down the countryside and concentrate to meet the Anglo–Portuguese challenge, and Wellington set out to exploit this weakness, which, together with their inadequate supply system, and the acrimonious relations between the members of the Marshalate serving in Spain, lay at the base of the French failure in the Iberian Peninsula. The popular resistance against the Gallic invader also provided Wellington with a mass of invaluable intelligence information that he was not slow to use. As a grand tactician, Wellington had few equals in his day; the skilled dispositions of his formations at such battles as Talavera, Salamanca or Vitoria proved him to be a master in battle-management, both in the defensive and the offensive role. And his mastery of minor tactics—particularly his skilled use of reverse-slope positions, light infantry screens, and well-sited battery positions—brought his army success after success. Above all, he knew his enemy. Before setting out for the Peninsula in 1808 he revealed that he considered the French 'new system' a bad one '. . . as against steady troops', and put his finger on the secret of French successes to that point when he declared that the Empire's opponents had as often as not been more than half-defeated by psychological domination, even before a shot was fired. 'I, at least, will not be afraid of them.' Here, if anywhere, lay the major secret of his success to date—but he had not yet had occasion to meet Napoleon on the battlefield.

Such, in barest outline, was the career to date of this outstanding soldier. Known as '*Monsieur Villainton*' to the half-admiring French, and as 'The Peer' to his officers, 'Old Hookey' (a reference to his nose) or 'the Bugger that beats the French' to his rank and file, Wellington was already overloaded with honours and titles bestowed by friendly governments and peoples. But now he was facing the ultimate test of his military career—a direct confrontation with 'Boney' in person.

The third commanding general whose reputation was at stake in June 1815 was Gebhard Leberecht von Blücher, commander-in-chief of all Prussian forces west of the Rhine. His temperament, for all his seventy-two and a half years, was still that of a blustering, tempestuous corporal of hussars; a stronger contrast with the egocentric dynamism and brilliance of Napoleon, or the cool and disdainful British Milord, would be hard to find. A contemporary described him as 'a rough, ill-educated man, but endowed with common sense, fiery energy and indomitable courage'. If he lacked the strategic grasp of a Napoleon or the tactical flair of a Wellington, Blücher shone as a leader who could inspire his officers and men, particularly the latter—the young and inexperienced conscripts who made up the great majority of his army. Blunt, intensely patriotic, rough and loyal, Blücher was known to them as '*Alte Vorwärts*' ('Old Forwards') or as 'Papa Blücher'. His inseparable pipe became a symbol, and his men would do anything he asked of them. He never overcame the 'Hussar-complex' developed during his early years in Frederick the Great's army, and this characteristic led him to both his greatest failures and his most notable successes.

Blücher's career stretched far back into the eighteenth century, and was filled with adventure and the vagaries of fortune. Born at Rostock in 1742, he joined a Swedish regiment at the age of sixteen, and this circumstance resulted in his being required to serve, during his first campaign, against his fellow-countrymen, who took him prisoner. Shortly thereafter, in typically easy-going eighteenth-century fashion, he was allowed to enter the Prussian army, with which he served for the remainder of the Seven Years War as an officer in the very hussar regiment that had captured him. Its colonel, Belling, extended his personal patronage over the young man. However, Blücher's fiery temper and dissolute habits—gambling, wenching and the bottle being his particular delights—caused him to be passed over for promotion; in 1772 he was told to 'go to the devil' by Frederick the Great, and resigned his commission. For

Blücher At Waterloo by A. Closs. Blücher's determination to honour his promise to march to Wellington's aid at Mont-St. Jean (the 'Waterloo' on the signpost is a piece of artistic license) proved a vital

contribution to ultimate victory. Here he is seen encouraging an artillery team to persevere through the rain and mud as he advances towards Plancenoit on the morning of 18 June

the next sixteen years he retired to live as a gentleman-farmer in Silesia, and achieved a notable degree of success. However, on the accession of Frederick William II in 1787, he returned to the colours with the rank of major. The years that followed established his reputation as a soldier, and earned him rapid advancement.

During the War of the First Coalition, he emerged as a dashing and able cavalry commander, and in May 1794 was promoted Major-General and entrusted with a command on the Lower Rhine in the new Prussian province of Münster, where he shared responsibility for its government with Baron Stein, the great political reformer of later years. By 1806 Blücher was a Lieutenant-General, and after the cataclysmic double defeat of Jena–Auerstädt he commanded the Prussian rearguard. But so ferocious was the French pursuit that he was compelled to surrender at Rakau near Lübeck as Prussian resistance was overwhelmed. This, his second captivity, proved short-lived, for within fourteen days he was exchanged for Marshal Victor. A number of appointments followed, including a spell in the Prussian War Ministry after Tilsit, and then a command of a district in Pomerania. But Napoleon had taken a distinct aversion to the Prussian leader, and he applied pressure upon a compliant Prussian government to secure Blücher's removal. Once again, therefore, he became a farmer, but from the seclusion of his estates lent what support he could express for the military reforms of Scharnhorst, whom he had first met during the cataclysmic days after Auerstädt. His patriotic fervour remained undimmed.

In 1813, following Prussia's defection from the French Alliance, the old war-horse was summoned from retirement and appointed commander-in-chief of the Army of Silesia. In this capacity he served with distinction at both Lützen and Bautzen, and gained great distinction by defeating Marshal Macdonald at Katzbach later the same campaign, taking 18,000 prisoners and 100 guns, thus clearing Silesia of the French once and for all. His services continued at the great, climacteric 'Battle of the Nations' around Leipzig in October—where he commanded in the northern sector and kept, with some difficulty, the Crown Prince of Sweden, Prince Bernadotte (a former French marshal), up to the mark. Next year he proved the major driving force and inspiration behind the Allied invasion of France, and his unwavering demand for a 'fight to the finish' rallied his weaker-hearted colleagues on several occasions. The victor of La Rothière, he rallied after a number of defeats in March to win

General Augustus Wilhelm, Graf Neithard von Gneisenau (1760–1831) by George Dawe. A brilliant staff officer, whose intellect complemented his commander's 'hussar complex', Gneisenau served as Blücher's chief-of-staff from 1813. Not noted for Anglophile attitudes, in Blücher's absence late on 16 June he was in favour of retreating towards the Rhine and leaving Wellington (whom he believed to have failed to march to the Prussian assistance at Ligny) to his own devices. Circumstances, however, dictated otherwise, and his decision to fall back on Wavre rather than Namur was one of the critical moments of the campaign. In later years he became Governor of Berlin, and died of cholera whilst suppressing a Polish insurrection

the battle of Laon against Napoleon himself, and thereafter helped mastermind the final drive on Paris, which he entered on 1 April. In due course he was created Prince of Wahlstadt for his considerable services. A sudden serious illness laid him low, but after recovery he visited England in June, where he was lionized wherever he went. The British press dubbed him 'Blücher the Immortal', and he was given the freedom of the City of London. It was about this time that he first met Wellington.

Once again he retired to his estates, only to be dragged back into harness yet again after news of Napoleon's return to France. His reaction was typical: 'It is the greatest piece of good luck that could have happened to Prussia. Now the war will begin again and the armies will make good all the faults committed at Vienna'—a reference to the unsatisfactory settlement, from Prussia's point of view, that appeared to be emerging from the Congress. This was an extreme and somewhat naïve view, but it reveals the extent of Blücher's patriotism: 'My country right or wrong.'

From at least 1806, Blücher waged what can only be termed as a personal vendetta against the French Emperor. In 1814 he spoke publicly of his ambition to capture Napoleon and hang him. This personal hatred for his opponent would explain several of his decisions during the forthcoming campaign. In sum, therefore, Blücher was a leader of men rather than a true *chef de guerre*. He was, however, aware of his limitations, and freely admitted his need for the expert assistance of Gneisenau to keep him along the right strategic lines. At Oxford to receive an honorary degree in 1814, he forthrightly remarked: 'If I am to be a doctor they should at least make Gneisenau an apothecary, for we go together.'

Such, then, were the three senior commanders vitally concerned with the forthcoming events. We must next turn from a study of the leaders to consider the men they led.

Chapter Three

The Rival Armies

The French *Armée du Nord* was in several ways the most experienced force Napoleon had commanded since 1807. It was largely composed of veterans; there were few raw conscripts and no dubious allies included in its ranks, and the leadership, up to *corps d'armée* level, was generally good. Somewhat paradoxically, however, it was at the same time potentially one of the least reliable armies that he had ever led. Like a rapier of imperfect steel, it was razor sharp but brittle. It contained a number of flaws that might well cause the blade to snap, however brilliant the passes and sword-play of its wielder.

The 128,000 men and 366 guns of its total, paper strength were split between 175 battalions, 180 squadrons, fifty batteries, and a number of garrison detachments. Until 6 June (when Napoleon ordered the general concentration around Beaumont) the troops were dispersed along a front of some 200 miles so as to preserve an appearance of normalcy and conceal the direction and force of the coming blow. General d'Erlon's I Corps was in position around Lille; Reille's II Corps was already in the Beaumont area; Vandamme's III Corps was in the vicinity of Mezières with Marshal Grouchy's cavalry reserve cantonned along the River Aisne. General Lobau's VI Corps was set slightly to their rear near Laon, and further south, Gérard's IV Corps was centred upon Metz. Finally, the Imperial Guard was located partly at Compiègne and partly in Paris.

Each of the five *corps d'armée* was a balanced force of varying total strength, comprising three or four divisions of infantry, one division of light or medium cavalry, several batteries of artillery, a contingent of sappers, supporting trains and medical services, and, last but not least, a headquarters formation—in

fact a miniature army with a flexible capacity. The cavalry reserve totalled four small corps, each of two cavalry divisions supported by batteries of horse artillery. The *corps d'élite*, the Imperial Guard, was made up of three infantry divisions—the Old, Middle and Young Guards—two divisions of Guard cavalry, heavy and light, and the Guard artillery, which, including the artillery reserve, totalled 118 pieces. To control and co-ordinate the movements of the whole army there was *Grand-Quartier-Général*, the Imperial General Staff, totalling almost 600 officers and men split between its various branches and departments.

Compared to the armies Napoleon had led in earlier campaigns this force was of only medium size. The *Grande Armée de l'Allemagne* of· 1805 had comprised 210,000 men; that of Russia, in 1812, all of 675,000 (reserves and communication troops included). Nevertheless its smaller size made it easier to control, and by 14 June the army had been drawn up in an area little more than thirty kilometres square around Beaumont, this sudden eight-day concentration being concealed by careful security measures implemented since the beginning of the month. On the eve of operations, the army was organized into three main columns behind the cavalry screen. On the left, ready to cross the Sambre through Marchienne and Thuin, waited d'Erlon's and Reille's corps, under the overall command of Marshal Ney once the campaign opened, but as yet still awaiting confirmation of this. On the right, waiting to advance on Charleroi itself, were Vandamme and Gérard, under the overall command of recently promoted Marshal Grouchy. Finally, in reserve behind the right wing, were the corps of Lobau, the Imperial Guard, and the heavy echelons of the cavalry reserve—forces which Napoleon kept under his own control.

So far, so good from the French point of view, but it is when we consider the key commanders under Napoleon that the first potential weakness becomes apparent. First, as chief-of-staff, Napoleon had appointed Marshal Soult, Duke of Dalmatia. He was not destined to shine in this unaccustomed role. At several critical moments in the days that lay ahead orders would be mislaid, forgotten or ambiguously expressed. Such errors were virtually unknown when Alexandre Berthier had carried out these functions, but the indispensable Berthier was dead, having fallen from a window in Bamberg on 1 June. Whether he slipped, jumped or was pushed remains a mystery; nor is it certain that he would have accepted his old post again, for he

General Honoré Charles Michel Joseph Reille, Count of the Empire (1775–1860) An experienced French soldier who had shared in many of Napoleon's campaigns and who played a large role in the Peninsular War, he was given command of the II Corps in 1815. His formation bore the brunt of the fighting at Quatre Bras, and two days later, thanks to the obstinacy of his subordinate, Prince Jérôme Bonaparte, he allowed almost half his strength to become tied down in an attritional struggle around the Château of Hougoumont for the entire battle

had passed through Brussels after leaving France in early April —that is to say after Napoleon's resumption of power. Soult was no replacement for Berthier, but he was a worthy soldier. It is hard to understand why Napoleon did not put him in command of the left wing of the army—the force that was likely to encounter Wellington, whom Soult had fought against time and again during the Peninsular War, particularly its later stages. A more suitable appointment for chief-of-staff would have been the superbly efficient Suchet, whom Napoleon had ordered to a command on the Upper Rhine.

The appointment of Marshal Grouchy, a hereditary aristocrat, to command the French right wing was also a strange decision. Grouchy was a notable cavalryman, and his original responsibility for the cavalry reserve was his true *métier*. In his own field, his reputation was second only to that of Murat—whom Napoleon refused to employ, partly on account of his defection

RIGHT *Marshal Emmanuel, Marquis de Grouchy* (1776– 1847) by Rouillard. Of aristocratic birth, he became established as an able cavalry commander. In 1815 he was the last officer to be appointed a Marshal of the Empire, and was given command of the right of the *Armée du Nord*. His success at Ligny was followed by his lesser one at Wavre, where his actions were much criticized. However, he capably rallied the survivors on 19 June

in 1814, and partly because of the premature offensive he had launched in Italy in March 1815. But Grouchy had never commanded a mixed force of horse, foot and guns, and would soon find himself out of his depth, at least at first. Both his corps commanders proved jealous and obstructive, not to say critical of his performance. This particular command, moreover, would have proved ideal for Marshal Davout, the hero of Auerstädt in 1806 and of the defence of Hamburg, 1813–14, who certainly had the measure of the Prussians and was both respected and feared by them. However, Napoleon chose to employ this very able soldier in the Paris area as we have already mentioned—indubitably a key political role, but one which would not allow him to display his great martial talents. There had always been an element of jealousy in Napoleon's attitude towards the Duc d'Auerstädt and Prince of Eckmühl, whose cold and austere personality allied to his proven military skills did not make him the easiest of subordinates.

A third key appointment was even more questionable—namely that of Marshal Ney to command the left wing. As we have seen, Soult would seem to have been the obvious candidate to pit against Wellington. Michel Ney, Duc d'Elchingen and Prince of the Moskowa, had never been famous for either brains or cool calculation. Napoleon had once unflatteringly likened his military knowledge to that '. . . of the last-joined drummer-boy'. For years he had depended upon the services of his brilliant Swiss chief-of-staff, Baron Jomini, in much the same way as Blücher relied on Gneisenau, but Jomini had joined the Allies in 1813. Moreover, ever since his valorous conduct of the rearguard during the retreat from Moscow, which had earned him the nickname of 'the bravest of the brave', Ney had been suffering from a form of battle fatigue. This made his actions unreliable—periods of almost total lethargy alternating with periods of great and often rash activity, traits that would play no small part in future events, as we shall discover. Nevertheless, there was considerable cunning in the Emperor's choice in this case. Ney was proverbially brave, and was the hero of the rank and file. It could be hoped, therefore, that his appointment would place an edge on the army's mettle. More, his return to imperial favour, given his former misconduct, would serve to persuade many another Frenchman who had co-operated with the Bourbons that 'all could be forgiven' in return for renewed loyal service. In other words, Ney's appointment was partly intended as a test-case demonstration of Napoleon's forgiving nature and generosity towards his former subjects, as well as a

Marshal Michel Ney, Prince of the Moskowa, Duke of Elchingen (1769–1815) 'The bravest of the brave' had led the mutiny of the marshals in April 1814 and then taken service under the restored

massive snub aimed at the Bourbons, whose commander-in-chief Ney had so recently been. On these grounds there was a great deal to be said in favour of his appointment. However, it was a practical mistake to fling him straight into his new command so abruptly on the first day of the offensive. He even had to borrow horses from another general, and he was certainly given no time to get to know his subordinates or feel his way into his new responsibilities. To this extent Ney deserves considerable sympathy, but he would prove responsible for several major errors, which some claim cost Napoleon the campaign, and with it his chance of survival as ruler of France.

Napoleon had as a general rule been very successful in choosing subordinates for key commands and responsibilities. This departure from the norm in 1815 can be explained in one of two ways. Either his powers of selection had suddenly atrophied—which is extremely unlikely—or, and here we are probably nearer the truth, the cunning and ruthless Corsican was deliberately fielding a second-rate team in order to throw his own brilliance into sharper focus. To secure his grasp over his people and to cow the opposition of the other crowned heads of Europe he knew he needed a tremendous demonstration of personal success. He did not wish to share the laurels of victory with such able subordinates as Davout or Suchet, notable commanders in their own right. In 1815 it had to be the Emperor's very own unquestioned success.

Enough of the commanders; what of the men? Here, once again, we find a strange contrast. In terms of accumulated experience and achievement, no army Napoleon had led had ever been so impressive on the surface. It was the nearest to a genuine army of volunteers he had ever led, and its junior and middle leadership could hardly be bettered. As Wellington himself admitted to Thomas Creevey, the quality of the French rank and file was potentially enormous. Asked if he counted upon receiving any French deserters he replied: 'Not upon a man from the colonel to the private in a regiment—both inclusive. We may pick up a marshal or two, perhaps; but not worth a damn.' But beneath the surface, the apparently imposing French army was irremediably and indeed fatally divided. For deep distrust stalked its splendid ranks. On the one hand, the 'old sweats' who had refused to serve under the Bourbons had little time for the turncoats who had chopped and changed in their allegiance: if it was one thing for Marshal Ney to behave in this way, it was quite another for ordinary officers and men. So the diehard Bonapartists regarded with both scorn and

Bourbons, so his appointment to command the left wing of the *Armée du Nord* came as a considerable surprise to many —not least himself. He only received his appointment on 15 June, and this fact, together with his 'shell-shocked' mental condition since the retreat from Russia in 1812, help explain his variable performance over the next three days. He mishandled Quatre Bras, failed to follow up Wellington's retreat promptly on the 17th, and was largely responsible for several fatal errors of judgement on the 18th itself. Courageous to a fault, this hot-headed 'soldier's soldier' vainly sought death on the battlefield, but fate was unkind. Instead, he faced a court martial of his peers on the orders of the Bourbon regime, and met his end bravely, his back to a wall, at the hands of a firing-squad in Paris

suspicion the units that had come from the Bourbon army, half expecting treachery. On the other hand, the former 'trimmers' loathed the superior airs and graces of the other half of the army, and secretly longed to see them cut down to size. This was potentially a serious morale problem, and indeed would prove the ultimate flaw in the *Armée du Nord* at the final crisis of the campaign, as we shall see. The rapier would ultimately prove too brittle for the strains put upon it.

Similarly, the army's weapons were not all of the highest quality. To re-equip the army at such short notice had strained the resources of France—and many muskets in particular were in need of repair or replacement. The supply organization was, as usual, behindhand and inadequate—an old failing. It was probably an awareness of these defects that helped dissuade Napoleon from attempting a protracted war of attrition in 1815.

The tactics of this army were also stale and stereotyped. As Wellington remarked after the battle: '... they have always

Drummers and bandsmen of the reconstituted *musique* of the *Garde Impériale* give a display at the *Ecole Militaire* in Paris, 1969. This institution had been the scene of Napoleon's officer-cadet training in 1784, and today is the Staff College of the French Army

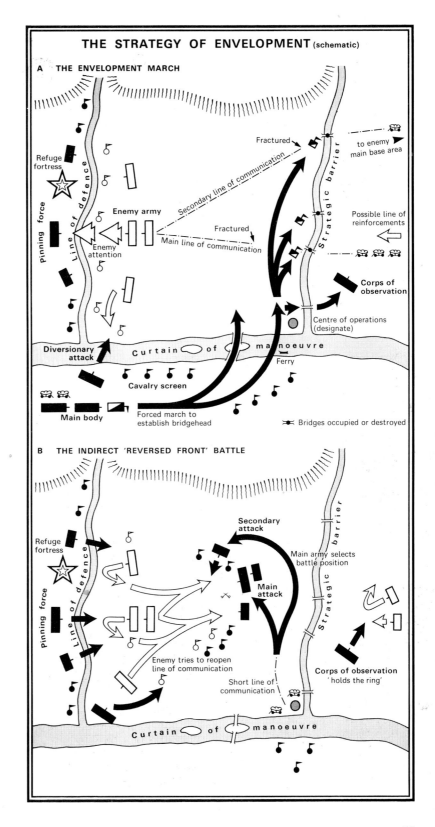

THE STRATEGY OF ENVELOPMENT (schematic)

A THE ENVELOPMENT MARCH

Refuge fortress

Pinning force

Line of defence

Enemy army

Enemy attention

Fractured

Secondary line of communication

Main line of communication

Fractured

Strategic barrier

to enemy main base area

Possible line of reinforcements

Corps of observation

Centre of operations (designate)

Diversionary attack

Curtain of manoeuvre

Ferry

Cavalry screen

Main body

Forced march to establish bridgehead

Bridges occupied or destroyed

B THE INDIRECT 'REVERSED FRONT' BATTLE

Refuge fortress

Pinning force

Line of defence

Secondary attack

Main army selects battle position

Main attack

Strategic barrier

Enemy tries to reopen line of communication

Short line of communication

Corps of observation 'holds the ring'

Curtain of manoeuvre

fought the same since I first saw them at Vimeiro.' On another occasion he stated that the French '. . . came on in the same old way and were repulsed in the same old way'. Thus the French had become very predictable at both the highest and lowest levels of military activity. In the strategic sense, Napoleon was known to favour '*la manoeuvre sur les derrières*', or sweeping envelopment, when he enjoyed a reasonable superiority of battle-power; alternatively, when outnumbered himself, his well-tried system of the manoeuvre based upon the central position, in which he sought to divide his opponents into parts and then to mass superior strength against each in turn to achieve a double victory, was also appreciated. Similarly, his battle plans tended to contain stereotyped features, whilst the tactical combination of skirmishers and troops in column, supported by cavalry and artillery, had varied hardly at all in twenty years. These facts did not make the French less redoubtable as individual opponents—and certainly nobody dared discount Napoleon's genius—but much of the old mystique and charisma had evaporated. Confidence born of knowledge of what the foe was likely to attempt probably lay behind Wellington's remark in early June: 'By God! I think Blücher and myself can do this business.' But it was to prove a 'near-run thing'.

Wellington's own command comprised many different nationalities, and British troops accounted for barely one-third of the whole. In early April only 14,000 had been available—mainly formations that had served under General Sir Thomas Graham, Lord Lynedoch, the previous year during the conquest of Holland and Belgium. Rapid steps had been taken to increase this force to more respectable proportions. The depots and county towns of England were emptied to find the necessary numbers, and not a few militiamen were persuaded to accept service in the line regiments. The Duke had demanded 15,000 cavalry, 40,000 infantry and 150 guns, but ultimately would only receive some 32,000 British troops in all, many of them far from being veterans except for the greater part of the Fifth Division, destined to be commanded by Sir Thomas Picton. Nevertheless some of his new formations were to prove of the finest mettle. These included the famous batteries of Sir Alexander Fraser's Royal Horse Artillery, a troop of which was under command of Captain Cavalié Mercer. On 8 April this officer received orders to take his men and guns from Colchester to Harwich, there to embark for Ostend, whence they had already been preceded by several battalions of the Guards. On

Lieutenant-General Sir Rowland Hill, first Viscount (1772–1842) by Salter. One of Wellington's most trusted subordinates during the Peninsular War, he was in command of the Allied II Corps in 1815. Nicknamed 'Daddy Hill', he was popular with the troops, and at Waterloo his men formed most of the right wing and extreme flank of the army. After Napoleon's second abdication he commanded the Army of Occupation in France. He subsequently became a full general (1825), and from 1825 until 1829 he was Commander-in-Chief in England

arrival there on 13 April, he found evidence of the new energy Wellington's arrival had infused into all parts of the services within one week of his taking over command. When Captain Hill, RN, began to supervise the hasty disembarkation of the unit with what appeared to be unseemly speed, he replied to Mercer's remonstrations: 'I can't help it, sir. The Duke's orders are positive that no delay is to take place in landing the troops as they arrive, and the ships sent back again. So you must be out of here before dark.' Another formation of great repute but little recent service were the North British Dragoons (or Scots Greys), who since 1801 had spent the wars serving in a quasi-military role in northern England in support of the civil power.

Indeed much of the British cavalry, and not a few militia-strengthened Regiments of Foot, were of unknown calibre. Lord Liverpool's government proved too slow in providing adequate resources for the Duke's taste. In his customary blunt way, on 9 May he described his command as '. . . an infamous army, very weak and ill-equipped, and very inexperienced staff. In my opinion they are doing nothing in England.' As for his senior officers, he was far from pleased with what he found awaiting him. The Prince of Orange's youthful inexperience has already been mentioned. Sir Hudson Lowe—destined to be Napoleon's jailer on St. Helena—was soon dismissed as a

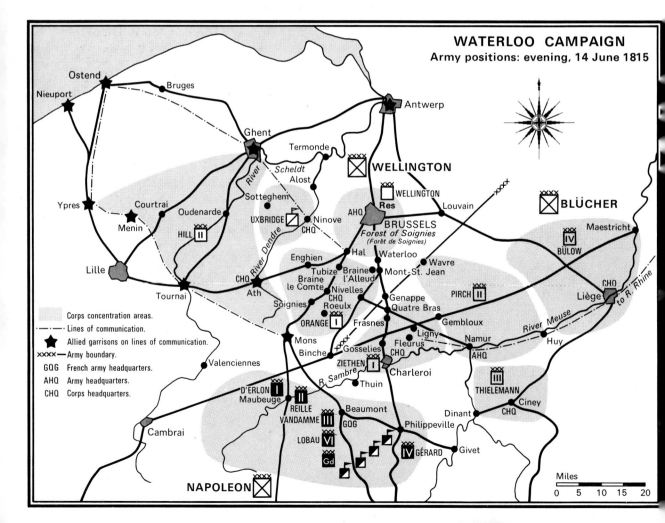

'damned old fool' by Wellington, who managed to have him replaced by Col. de Lancey as Quartermaster-General. The Horseguards made numerous questionable appointments to fill the vacancies in the higher echelons left by the absence of so many experienced officers in North America. To command the cavalry in Flanders they sent out Lord Uxbridge, for example, hardly a tactful appointment in view of his elopement with Lady Charlotte Wellesley, Wellington's sister-in-law, although in fact the Duke made light of the affair and Uxbridge would give him good service. However, to balance the inexperienced and the unsuitable officers were a number of generals well known and respected by the Duke, including Lord Hill and Sir Thomas Picton.

If the Duke had some reason to be doubtful about the quality of some of his British officers and men, he had even greater justification at looking critically at much of the remainder of his hybrid command. By mid-June, the 106,000 men that made up his 133 battalions, 109 squadrons and thirty-four batteries were nationally distributed as follows:

	Infantry	Cavalry	Artillery	(Guns)	Total
British troops	23,543	5,913	5,030	(102)	34,486
King's German Legion	3,301	2,560	526	(18)	6,387
Hanoverians	22,788	1,682	465	(12)	24,935
Brunswickers	5,376	922	510	(16)	6,808
Nassauers	2,880	—	—	—	2,880
Dutch & Belgian	24,174	3,405	1,635	(56)	29,214
Engineers, train & Staff Corps (British)....................		—	1,240	(12)	1,240
Totals:	82,062	14,482	9,406	(216)	105,950

Of these troops, many of the Dutch, Belgian and German detachments had until recently been allies or subjects of Napoleon, and consequently their loyalty was to some degree suspect, and this, together with the inexperience of many of the British troops, perhaps explains the Duke's unflattering description of his army already quoted. Several detachments, particularly the Dutch, were far below the strength that had been promised. Nevertheless, the Duke also declared he resolved to '. . . do the best I can with the instruments which have been sent to assist me'.

The deployment of these troops on the eve of campaign requires description. Some 13,000, of various nationalities and with twenty-six guns, were told to garrison Antwerp, Ypres,

Ghent, Tournai, Mons, Ath, Nieuport and Ostend, thus protecting the main Allied lines of communication running towards the English Channel and the Scheldt. The remaining 89,000 were divided into two corps, the cavalry and the reserve. The young Prince of Orange commanded I Corps from his headquarters at Braine-le-Comte; this consisted of two pairs of British and Dutch–Belgian divisions, commanded respectively by Generals Cooke, Alten, Perponcher-Slednitsky and Chassé, some cavalry and sixty-four guns—perhaps 31,500 men in all—scattered in cantonments stretching from Binche in the south to Soignies, Enghien and Nivelles. Even more spread out were the Allied troops of II Corps, commanded by General Hill, occupying a vast triangular sweep of territory from Mons in the south-east to Menin and Courtrai in the north-west and to the approaches of Ghent in the north, with headquarters situated at Ath. This force comprised three infantry divisions made up of British, Hanoverian and Dutch–Belgian troops under Generals Clinton, Colville and Stedman, a brigade of Hanoverian cavalry and forty cannon, totalling rather more than 27,000 men in all. Lord Uxbridge's cavalry reserve command—comprising two heavy and five light brigades (under Somerset and Ponsonby in the case of the former, and Vandeleur, Grant, Dornberg, Vivian and Arentschildt in those of the latter)—were massed, with thirty guns of the horse artillery, along both banks of the River Dendre, headquarters being at Ninove. The cavalry reserve mustered perhaps 11,800 sabres and horse gunners. Finally, in the immediate vicinity of Brussels, the site of General Headquarters, were disposed the forces of the General Reserve. There was talk of forming a third corps for the Duke of Richmond to command, but in the event this never materialized, and Wellington kept the Reserve under his own hand. It was made up of Anglo–Hanoverian divisions commanded by Picton and Cole, the Nassau contingent under Kruse, the Brunswicker detachments (both horse and foot) under their own Duke, and fifty-six guns—a force of 23,000 men. Such were the general dispositions of Wellington's Allied Army up to the evening of 14 June.

As well as being hybrid in respect of personnel, so was this army in terms of equipment. The British artillery, for example, mainly comprised 9- and 6-pounder guns with a number of $5\frac{1}{2}$-inch howitzers. Several of the Allied detachments, however, were still equipped with guns modelled along French lines, namely 4-, 6-, 8- and 12-pounders and a proportion of $6\frac{1}{2}$-inch Gribeauval howitzers. The Dutch and Belgians, for instance,

A selection of the 'Waterloo guns' on display at the Royal Military Academy, Sandhurst. TOP: the near gun is a British brass 6-pounder Horse Artillery piece; the further cannon is a British brass 9-pounder—the standard gun of the British Army in 1815. BELOW: a French bronze 12-pounder cannon, captured at Waterloo, sternly guards the Yorktown Gate. Nicknamed 'the Emperor's beautiful daughters', guns of this calibre formed part of the Great Battery, and were also attached to the Corps and the Artillery Reserve

had only 6-pounders. Similarly, some of the Allied infantry were armed with French '1777' model flintlock muskets, Prussian Potsdam weapons and a proportion of British 'Brown Besses', the standard weapon of the British line infantry with a .75 calibre and firing a one-ounce ball; but the British 95th (later the Rifle Brigade), and King's German Legion light formations were armed with the Baker Rifle, and some Hanoverian, Brunswicker and Nassauer units carried Jaeger-type hunting rifles. This profusion of weaponry complicated the ammunition and repair aspects of the logistical support of the Allied army.

Similarly, there was great variation in the organization and composition of formations in the Allied Army. The average size of a battalion was about 600 men, but a brigade might hold as few as two or as many as six battalions; cavalry brigades held two, three or four regiments of horse or dragoons, each of which might contain three or four squadrons. The British infantry fought in two-deep linear formations; many of their Allies in columns or four-deep lines, like the French. Thus there was an almost total lack of uniformity throughout Wellington's command; and his wisdom in brigading British and Allied formations into composite divisions would soon be convincingly demonstrated.

Blücher's Prussian army was more homogeneous in terms of nationality, but, as we have already mentioned, of largely untried mettle. It comprised four corps (designed after the French model) under immediate command, and one on detachment. To

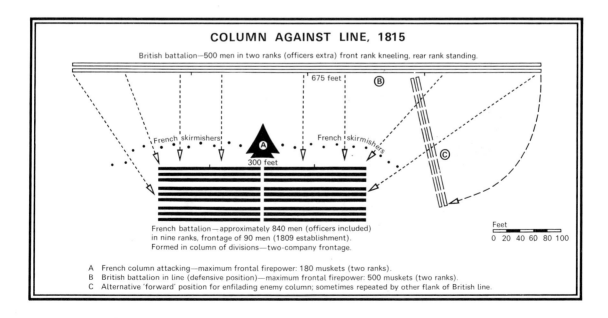

COLUMN AGAINST LINE, 1815

British battalion—500 men in two ranks (officers extra) front rank kneeling, rear rank standing.

675 feet

Ⓑ

French skirmishers   French skirmishers

Ⓐ

300 feet

Ⓒ

French battalion—approximately 840 men (officers included) in nine ranks, frontage of 90 men (1809 establishment). Formed in column of divisions—two-company frontage.

Feet
0 20 40 60 80 100

A French column attacking—maximum frontal firepower: 180 muskets (two ranks).
B British battalion in line (defensive position)—maximum frontal firepower: 500 muskets (two ranks).
C Alternative 'forward' position for enfilading enemy column; sometimes repeated by other flank of British line.

deal with the latter first (as it took scant part in the events which most concern us), General Kleist von Nollendorf commanded some 25,000 men in the vicinity of Luxemburg, serving in effect as a link between Blücher's main army and the more southerly Allied formations beginning to form on the Rhine. Turning to the main field army, I Corps, under Lieut.-General Hans Ernst Karl, Graf von Ziethen, was holding a sector close to the Sambre, with its headquarters in Charleroi. This formation, some 32,500 strong, was thus placed directly in line with Napoleon's intended blow, and would accordingly take the brunt of the initial fighting. It comprised four 'brigades' (see below), commanded by von Steinmetz, von Pirch II, von Jägow, and von Donnersmarck, controlling between them some thirty-four battalions or 27,887 infantry. They were supported by Major-General von Röder's two brigades of cavalry—thirty-two squadrons, amounting to almost 2,000 cavalry men in all. The attached artillery—a dozen batteries or ninety-six guns in all—was under Colonel Lehmann, and together with two companies of engineers made up a force of 1,220 men.

Immediately in rear of this major formation was stationed the Prussian II Corps, under Major-General George Ludwig von Pirch I, which was some 33,000 men strong, occupied an area from Wavre in the north to Hannut and Huy in the east, and had its headquarters at Namur at the confluence of the rivers Meuse and Sambre. It comprised four infantry 'brigades', led by von Tippelskirch, von Krafft, von Brause and von Bose (other accounts say Langen) respectively. Amounting to thirty-two battalions, it held some 27,000 infantry, besides 4,500 cavalry (thirty-six squadrons) under Major-General von Wahlen-Jürgass and 1,600 men in Colonel von Röhl's ten batteries (eighty guns) and two sapper companies. Still further east stood General Friedrich Wilhelm Count Bülow von Dennewitz's IV Corps, some 32,000 men strong, grouped around headquarters established at Liège. Like the other corps, it comprised four 'brigades' (von Hacke, von Ryssel, von Losthin and von Hiller), Prince William of Prussia's cavalry, and Major von Bardeleben's eleven batteries of guns. The infantry component of thirty-six battalions made up 27,500 men, the forty-three squadrons comprised 3,300 cavalry, and the gunners and engineers totalled 2,000 men.

Lastly, situated to the south of II Corps with headquarters at Ciney, was Lieut.-General Johann Adolf Freiherr von Thiele-mann's III Corps, some 25,000 men strong. Its four 'brigades' were commanded by von Borcke, von Kampfen, von Luck and von Stülpnagel and held about 21,000 infantry in thirty battalions. Its twenty-four squadrons of cavalry under Major-General von Hobe numbered 2,400 sabres; its six batteries of artillery (forty-eight guns) and two companies of engineers added a further 1,100 men. The strength of III Corps was considerably less than that of the others, and, like IV Corps, a large proportion of its formations were *Landwehr* (or militia).

The Prussian army contained a number of special features. First, its staff organizations were very economical in contrast to those of the French. The Army Headquarters amounted to only fifty-eight officers, and Major-General von Grölmann, the chief of the general staff (not to be confused with von Gneisenau, who was Quartermaster General and chief-of-staff to Blücher), was aided by only six officers. At corps level the staff consisted of perhaps twenty officers, and at 'brigade' level only of five. Next, the term 'brigade' needs definition. It will have been noticed that there has been no mention of Prussian 'divisions' in the above paragraphs. In fact, the Prussian 'brigade' was the equivalent of a French division, containing on average three infantry regiments, each of which was made up of three battalions. Each of the battalions had a strength of about 730 men, divided between four companies. The Prussians also organized their cavalry into these so-called 'brigades'. They habitually attached two squadrons to each infantry 'brigade', and retained the remainder in a divisional role. As for their guns, the great majority were 6-pounders with a sprinkling of 12-pounders and a small proportion of howitzers. It is also noticeable that the Prussians did not retain a force of cavalry and guns to serve as an Army reserve; all their resources were deployed in the corps. This constituted a grave weakness in their otherwise very well-organized army. They were also short of heavy cavalry and gunners.

As for Prussian equipment, much of it was of French pattern, and a considerable further amount was of British origin. Many stands of muskets and thousands of shakos and other equipment were supplied by Great Britain from 1813 onwards. The Prussian army also contained a large number of middle-class volunteer *Jäger* units and militia-type peasant-based *Landwehr* formations. These were built around cadres of experienced officers and NCOs, but the ranks contained many boys of less than seventeen or older men of over forty-five. Thus in 1815 the four corps we have described above contained a total of twenty-six regular infantry units and twenty-two *Landwehr* regiments. As might be expected, many of the latter tended to be under-equipped, and were often short of rations, clothing and even shoes. In the cavalry the proportion of recently raised formations was even higher—only twenty-two out of forty-nine regiments being regulars. As for tactics, the Prussians had largely modelled their ideas on French lines since 1807, fighting in columns and light infantry screens rather than in lines. The army's discipline was far inferior to the draconian standard demanded by Frederick the Great in the middle years of the previous century and earned a bad reputation for looting. It was very much of a national, people's army, led by the local aristocracy and squirearchy rather than the great nobles, and presented a great contrast with the 'walking muskets' of the pre-1806 army. Great reforms had been carried out following the double cataclysm of Jena–Auerstädt in late 1806, and between them Stein and von Scharnhorst had wrought a total transformation, creating a system of reservists which enabled them to build up a reservoir of reasonably trained troops without breaking the letter of the size restrictions imposed by France in 1807. In early 1813 Prussia deserted the unpopular French Alliance and declared war.

Although the Prussian army of 1815 contained a high proportion of conscripts and recalled reservists, and although its overall standards of discipline, experience and training left something to be desired, there was no denying the generally high level of morale that pervaded its ranks. This was partly the product of the considerable successes won by Prussian arms at such battles as Dennewitz and Leipzig, and partly due to the warm admiration and even affection felt by the men in the ranks for '*Alte Vorwärts*'. 'Father Blücher' would habitually address them as his *Kinder*, or 'children', but this is not to imply that the Prussian army was unduly soft or paternalistic. Its leaders could be ruthless and overbearing, and new recruits were very roughly treated in order to lick them into some sort of battle-worthiness. But the army had a spirit born of a firm patriotic loyalty to King Frederick William III leavened by the spread of more liberal ideas than had been permitted in eighteenth-century Prussia. How well it could fight will be discovered in later pages.

Chapter Four

The Campaign Opens

At 2.30 a.m. on 15 June, the French troops around Beaumont were roused from their bivouacs. As the formations began to fall into their pre-arranged positions, ready to take to the roads leading over the frontier, twelve regiments of cavalry jingled and clattered off through the darkness to form the spearhead of the invasion of Belgian soil. The critical phase of the campaign of Waterloo had begun.

In earlier chapters we have described both Napoleon and the *Armée du Nord* he was now about to lead into action, and also his broad intentions. Now it is necessary to examine his plan in rather more detail, and to describe the strategic method upon which it was based. First let us look at the principles—then at the example.

The campaign of 1815 was based upon Napoleon's 'Strategy of the Central Position'. This method was far from new—indeed, as far back as April 1796 he had based the initial phase of his very first campaign as commander-in-chief upon the same principles he was now about to re-employ. It was a method designed to make the most of surprise, speed and carefully co-ordinated manoeuvre to offset the disadvantages of facing numerically superior opponents. As always with Napoleonic warfare, whether he was outnumbered or not the Emperor insisted on boldly seizing the initiative from the outset. In 1796 he had been badly placed with his back to the Mediterranean, clinging on to the narrow plain of the Ligurian coast, facing two enemy armies—the Piedmontese and the Austrian—who between them enjoyed a substantial advantage in strength and were, moreover, in possession of all the high ground of the coastal mountain ranges. Now, in 1815, Napoleon was not so disadvantageously placed in geographical terms: instead of an active and hostile Royal Navy operating behind him, he was backed by his own country, and there certainly were no mountains over the Belgian frontier. On the other hand, there was no denying his numerical disadvantage: between them, Wellington and Blücher commanded in the field (ignoring garrisons and such distant detachments as Kleist's Corps) all of 210,000 men supported by almost 500 field guns. Napoleon could at best only deploy a total of 128,000 men and 366 guns.

To fight a united Allied and Prussian army would therefore be to court disaster, just as it would have been to take on Colli's 25,000 and Beaulieu's 22,000 with the 37,600 French troops of the Army of Italy on a single battlefield nineteen years earlier. But Napoleon, from his study of military history, had devised a method of solving this problem—or rather he had borrowed a concept which had been known to able leaders from Caesar to Frederick, and breathed a new ruthless energy and sense of purpose into its application. In the simplest terms, his 'inferiority' strategy was based on the ancient Roman adage, *divide et impera*—'Divide and rule'.

The Strategy of the Central Position was designed to place the French army (smaller in overall terms) in such a position that it could fight and defeat smaller or larger detachments of the enemy *in turn*, with sufficient local French superiority to ensure success on each successive battlefield. This was easier to attempt than to achieve, but Napoleon's practical genius and computer-like mind were ideally suited to accepting this type of challenge—one which would have daunted most commanders of his day. To have a chance of success, two prerequisites were vital: surprise and security. If the foe was to guess his intention, he could mass his forces before the blow fell and present a united front to Napoleon's onslaught. The French attack therefore had to be launched without affording the enemy warning; it was equally important that he should have no accurate idea of the number of French troops opposing him. Napoleon therefore had to mass his force in secret, and then choose the right time and place to attack. To judge the latter imponderables correctly, he relied on good information and military intelligence—spies, patrols and intercepted enemy letters and despatches. To secure his own army's safety during the vital pre-action moves, he depended upon the effective use of natural cover—mountain ranges, river lines or forests—supplemented by a moving screen of cavalry serving to delude the foe into expecting attacks from what would prove to be irrelevant quarters.

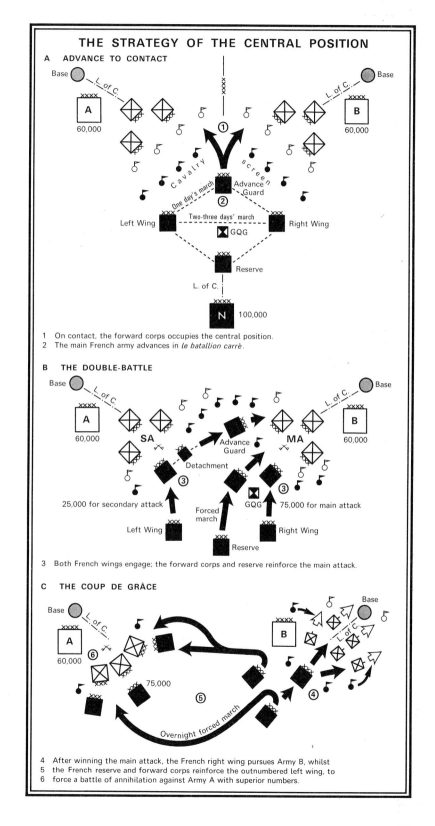

THE STRATEGY OF THE CENTRAL POSITION

A ADVANCE TO CONTACT

Base

A
60,000

Base

B
60,000

Cavalry screen

Advance Guard
②

One day's march

Left Wing

Two-three days' march

GQG

Right Wing

Reserve

L. of C.

N 100,000

1 On contact, the forward corps occupies the central position.
2 The main French army advances in *le batallion carrè*.

B THE DOUBLE-BATTLE

Base

A
60,000

Base

B
60,000

SA

Advance Guard

MA

Detachment

③

③

25,000 for secondary attack

GQG 75,000 for main attack

Left Wing

Forced march

Right Wing

Reserve

3 Both French wings engage; the forward corps and reserve reinforce the main attack.

C THE COUP DE GRÂCE

Base

A
60,000

Base

B

⑥

75,000

⑤

④

Overnight forced march

4 After winning the main attack, the French right wing pursues Army B, whilst
5 the French reserve and forward corps reinforce the outnumbered left wing, to
6 force a battle of annihilation against Army A with superior numbers.

Napoleon's aim then, in this type of operation, was to seize and exploit the initiative from the beginning in order to occupy the central position between the various components of his enemy's force, from which he could set out to defeat him in detail. To achieve this required a careful orchestration of all moves and operations. The French army, in such a campaign, would usually be organized into a forward cavalry screen (serving as an advance guard), two wings (each comprising several corps all within supporting distance of one another) and a reserve held a little way to the rear of the rest. The role of the cavalry was to probe ahead, and eventually to locate and report back to headquarters the exact positions of the enemy's major forces. As soon as these were plotted on the map, the Emperor would order each of his wing commanders to engage the nearest enemy force, heedless of the odds they might initially be accepting. Thus two engagements would begin, often miles apart.

To understand what was to follow, it is necessary to appreciate the versatility and toughness of the French *corps d'armée*, which

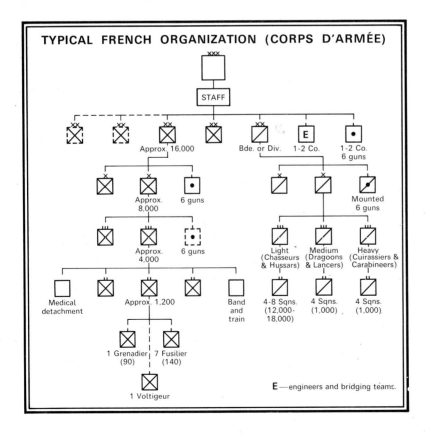

may be described as Napoleon's 'secret weapon'. Although individual corps varied in size enormously, they all shared one thing in common: each was a balanced, all-arm force of infantry, cavalry and guns, equipped with trains and a staff—in fact a miniature army. Heedless of numerical disadvantage, therefore, such forces, acting alone or in concert, could take on several times their own number for a limited period. As Napoleon wrote to his stepson Eugène de Beauharnais, in 1809, '. . . a corps of 25,000–30,000 men can be left on its own. Well handled it can fight or alternatively avoid action . . . an opponent cannot force it to accept an engagement, but if it chooses to do so it can fight alone for a long time.' Here was a major secret of Napoleon's warcraft: he could use these self-reliant corps to pin down larger numbers of opponents whilst the master used his remaining forces to plot and encompass their doom. *Corps d'armée* could therefore be left to move on their own, greatly easing the traffic on any particular set of roads and also facilitating 'living off the countryside' by spreading the logistical load over a wide area. This was one way in which the French managed to move so fast on campaign.

The central importance of the *corps d'armée* system to the strategy of the Central Position now becomes easier to understand. Napoleon, having made firm contact with the surprised foe, could use a mere part of his total force to tie down and occupy the attention of each enemy force, however powerful. Then, still retaining the initiative, he could move his reserve, and if necessary part of a wing, to build up a local superiority on one battlefield or the other. Then, after defeating the first foe, Napoleon would leave a small force to pursue the survivors and counter-march with the remainder and the reserve to repeat the process on the second battlefield. Of course, correct timing was essential. If too long elapsed before the reserve could reach the second battlefield, the embattled French pinning force might well go under, and the victorious foe swing forward to envelop the French rear. But Napoleon calculated that providing he could reinforce his detachment commander within twenty-four hours of the battle's opening, all would be well.

This method had been used in various combinations in many a campaign since 1796. That it was what he was attempting in 1815 cannot be doubted. Not only have we the historical facts to show it, we also for once have documentary evidence. Writing to Ney on the 16th, the second day of the campaign, Napoleon stated the following: 'For this campaign I have adopted the following general principle—to divide my army

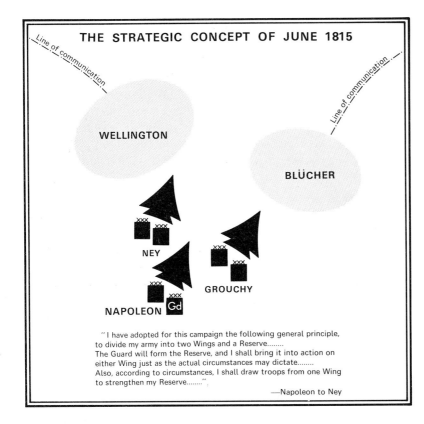

THE STRATEGIC CONCEPT OF JUNE 1815

Line of communication

Line of communication

WELLINGTON

BLÜCHER

NEY

GROUCHY

NAPOLEON Gd

"I have adopted for this campaign the following general principle, to divide my army into two Wings and a Reserve........
The Guard will form the Reserve, and I shall bring it into action on either Wing just as the actual circumstances may dictate........
Also, according to circumstances, I shall draw troops from one Wing to strengthen my Reserve........"

—Napoleon to Ney

into two wings and a reserve. The Guard will form the Reserve, and I shall bring it into action on either wing just as the actual circumstances may dictate. Also, according to circumstances, I shall draw troops from one wing to strengthen my reserve.' Here, in three brief sentences, lies the French plan of campaign for 1815. Unfortunately for the French, however, the enemies on this occasion would eventually become fully aware of what Napoleon was attempting. Familiarity breeds contempt and, in the realms of strategy, produces military counter-ploys and antidotes. Nevertheless, as we shall see, the Emperor came within a hairsbreadth of bringing off a major success by using this system. It might not be exactly new, but it was being operated by a great master of strategy.

We must now relate this theoretical plan to the exact circumstances of June 1815 on the French north-eastern frontiers. Napoleon, as we have seen, was facing two enemy armies, separately inferior to the *Armée du Nord*, but far superior when combined. Obligingly, however, the Allies had drawn their respective armies up in two separate areas—partly for logistical reasons, partly to cover as much of Belgium as possible. Furthermore, the component parts of each army were spread over a considerable area. All this Napoleon knew, so good was his military intelligence based upon the numerous secret French supporters living in every Belgian town and village. He knew that the inter-army boundary ran from west of Charleroi away to the north-east: here, then, lay the 'Central Position'. Even more important, he knew that the Allies had built up two *divergent* lines of communication and supply—those of Wellington stretching west towards Ostend and the Channel coast, those of Blücher to the east, towards Liège and the distant Rhine—the direction of Prussia.

From this information, his staff built up certain deductions and calculations. First, that each enemy army would need at least a dozen hours to complete its concentration, so scattered were the various components. Second, that it was likely to take all of three days for the two Allied forces to mass in a single body. And third, that a drubbing meted out to either opponent was almost certain to widen the distance between them, rather than induce them to move closer together, because the natural course of action for the defeated commander would be to retreat along his lines of communication to seek the reinforcements and safety of his bases. Thus, if Napoleon could gain sufficient time at the start of his offensive, his foes would never be afforded time to mass their superior forces—or to recover from the blows he inflicted.

And so the plan emerged, designed to exploit the known details of the enemy dispositions and to make the very most of the primordial elements of Napoleonic warfare—namely surprise and speed. First, the massed *Armée du Nord* was to secure a crossing over the Sambre and establish a bridgehead around Charleroi, Thuin and Châtelet. Next it was to advance along two axes—the French left wing under Ney towards Frasnes and Quatre Bras, their right under Grouchy towards Fleurus and Sombreffe. Napoleon would thus drive a wedge between the two Allied armies by seizing the area linking their respective areas of responsibility, and by keeping his reserve massed near Charleroi he would be in a position to reinforce either of his wing commanders to battle-winning strength whichever foe first presented himself. The Emperor expected that this was more likely to be Blücher, whose 'hussar complex' he was determined to exploit, for he deemed Wellington to be both more cautious and slower in movement. Next, the French would take possession of the significant lateral road, running through Quatre Bras towards Sombreffe: this highway in French hands would

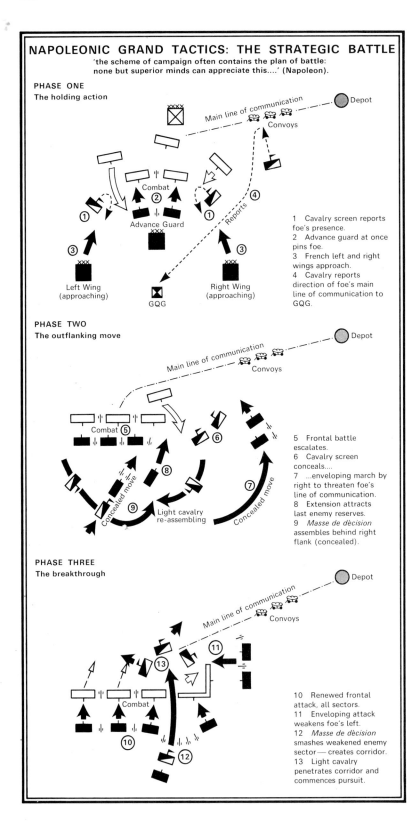

NAPOLEONIC GRAND TACTICS: THE STRATEGIC BATTLE

'the scheme of campaign often contains the plan of battle:
none but superior minds can appreciate this....' (Napoleon).

PHASE ONE
The holding action

Main line of communication

Depot

Convoys

Reports

Combat

Advance Guard

1

2

1

4

3

3

Left Wing
(approaching)

Right Wing
(approaching)

GQG

1 Cavalry screen reports
foe's presence.
2 Advance guard at once
pins foe.
3 French left and right
wings approach.
4 Cavalry reports
direction of foe's main
line of communication to
GQG.

PHASE TWO
The outflanking move

Main line of communication

Depot

Convoys

Combat 5

6

8

7

9

Concealed move

Concealed move

Light cavalry
re-assembling

5 Frontal battle
escalates.
6 Cavalry screen
conceals....
7 ...enveloping march by
right to threaten foe's
line of communication.
8 Extension attracts
last enemy reserves.
9 *Masse de décision*
assembles behind right
flank (concealed).

PHASE THREE
The breakthrough

Main line of communication

Depot

Convoys

11

13

Combat

10

12

10 Renewed frontal
attack, all sectors.
11 Enveloping attack
weakens foe's left.
12 *Masse de décision*
smashes weakened enemy
sector — creates corridor.
13 Light cavalry
penetrates corridor and
commences pursuit.

greatly assist co-operation between the French left and right wings: even more important, its denial to the Allies would severely curtail the ability of Wellington to aid Blücher, or *vice versa*—their only means of inter-communication would be back through Brussels, by way of the dense Forest of Soignies and then through the very broken and badly roaded terrain leading through Wavre towards Fleurus and the neighbouring hamlet of Ligny. Next would occur the two battles, which would result, if Napoleon's calculations proved correct, in the repulse of one foe and the near destruction of the second, and the subsequent French triumphal entry into Brussels.

Much, of course, depended on achieving initial surprise and in fooling the enemy into false deductions about the French threat. But Napoleon was a past-master at such schemes. He gave the most positive orders to his subordinates that all the eastern frontiers of France were to be sealed: no travellers were to cross, fishing boats sail or couriers ride: the mail was to be stopped: all this from 7 June. Under cover of this blackout, the French corps could mass around Beaumont, their original places being taken by the unobtrusive substitution of National Guard units. Next, the garrisons of Lille and Dunkirk were to make aggressive moves towards the frontier as if presaging a major onslaught designed to isolate Wellington from Ostend and thus from distant England. Ideally, this would induce the Duke to draw off westwards, thus widening the interval dividing him from Blücher—and it was occupation of that gap and the 'central position' it represented that was Napoleon's first strategic priority once his real movement began.

And so the final moves prior to the attack began. They proved brilliantly successful. The Emperor and the Guard reached Beaumont on the 14th without any clear indication of what was planned reaching the Allies beyond the frontier. On the night of 13 June Prussian patrols reported a mass of camp-fires burning around Beaumont, but Ziethen at Charleroi took scant heed, ordering only local precautions. As for Wellington, he spent the 13th attending a cricket match with a fair companion, sixteen-year-old Lady Jane Lennox. The next day brought nothing but rumours to Allied ears—and even on the 15th, when the French attack began, it would be only at 3 p.m., nine hours after the first blatant moves over the frontier, that Wellington learnt that Ziethen had been attacked near Thuin. Thus the campaign would get off to a brilliant strategic start, and Napoleon would acquire a great strategic advantage almost before the first shot had been fired.

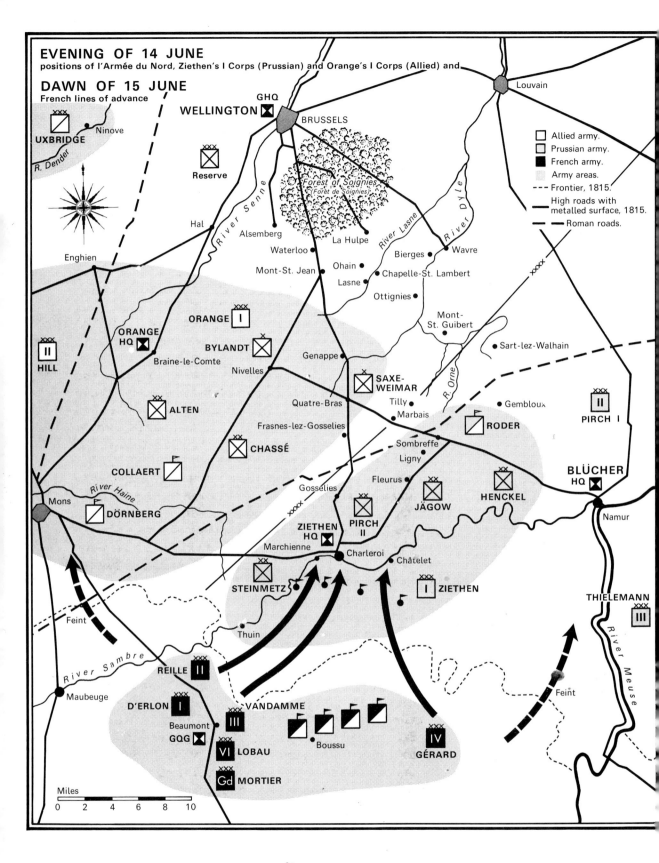

EVENING OF 14 JUNE

positions of l'Armée du Nord, Ziethen's I Corps (Prussian) and Orange's I Corps (Allied) and

DAWN OF 15 JUNE

French lines of advance

UXBRIDGE
Ninove

R. Dender

WELLINGTON GHQ
BRUSSELS
Reserve

Forest of Soignies
(Forêt de Soignies)

☐ Allied army.
☐ Prussian army.
■ French army.
Army areas.
--- Frontier, 1815.
━━ High roads with metalled surface, 1815.
━━ Roman roads.

Hal
Alsemberg
Waterloo
La Hulpe
Bierges Wavre
Mont-St. Jean
Ohain
Lasne Chapelle-St. Lambert
Ottignies

Enghien

River Senne

River Lasne

River Dyle

ORANGE I

BYLANDT

ORANGE HQ
Braine-le-Comte

HILL

Genappe
Nivelles

SAXE-WEIMAR

Mont-St. Guibert

Sart-lez-Walhain

PIRCH I

ALTEN
Quatre-Bras
Tilly
Marbais

R. Orne

Gembloux

CHASSÉ
Frasnes-lez-Gosselies

RODER

COLLAERT
Gosselies

Sombreffe
Ligny
Fleurus

JÄGOW

HENCKEL

BLÜCHER HQ

Mons
River Haine
DÖRNBERG

PIRCH II

ZIETHEN HQ

Namur

Marchienne
Charleroi
Châtelet

THIELEMANN

STEINMETZ

I ZIETHEN

River Meuse

Feint

Thuin

REILLE II

D'ERLON I

Maubeuge

VANDAMME

Feint

Beaumont
GQG

III

Boussu

GÉRARD IV

VI LOBAU

Gd MORTIER

Miles
0 2 4 6 8 10

80

General Maurice Etienne Gérard, Count of the Empire (1773–1852) An experienced divisional and corps commander, he resented being placed under Grouchy's orders in June 1815. He fought well at Ligny, but on the 18th his tactless demands that his superior should abandon the Wavre operations and 'march on the sound of the cannon' to the west only hardened Marshal Grouchy's determination to execute to the letter his last-received orders from Napoleon—namely to attack the Prussians to his front. Gérard was severely wounded at the head of his IV Corps at Limale near Wavre. He survived, and years later was made a Marshal of France

In actual fact, however, the French offensive did not get off to quite as successful a start at the tactical level early on the 15th, despite these brilliant preliminaries. The initial movement of Reille, d'Erlon and the massed cavalry of the designated left wing towards Thuin and Marchienne, and that of Vandamme, Gérard, Lobau and the Guard towards Charleroi, was hampered by considerable confusion and delay. Vandamme's Corps was a little late taking to the road owing to a delayed order, and as a result Lobau's VI Corps ran into its bivouacs, and it took time to extricate the two formations. To try and clear the log-jam, Napoleon ordered Gérard to march his Corps to cross the Sambre at Châtelet. But the situation at Charleroi was far from the Emperor's liking. According to the plan, Vandamme's III Corps was supposed to be in the outskirts by 10 a.m., but in the event his leading units only made an appearance at 3 p.m. This meant that for most of the morning the only troops fighting the Prussians were Pajol's cavalry of the forward screen, but at 11 a.m. Napoleon appeared in person at the head of part of the Guard and soon after Ziethen decided to obey his contingency orders and fall back towards Fleurus. It was indeed fortunate for the French that the Prussians did not destroy the Sambre bridges in the process, and that there were not more men close at hand to contest the crossing.

The same pattern of delay and confusion was repeated elsewhere. Gérard reached Châtelet safely, only to have the commander of his leading division, General Bourmont, desert to join the Prussians, which caused his troops considerable dismay. Similarly, although Reille's Corps was the only formation to reach its deadline exactly at the prescribed time, the Prussian force defending Marchienne put up such a staunch defence that it was only firmly in French possession by midday, and further tough fighting took place around Gosselies as General Steinmetz fell back.

Despite these complications and disappointments, there was no denying that Napoleon had scored a substantial strategic surprise. Of course Ziethen, with Bourmont to help fill in the details, hastened to inform Blücher at Namur of what appeared to be afoot, but valuable time was already lost. Nevertheless Blücher at once ordered his II, III and IV Corps to concentrate forward on Sombreffe—and reached that place in person at 4 p.m., but in itself this was a very dangerous move given the proximity of Napoleon's main force and the time it would take for the furthermost Prussian formations to reach the scene. I Corps, for example, received a very vague order from Gneisenau.

As for Wellington, when he at last heard that an attack had been made at Thuin, he complied with Napoleon's wishes to an extent the Emperor could never have hoped for. Completely deluded by the apparent threat to his links with Ostend and the Channel, the first orders Wellington issued that afternoon (he had heard nothing from Blücher) were for the Allies to take up prearranged positions and in the process to draw off some little way to the *south* and *west* of Brussels—that is *away* from the true crisis point—rather than towards the inner flank from which they could have assisted the Prussians. Thus in the very first round of the contest the Allies committed two major blunders of judgement. Normally, one enemy error was all that Napoleon required.

It was only at 3.30 p.m. that Marshal Ney arrived at the front, as the army strove to consolidate its position on both banks of the Sambre. Napoleon hastened to appoint him to command the left wing, namely I and II Corps, and Lefebvre-Desnouëtte's cavalry of the Guard, with orders to advance up the Charleroi to Brussels highway forthwith. Marshal Grouchy was similarly ordered to head for Sombreffe on the road to Fleurus, his right wing consisting of III and IV Corps and more cavalry. The Army Reserve, namely VI Corps and the Imperial Guard, was to close up around Charleroi once Grouchy's wing was clear of its streets. There is no evidence one way or the other to demonstrate whether Napoleon specifically mentioned the desirability of Ney's reaching Quatre Bras that evening, but the Order of the Day issued later that night claimed that Ney '. . . this very evening established his headquarters at Quatre-Chemins on the Brussels road'.

First let us describe what befell the right wing's advance. Initially, it did not make very fast progress. Of course it was facing the main body of Ziethen's retiring Prussians, and Grouchy was not accustomed to his new role, but so frustrated did the Emperor become with the slow progress on this wing that he rode forward in person to infuse a little more life into operations at about 5.30 p.m., joining Grouchy near Gilly. An immediate improvement became manifest, and by last light III Corps had fought its way into the outskirts of Fleurus, whereupon a halt was called for the night. Thus the right wing had covered some nineteen miles during the 15th.

Meanwhile, Marshal Ney was also pressing ahead up the Brussels road, several miles to the west of Grouchy's line of advance. Initially the French left wing made considerably faster progress than its neighbour, and cleared the last Prussians out of Gosselies by late afternoon. Then its impetus died away. Lefebvre-Desnouëttes' cavalry probed ahead towards the small village of Frasnes, and when just short of the village it came under fire from infantry outposts, which retired through the houses. The cautiously following cavalry then suddenly came under fire from eight cannon drawn up beyond. Their commander pulled back, and referred to higher authority for further orders and reinforcements. An infantry battalion was sent forward to join the cavalry, but it could see little because of the high standing corn near Frasnes and the failing light of evening. Ney, mindful of Wellington's trick of concealing his troops, decided to play safe, and ordered his men to bivouac for the night at about 8 p.m. His force had covered over twenty-two miles during the day and were weary. Thus both wings of the *Armée du Nord* suspended operations for the night, being linked by a force of cavalry at Heppignies and Girard's division of II Corps at Wangenies.

About 9 p.m. Napoleon rode back to Charleroi to spend the night there. In overall terms, he had some reason for satisfaction with the way affairs had worked out during the day after the chaotic opening. It was true that no final objective had been taken, but his army was well and truly in possession of the Central Position, and he had news that Blücher's main force was still obligingly advancing towards Sombreffe—straight into the arms of the waiting French.

Unbeknown to either Napoleon or Ney, a far more important prize—namely Quatre Bras and with it control of the lateral road—had also been theirs for the taking. Indeed, the Emperor may have been under the impression for the earlier part of the night that Ney was in possession of this critical point. However, as we have seen, the Prince of the Moskowa had halted his advance at Frasnes, some two miles short of the objective, convinced that he faced a substantial force of opponents.

Nothing, in fact, could have been further from the truth. The entire force that Ney's imposing column of almost 50,000 men had run into near Frasnes totalled just 4,000 infantry and a single battery of eight guns. That this numerically insignificant force was present at all was not due to any foresight or volition on the part of the Duke of Wellington. Indeed, Prince Bernard of Saxe-Weimar, commanding this isolated brigade of Nassauers, was acting in direct contravention of the latest orders when he decided to hold his ground and offer opposition to the French cavalry, after drawing back from Frasnes to about one kilometre south of Quatre Bras. In this act of intelligent disobedience he

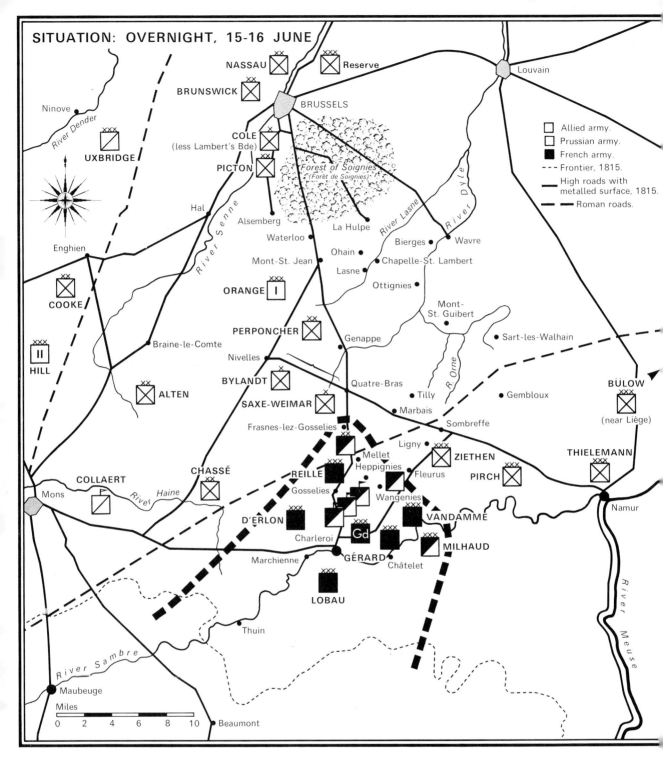

SITUATION: OVERNIGHT, 15-16 JUNE

Allied army.
Prussian army.
French army.
– – – Frontier, 1815.
––––– High roads with metalled surface, 1815.
▪ ▪ ▪ Roman roads.

Ninove
River Dender
UXBRIDGE
Enghien
COOKE
HILL
Hal
Braine-le-Comte
Nivelles
BYLANDT
ALTEN
SAXE-WEIMAR
Frasnes-lez-Gosselies
CHASSÉ
Mons
COLLAERT
River Haine
D'ERLON
Charleroi
Marchienne
Gosselies
REILLE
Mellet
Heppignies
Gd
GÉRARD
Châtelet
LOBAU
Thuin
River Sambre
Maubeuge
Miles
0 2 4 6 8 10
Beaumont

NASSAU
Reserve
BRUNSWICK
BRUSSELS
Louvain
COLE
(less Lambert's Bde)
PICTON
Forest of Soignies
(Forêt de Soignies)
River Dyle
Alsemberg
Waterloo
Mont-St. Jean
ORANGE I
PERPONCHER
Genappe
La Hulpe
Ohain
Lasne
River Lasne
Bierges
Wavre
Chapelle-St. Lambert
Ottignies
Mont-
St. Guibert
Sart-les-Walhain
Quatre-Bras
Tilly
Marbais
Sombreffe
Ligny
ZIETHEN
Fleurus
PIRCH
Wangenies
VANDAMME
MILHAUD
Gembloux
R. Orne
BÜLOW
(near Liège)
THIELEMANN
Namur
River Meuse

was not entirely alone. The Prince of Orange's chief-of-staff, General Constant de Rebecque, had been responsible for the original placing of Saxe-Weimar, earlier in the afternoon. As soon as he learnt of the engagement opening, he authorized

General Bylandt's Brigade to move off to support the Nassauers. At this juncture, Wellington's afternoon order arrived, which instructed the whole of General Perponcher-Sedlnitzberg's Division (of which the two brigades already mentioned were the major components) to concentrate at once at Nivelles—almost nine miles away from Quatre Bras. The chief-of-staff and divisional commander thereupon decided on the bold course of ignoring this instruction on the grounds that they were in possession of information not available to the Allied commander-in-chief. So Saxe-Weimar was ordered to hold his ground, and Bylandt told to move to his assistance. This decision was the fulcrum on which much of the outcome of the whole campaign would hinge, as later events would soon prove.

By this time Brussels was full of rumours and considerable disquiet. Wellington decided to try to calm the incipient panic by attending a ball given by the Duchess of Richmond. Before leaving for this social engagement, at 9 p.m. he at last received a message from Blücher indicating that the Prussians were marching on Sombreffe and another from Dornberg reporting that all was quiet around Mons. An hour later, the Duke adjusted the gist of his orders of the afternoon, ordering a movement towards the inner flank, and alerting the Reserve to be ready to move to Mont-St. Jean the next morning. But he still knew nothing of what had transpired south of Quatre Bras, and still suspected that the main French line of attack would prove to be well to the west. However, it was not long before he would realize the mistake he was labouring under—and its gravity. At the height of the ball, an urgent message was brought to the Duke early on the 16th. For twenty minutes he remained amidst the *monde*, and then made as if to leave for bed. As he wished his host goodnight he '. . . whispered to ask him if he had a good map in the house. The Duke of Richmond said that he had, and took him into his dressing room. . . . . The Duke of Wellington shut the door and said: "Napoleon has humbugged me, by God! He has gained twenty-four hours' march on me." The Duke of Richmond said, "What do you intend doing?" The Duke of Wellington replied: "I have ordered the army to concentrate at Quatre Bras; but we shall not stop him there, and if so, I must fight him here" (at the same time passing his thumb-nail over the position of Waterloo).'

The cat was now out of the bag. Soon a further set of orders was being rushed through the night to the major formations, reinforcing their earlier instructions and demanding that they conduct a forced march towards the inner flank—and Quatre

Bras. But Wellington was aware that his troops might arrive too late to stop the French left wing: some units were already so distant as to be incapable of coming up before the evening of the 16th. A very great deal therefore depended on the events of the next morning. If Ney bestirred himself in reasonable time, and made a serious probe towards Quatre Bras, he would realize the bluff constituted by Saxe-Weimar and the remainder of Perponcher-Sedlnitzberg's Division. Then Wellington's main reinforcements would arrive too late to save the day. It would be a race against time. The bugles blared in the streets of Brussels, and by dawn the Reserve was marching south, followed by the Duke and his staff at about 7.30 a.m.

Intelligence of the Battle of Ligny by J. C. Stadler. In fact the Duke played it very cool, for he was determined to avoid a panic of the type the imaginative artist portrays here, with Wellington striking heroic and manly poses while the ladies have fits of the vapours and a miniature riot develops in the back of the hall

Chapter Five

The Fluctuations of Fortune

At much the same time as Wellington was learning of the events of the previous evening while attending the Duchess of Richmond's ball, the Emperor received a visit from Marshal Ney at Charleroi. Only then did Napoleon learn that Quatre Bras remained in Allied hands. Weighing up all the circumstances, the conviction grew upon him that Blücher would retire from his exposed position around Sombreffe, and that the best plan would be to try conclusions with Wellington first and occupy Brussels before turning all the might of the *Armée du Nord* against the Prussians. At the same time, as it was important that Blücher should not be in a position to transfer aid to his colleague by way of the lateral road, Napoleon determined to mount preliminary operations with Grouchy's wing against Gembloux and Sombreffe—mainly as a precaution. Thus, by the time Ney left for his own headquarters, he was probably under the impression that Napoleon and the Reserve would be soon on the move to support his left wing on the Brussels road.

In fact, events were to prove very different, but only such a belief can explain Ney's extraordinary conduct during the morning of the 16th—namely his complete lack of any aggressive movement towards the key cross-roads. An ambiguous phrase in the orders he received about 10 a.m. also implied that he was to await the Reserve's arrival, and in the meantime merely hold six of his divisions in readiness to march after sending one out to the north-west of his position as a flank-guard and another to the east towards Marbais to serve as a link with Grouchy. Yet it seems inconceivable that Ney took no steps to secure Quatre Bras soon after first light—when Perponcher was the only opponent. As it transpired, however, Ney would not launch any attack until 2 p.m., by which time the Allied Reserve would be drawing close to reinforce Perponcher from Brussels. Indeed, the inexplicable lack of any action towards Quatre Bras caused Napoleon to send off a curt hand-written note to Ney at 1 p.m. commanding him to attack immediately.

As for Napoleon, by mid-morning he was on the point of switching the direction of his main attack. News arrived from Grouchy that dense Prussian columns were deploying around Sombreffe. Still not quite crediting the reliability of these reports, Napoleon rode over accompanied by his battle head-quarters staff to see for himself. By 11 a.m. he had joined Vandamme's Corps facing Ziethen's troops near St. Amand. What he could then perceive through his spy-glass convinced him that even if the main Prussian force was not present there were enough enemy troops obligingly marching into range to justify a reversion to his earlier plan. Thus he decided that Ney's advance towards Brussels should be subordinated to a major action against the Prussians—but Ney would not comprehend this switch of emphasis until mid-afternoon, as we shall see. However, there was no question of attacking at Ligny imme-diately; time was needed for Gérard's Corps to come up into line, and for the Guard to come up in rear. Besides, the Em-peror's plan conceived of a large part of Ney's command coming into action at the critical moment on the Prussian right flank and rear after a march from Quatre-Bras—the Emperor assum-ing that his subordinate would be in a position to use the lateral road for this purpose during the afternoon period. Exclusive of this force, Napoleon planned to mass 68,000 men (including 12,500 cavalry) and 210 guns for the battle of Ligny, but this full force could not be deployed before approximately 2 p.m.

Field-Marshal Blücher, meantime, was equally determined to hold his ground. He had reached the area of Sombreffe by 4 p.m. on the previous afternoon, and by noon on the 16th had three corps either present or on the point of arriving. Ziethen's I Corps was occupying a salient along the line of the Ligny Brook with some 32,000 men, the left holding the village of Ligny, the centre St. Amand, and the right hinging upon Wagnelé. Next to arrive was Pirch's II Corps, which was placed in rear of I Corps, and then at about 3 p.m. Thielemann's III Corps marched up to be placed between Sombreffe and Mazy on the left. By this time there were all of 84,000 Prussians present (including 8,000 cavalry) and 224 cannon, holding a seven-mile front along the marshy banks of the Ligny Brook (only a minor obstacle in itself) and occupying all of ten villages

This previously unknown order to Marshal Ney on 16 June in Napoleon's execrable handwriting was auctioned at Sotheby's in 1970. Dated '1 hour after midday', it informs the Prince of the Moskova of Napoleon's surprise that his imperial orders were not being obeyed, and stresses the need for Ney to attack without further delay 'all that is before you with the greatest impetuosity'. The Emperor ends by reminding his subordinate that 'the fate of France is in your hands'. Had Ney attacked before 2 p.m. he must have achieved a considerable and even possibly a decisive success over Wellington, whose troops were mostly distant from the field and in the process of assembling. As it was, it appears that this order—one of several dispatched—only reached Ney in the late afternoon, when he was already hotly engaged. The Marshal certainly used the final phrase from the order when briefing General Kellerman to make a desperately dangerous cavalry charge at about 5 p.m. The message was later authenti-cated by Baron Gourgaud, the aide-de-camp who accompanied the Emperor into exile on St. Helena

Monsieur le prince de la Moskowa — je suis
surpris de votre grand retard a executer
mes ordres — il n'y a plus de tems a perdre
attaquez avec la plus grande impetuosité
tout ce qui est devant vous — le sort
de la patrie est dans vos mains

1 heure apres midi

J'attaquer la position de quatre Bras

Ordre l'écrit de la main de L'Empereur Napoléon le seize
Juin mil huit Cent quinze pour le Marechal Ney
Le Général Aide de Camp de L'Empereur
Le Baron Gourgaud

and hamlets. Blücher, from his headquarters established at the
Mill of Bussy on a hillside overlooking his centre and right
wings, believed that the marshy nature of the Ligny valley
could force the French to attack at one or more of the four

available bridges, all of which were dominated by Prussian-held villages. He also hoped for the arrival of Bülow's IV Corps to reinforce his front, but in fact this formation was too far distant to be able to take an active share in the events of the 16th—largely as a result of an over-politely phrased order sent out by Gneisenau. As for the troops already present, they were drawn up along the exposed forward slopes of the overlooking hillsides. This was to invite casualties—and the French artillery would not ignore the opportunity.

The Duke of Wellington, after finding everything surprisingly quiet around Quatre Bras (which he had reached at 10 a.m.), rode over to visit Blücher, arriving at about 1 p.m. He pointed out to his colleague the advantages to be gained by putting more troops behind cover, but Gneisenau riposted that Prussian troops liked to have a plain view of their enemy. Wellington then promised that he would bring at least part of his army over to Ligny '. . . provided I am not attacked myself', before setting off back towards Quatre Bras. In fact he would be in no position to redeem that promise, as events would soon prove.

As for Napoleon, after a detailed reconnaissance of the area he was soon convinced that the Prussians were indeed present in greater strength than he had at first thought. It confirmed his intention of trying conclusions at Ligny rather than at Quatre Bras. His orders were soon issued. Pajol's and Exelmann's cavalry corps were to take post on the French right, and keep the Prussian left wing in play, whilst Vandamme and Gérard (now coming into position near Fleurus at 1 p.m.) attacked Blücher's centre and right by means of direct frontal attacks over the Ligny. The impressive formations of the Imperial Guard, both foot and horse (Lefebvre-Desnouëttes' Guard cavalry had been recalled from Ney earlier in the day, being replaced by Kellermann's cavalry corps) would form the battle reserve, ready to advance and deliver the decisive blow once a substantial part of Ney's command had materialized from the west to fall on the Prussian left at about 6 p.m. Napoleon envisaged a great success that would scatter two-thirds of Blücher's army, and hurl it back along its line of retreat towards Namur and Liège—thus away from Wellington's army, which would then become the sole object of the Emperor's attentions on the 17th. This was all a convincing demonstration of the flexibility—in theory—of the French formation of 'two wings and a reserve'. In practice it would not work out so well on this occasion. 'If Ney carries out his orders thoroughly, not a gun of the Prussian army will get away; it is taken in the very act,'

General Maximilien Sebastien Foy, Count of the Empire (1775–1825) by A. Tardieu. A soldier with much experience of fighting the British in the Peninsular War, Foy commanded a division in Reille's II Corps in 1815, and at its head played a prominent part at both Quatre Bras and Waterloo. His efforts on the 18th were however compromised by his fellow divisional commander's (Jérôme Bonaparte) rash handling of the French attacks against Wellington's outpost at Hougoumont. The wars over, Foy turned military historian, and started a notable History of the Peninsular War. Unfortunately, he died when his work was only complete to the year 1810

declared Napoleon, carried away by his enthusiasm for the plan.

But in Ney's performance of his orders would lie the rub. Soult drafted his new definitive instructions at 2 p.m. In part these enlarged upon Napoleon's 1 p.m. note, declaring that Ney should '. . . attack whatever force is before you, and after vigorously driving it back, you will turn in our direction, so as to bring about the envelopment of . . . [Blücher's] . . . troops.' Napoleon had already described the broad principles of the campaign, so Ney should have been aware of the general scheme. Unfortunately, as late as 4 p.m. he was labouring under the misconception that *his* battle area around Quatre Bras was to see the day's main effort by the French army. In this miscalculation lay the seeds of the outcome of the day—and possibly of the whole campaign.

Owing to the need to deploy Gérard's Corps, it was only after 2.30 p.m. that the battle at last opened around Ligny. Half an hour earlier, the battle of Quatre Bras, about seven miles away, had at last begun. Ney had allowed six precious hours to slip away before he ordered Reille's II Corps to advance. Even at 2 p.m. the Allies at the cross-roads only totalled 8,000 men and sixteen guns, and Wellington himself was still absent, being in the process of riding back from his meeting with Blücher. Reille alone commanded all of 20,000 men and sixty guns, but fortunately he was a cautious commander, and dreaded being drawn into a 'Spanish battle'—believing that large numbers of Wellington's troops already lay concealed in the battle area. This was not, in fact, the case. The thick woods to the west of the Brussels highway were only very sparsely held, and the same was true of the subtantial farmsteads to the south of Quatre Bras—namely Piraumont, Pierrepoint and Gemioncourt. The Allied Reserve was approaching from Mont-St. Jean, but could not be in position before 3 p.m. Ney decided to await the arrival of d'Erlon's forces from the direction of Charleroi.

Nevertheless, the die was cast. Shortly after 2 p.m., fourteen French guns blazed into action, and forward went General Piré's cavalry followed by the infantry divisions of Bachelu and Foy, supported by Jérôme Bonaparte (Napoleon's youngest brother, the former King of Westphalia). The height of the standing corn and the dark recesses of the woodland obscured the French view, and their advance was cautiously pressed despite the comforting presence of another 20,000 men behind them. Consequently against all the odds Perponcher was able to hold on to his main position, although by 3 p.m. Bachelu's Division had captured Piraumont Farm from Perponcher's

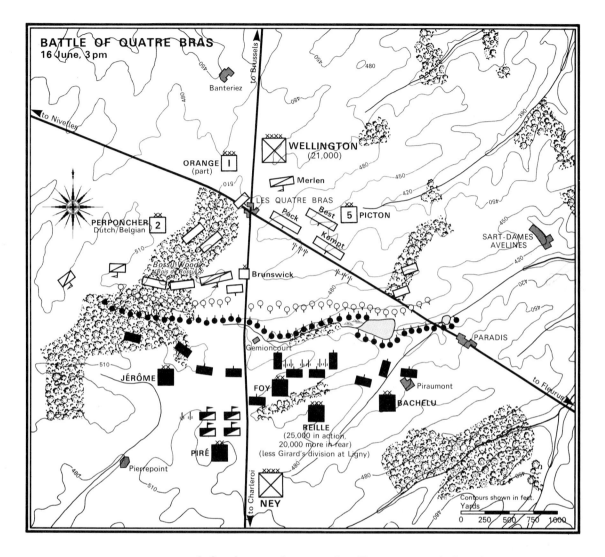

left wing, and soon after Foy captured Gemioncourt in front of his centre. The Dutch troops broke and fled for Bossu Wood, pursued by Piré's cavalry. Foy was less successful against Pierrepoint Farm near the edge of Bossu Wood, and it took the intervention of Prince Jérôme's 8,000 men and eight guns to capture this strongpoint. Only then could the time-consuming wood-clearing operation against the Nassauers holding Bossu Wood commence.

Timely assistance came to help relieve some of this intense pressure on General Perponcher. General van Merlen's Belgo-Dutch cavalry brigade was first to join him from the direction of Nivelles, and shortly thereafter the 8,000 men of Picton's veteran division, with twelve guns, arrived to redress still further

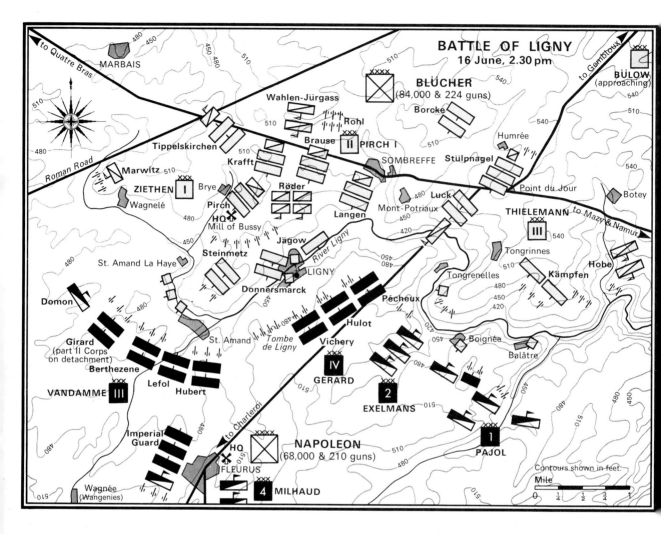

the unfavourable balance. The Duke and the Prince of Orange
were now both on the scene—but the latter's cavalry counter-
attack to assist Perponcher received short shrift from the French,
resulting in the loss of half a dozen cannon and at one point
Wellington had to ride for his life to seek shelter within a square
formed by the 92nd Highlanders. Fortunately Picton's men were
at hand to reinforce the perilously thin line on its left flank and
secure the cross-roads, and now the Duke of Brunswick
materialized with 4,000 more men. Thus the Allies were fielding
some 21,000 men against Ney's 25,000 committed to action.
So the struggle for possession of Quatre Bras continued to
escalate.

Meantime, the battle of Ligny had sprung to life. At 2.30 p.m.
Grouchy's cavalry began to manoeuvre in order to tie down the

Prussian left, whilst Vandamme led forward four divisions to attack the village of St. Amand. At the same time, Gérard sent two of his divisions against Ligny to perform the main pinning role and attract Prussian reserves into action. The French batteries thundered out death to the Prussian reserves drawn up on the facing hillsides. Soon a titanic struggle was raging along the line of the Ligny brook, amidst the hedgerows and outlying houses. Losses were heavy on both sides: the French 30th Line Regiment lost two-thirds of its fighting strength during this day, to cite but one example.

Napoleon had hoped to hear news that Ney was marching towards the Prussian flank by this time, but no such tidings had arrived. Consequently at 3.15 p.m. a further message was sent by Soult; Ney was again told that 'the fate of France is in your hands', and was enjoined to attack the heights of Brye and St. Amand without delay. But hardly had this message been sent off than news at last arrived from Quatre Bras which revealed that battle had already been joined there against some 20,000 Allies. It was clear, therefore, that there was little chance of Ney arriving near Ligny in force, so it appears that a further pencilled note was scribbled requiring the commander of the French left to send over only d'Erlon's Corps. At the same time the Emperor remembered the 10,000 men of Lobau's neglected VI Corps still awaiting orders near Charleroi, and very belatedly required them to march towards Fleurus to add further weight to the French *masse de décision*. As the messengers rode off, the struggle for St. Amand-la-Haye and Ligny reached new heights. It took the French five attacks to secure even a foothold in the outskirts of the latter, and General Girard, commanding the detached division of Reille's Corps, which was serving under Vandamme this day, was killed at St. Amand. But this notwithstanding, Napoleon's overall plan was beginning to take effect, for more and more Prussian reserves were being sucked into the battle. By 5 p.m., some 58,000 French troops were successfully tying down 84,000 Prussians—and the Emperor still had the Guard in hand.

An hour later Napoleon believed the time had come for the *coup de grâce*. Imagining that he could hear the roar of d'Erlon's cannon in the distance, and selecting Ligny as the target, he ordered the Imperial Guard to prepare to attack the smoke-shrouded Prussian line. They were about to advance when the commander of III Corps hastened up, reporting that his staff had spotted a strong column of unidentified troops moving on the *French* left flank. As d'Erlon was expected to appear far

OVERLEAF It was not only Napoleon who encountered problems of communication during the Waterloo campaign. This touching (but unfortunately wholly unauthenticated) story of the Duke entrusting a vital message to an English gentleman who just happened to be passing is typical of the legends that grew around the great battle. Perhaps the title of the source of this story should give a clue to its reliability or otherwise

THE DUKE AND THE TRAVELLER.

FOR a quarter of an hour, during one of the greatest crises of the Battle of Waterloo, when the Duke of Wellington had sent all his *aides-de-camp* with orders to the different divisions of the army, he found himself alone at the very moment when he most needed help. While watching the movements of his troops through his field-glasses, he saw Kempt's brigade beginning a manœuvre which, if not promptly countermanded, would probably lead to the loss of the battle. But there was no officer at hand to convey his orders. Just then he turned round in his saddle, and saw not far off a single horseman, rather quaintly attired, coolly watching the progress of the strife. The instant the Duke caught sight of him, he beckoned to him, and asked him who he was, why he was there, and how he had passed the lines.

He answered: 'I am a traveller for a wholesale button manufactory in Birmingham, and was showing my samples in Brussels when I heard the sound of the firing. Having had all my life a strong desire to see a battle, I at once got a horse, and set out for the scene of action; and, after some difficulty, I have reached this spot, whence I expect to have a good view.'

The Duke, pleased with his straightforward answer, determined to turn his sense and daring to good account, and addressed him as follows: 'You ought to have been a soldier. Would you like to serve your country now?'

'Yes, my lord,' said the other.

'Would you take a message of importance for me?'

Touching his hat in military fashion the traveller replied, 'Were I trusted by you, sir, I would think this the proudest day of my life.'

Putting his field-glass into the man's hands, the Duke explained to him the position of the brigade that had made the false move, and added: 'I have no writing materials by me; see, therefore, that you are very accurate in delivering my message.' He then entrusted to him a brief, emphatic order, which he made him repeat, that there might be no mistake.

The orders were barely delivered before the stranger was off at the top of his horse's speed, and soon disappeared amid the smoke of the battle. After a few minutes' interval, the Duke turned his glass in the direction of the brigade which was at fault, and exclaimed, in a joyful tone, 'It's all right, yet. Kempt has changed his tactics. He has got my message, for he is doing precisely as I directed him. Well done, Buttons!'

The Duke used to say he considered the alteration of Kempt's original movement the turning-point of the battle. Wishing to reward our hero for his intelligence and courage, he caused inquiries to be made for him in every direction, but in vain. It was not till many years afterwards that he accidentally heard of the man's whereabouts, and managed to secure for him a good appointment in the West of England, in recognition of his services.

" 'Would you take a message of importance for me?' "

No. XXI.

further north than this there were fears that this force might turn out to be part of the Allied army. The Guard's attack was at once suspended, and officers were sent off to investigate the newcomers. This delay gave the hard-pressed Blücher a welcome respite, and it was half an hour before Napoleon learnt that the enigmatic column was indeed French. He at once ordered a message to be sent to d'Erlon ordering him to manoeuvre his men towards Wagnelé, but was soon after astounded to learn that the column was now marching back in the direction from which it had come, returning towards Quatre Bras.

To understand the reasons for this peculiar development we must retrace our steps and consider events at Quatre Bras some little time earlier. Marshal Ney had at last received Soult's 2 p.m. order at about 4 p.m. Using Jérôme's newly deployed division supported by forty-two guns, he at once launched a new onslaught on Bossu Wood and captured part of it, but Picton repulsed a similar attack to the east of the Brussels highway. Eager to clinch the action and take possession of the crossroads, Ney decided to send into action his reserve corps—namely d'Erlon's—only to discover that this 20,000-strong formation was marching away to the east! This movement was being made without Ney's authorization and he was not unnaturally furious. What had happened was this: Napoleon's aide, General de la Bedoyère, bearing Napoleon's *pencilled* message, rode through I Corps as he sought out Marshal Ney, and on his own authority ordered the leading division to swing to the east straight away. He then, after an interval, found d'Erlon, and told him what had to be done, and the commander decided to obey de la Bedoyère, who was acting 'in the Emperor's name', although such a radical change in orders should have been taken to Ney in the first instance. The reason why d'Erlon headed for the French, rather than the Prussian, flank at Ligny has still to be explained—or rather an explanation suggested for this is still a matter for debate. Here the explanation may lie in the pencilled note—and Napoleon's notoriously bad handwriting. The fact that the head of d'Erlon's column appeared near the village of Wagnée (as it appears on old maps) instead of at Wagnelé, might suggest that it was simply a matter of a badly written, or a misread, note. That would at least be a logical and simple explanation. Less easy to explain is the failure of d'Erlon to push out patrols ahead of his main column—the usual practice—which would have enabled Napoleon's staff to identify the newcomer near Wagnée more quickly.

Ney had just realized that I Corps was disappearing over the

horizon when another imperial aide, bearing Napoleon's
3.30 p.m. message, appeared before him. This officer, Colonel
Forbin-Janson, only had time to deliver Napoleon's verbal
message that Ney was to take Quatre Bras without further delay
before he received the full vent of the Marshal's pent-up wrath.
He was so stunned by this, that he quite overlooked to hand over
the written message, which would have explained what was
happening. Instead, he was sent galloping back whence he had
come with Ney's message that he would hold on where he was,
but '. . . as d'Erlon has not arrived, I cannot promise any more'.
Immediately thereafter, General Alten and the newly arrived
3rd Division, launched a strong attack against Reille's Corps,
and Ney decided on the spur of the moment that if a possible
defeat was to be averted d'Erlon must be instantly recalled. The
I Corps had almost reached Ligny, as we have already related,
when Ney's strongly worded message reached its commander,
who philosophically began to retrace his steps without sending a
messenger to the Emperor to explain his reason. So it was that
20,000 men, whose active presence on either field of battle
would have been decisive, spent the afternoon and evening
marching and counter-marching between the two scenes of
conflict and achieved nothing. This amounted to another lost
opportunity for the French, and was largely due to shoddy staff
work and 'the fog of war'. Its effect on the campaign was
incalculable.

The battle for Quatre Bras reached a new intensity as French
lancers severely mauled the 42nd Highlanders and 44th
Regiment, but the opportune arrival of Alten's troops built up
Wellington's strength to 26,000 men and forty-two cannon. At
last he was marginally superior to Reille and the French cavalry.
Ney, despairing of d'Erlon's arrival, decided that an 'all-or-
nothing' effort was required, and ordered General Kellermann
to lead a hell-for-leather *cuirassier* charge towards the elusive
cross-roads. Despite the odds involved, this attack by a single
brigade of French 'heavies' at about 5 p.m. almost succeeded:
thanks to an injudicious intervention by the Prince of Orange,
who ordered its commander to remain in line rather than form
square, the 69th Regiment was overrun and its King's colour
captured. The 33rd Regiment was next driven in some disorder
into the woodland, and the French *cuirassiers* reined in actually
upon the contested cross-roads. But in a trice the heavy fire of a
battery manned by the King's German Legion and some telling
volleys from neighbouring British regiments brought men and
horses crashing down, and Kellermann himself narrowly

OVERLEAF *The 'Black Watch' at Bay at Quatre Bras* by W. Wollen. At the height of the battle of Quatre Bras the French cavalry almost broke through Wellington's position. One regiment—the 69th—was decimated and lost its Colour as it tried to form square. Another—the 42nd—received a terrible mauling as depicted here, but survived

escaped death or capture after being dismounted by clinging to the bits of two of his cavalrymen's steeds. And so this attack, in its turn, was eventually repulsed.

Only after 6 p.m. did a duplicate copy of Napoleon's 3.30 p.m. order reach Ney—and it was then practically too late to hope for a success that day. It caused the Marshal to fling himself in person into the front-line fighting, but this achieved nothing. Moreover, by 6.30 p.m. Wellington's strength had risen to over 35,000 men and seventy guns, thanks to the arrival of Cooke's Guardsmen—and 'the Peer' at once launched a triple counter-attack against Bossu Wood and Gemioncourt and Piraumont farms. By 9 p.m., when the fighting at last died

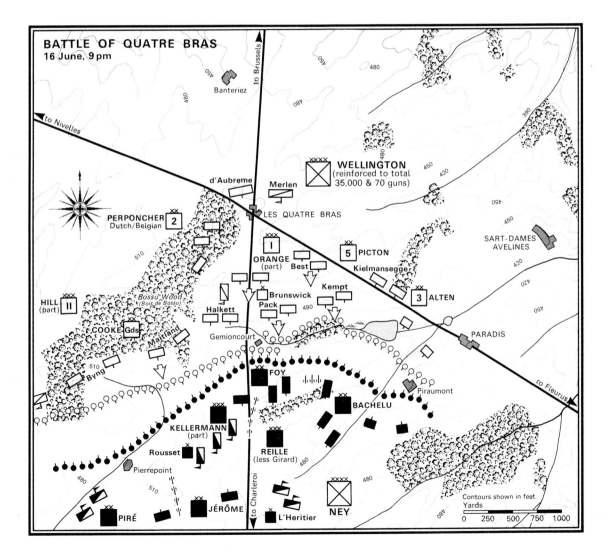

away, almost all of Perponcher's original position had been regained. By that time the Allies had lost almost 5,000 casualties —including the Duke of Brunswick, struck down shortly before Kellermann's charge. The French had lost some 4,000 killed and wounded since 2.30 p.m., and as we have seen had very little to show for it: the key cross-roads remained in Allied hands, Wellington had been permitted to reconcentrate his army, and the French had never been able to bring their full strength to bear against it thanks to the peregrinations of I Corps. Responsibility for these French disappointments lies partly with Marshal Ney, whose tardy opening of the engagement robbed him of an easy victory, partly with Marshal Soult and the imperial aides, who failed to communicate their master's wishes to the Marshal before it was too late to implement them, and partly with de la Bedoyère, whose well-meaning but fatal tampering with Ney's original order to d'Erlon led to much confusion. Nor can the author of the pencilled note be deemed blameless. All along Napoleon had discounted the scale of the opposition building up at Quatre Bras, so engrossed was he with the struggle against Ligny, and his error in ignoring Lobau's VI Corps until the mid-afternoon also robbed him of a part of his reserve.

The outcome at Ligny, however, was far more satisfactory for the French, even if incomplete, than the outcome at Quatre Bras. Not that it had proved anything of a walk-over. Profiting from the temporary suspension of the French onslaught at six p.m., Blücher had launched a counter-attack against Vandamme's weary troops which recaptured part of St. Amand, only to be driven out again for want of supporting troops by a division of the Young Guard. As a result it was only at 7.00 p.m. that the French grand attack was ready to be delivered once again. Forward went the Imperial Guard against Ligny in two columns. They were supported by Milhaud's cavalry on their left and by the fire of sixty guns and followed by squadrons of the Guard heavy cavalry, whilst the rain poured down. Half an hour later the Prussian line, exhausted after six hours of fighting, buckled and broke.

The French now scented victory—but into the gap torn in the Prussian line spurred the gallant Field-Marshal at the head of thirty-two squadrons of cavalry. They achieved little except to gain some time for their surviving infantry to withdraw, and by 9 p.m. the last Prussian cavalry were driven off after a final engagement near the Mill of Bussy. Into the gathering darkness retired the battered Prussian columns leaving 16,000 dead and

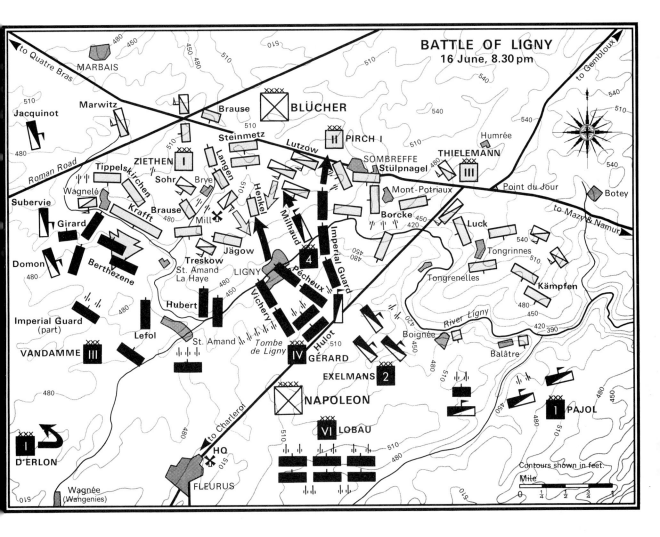

BATTLE OF LIGNY
16 June, 8.30 pm

Contours shown in feet.
Mile

wounded and twenty-one guns on the field of battle. Unbeknown to them they also left their commander-in-chief. At the height of the last cavalry action by the 7th Uhlans he had been pinned beneath his wounded horse and badly shaken. Twice thereafter he—and one aide who faithfully stayed at his side—were ridden over by waves of French cavalry who in the gloom did not recognize the prize within their grasp. Once all was quiet the aide found a horse, freed the semi-conscious Field-Marshal from beneath his dead mount, and led him away to the north, still unrecognized.

Napoleon himself was far from well on this particular evening. Instead of busying himself organizing an immediate pursuit of the Prussian army, he set up his quarters in a large farmstead in Ligny. This was to prove another major mistake from which great consequences would flow. He believed that he had shattered the Prussian army beyond repair, and that their one thought would be to retire towards Namur and Liège. The French army was itself exhausted. All of 11,500 casualties had been sustained at Ligny. As a result no immediate attempt was made to follow-up the Prussians, and the resulting break in contact would have dire results for the French before a further forty-eight hours were out.

Nevertheless, Ligny deserves to be ranked as a major French battle success—and no doubt it would have been recognized as such but for the even greater battle two days later that over-shadowed it. But for the failure of d'Erlon to intervene—which would have made it impossible for most of the Prussians to escape—and for the failure to pursue immediately, Ligny would have been an even greater victory. Nevertheless, Napoleon had reasonable cause for some satisfaction that night. The *Armée du Nord* had successfully kept the two Allied armies apart, defeated one heavily and at least held the other to a draw. Two French corps—the I and VI—were still untouched. Thus the morrow might still see a complete French victory.

No such complacent thoughts can have been in the minds of either Wellington or Blücher that night. Only at 7.30 a.m. on the 17th did the Duke learn of what had befallen the Prussian army and come to realize fully the peril facing his own army. For overnight the Prussians had been in full retreat, resulting in the left wing of Wellington's army becoming increasingly exposed to a possible French out-flanking attack from the direction of Ligny. Even more important than this, however, was the direction in which they had retreated, for instead of moving away towards Namur and their bases beyond (that is to say to the south-east), the Prussians had marched north towards Wavre. This had come about more by chance than deliberate design. With Blücher's whereabouts—or even survival—still unknown, Gneisenau had held a roadside conference with his corps commanders to decide their actions. Great difficulty had been experienced in reading their maps by the light of flickering torches, and the only town name all could find was Wavre. It was therefore decided that the Prussians would withdraw there as a first step in order to re-form before heading away towards Liège and the distant Rhine.

Gneisenau had little intention of staying to support Wellington, but in fact he had arbitrarily taken the one course of action that would make that support possible, for instead of drawing away to the south-east (as Napoleon assumed they would have

The Perilous Situation of Marshal Blücher in the Battle of Ligny by G. Jones. As dusk fell at Ligny, Field-Marshal Blücher led one last, desperate charge to try and win a respite for his battered infantry to disengage. His horse was killed, and for

some time he lay trapped beneath his steed whilst friendly and hostile cavalry swirled, charged and counter-charged unknowingly over his prostrate body. One aide remained nearby, and in due course rescued his Commander-in-Chief.

done) the Prussians had abandoned their lines of communication and were falling back parallel to the Allies and Brussels, and were thus closer to both than ever before, although still not in direct contact. Some time later Field-Marshal Blücher at last materialized at Mellery, and rejoined his headquarters. Although badly shaken by his experiences, he soon recovered sufficiently with the aid of liberal dosages of gin and garlic to resume control over the destinies of the Prussian army. He forthrightly opposed Gneisenau's suggestion of a continuing retreat towards Liège, and insisted that honour demanded that the Prussians should back Wellington to the uttermost. This, as it proved, was the most important decision taken throughout the campaign. It alone made possible the outcome of the battle of Waterloo on the 18th.

As the Prussians had broken contact with the French, the main centre of crisis now inevitably shifted to Wellington's sector. His belated tidings of Ligny and the subsequent Prussian movements convinced him that he must lose no time in retreating as well from Quatre Bras. 'I suppose in England they will say we have been licked. I can't help it; as they are gone

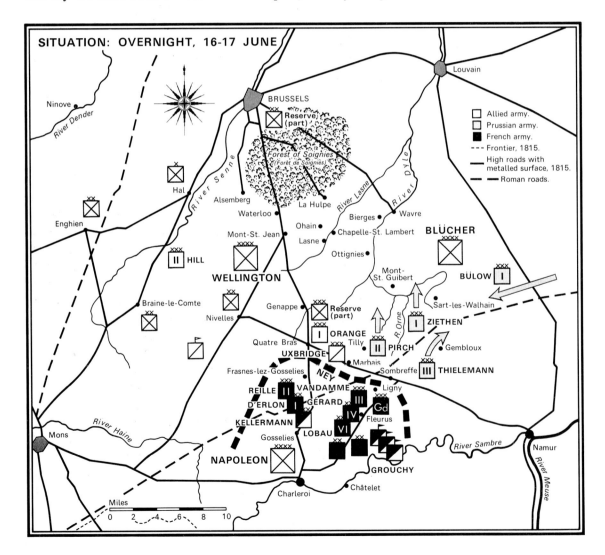

back, we must go too.' He at once sent off a message to Blücher announcing that he intended to stand and fight at Mont-St. Jean if the Prussians could provide the aid of a single corps—for Wavre was only some ten miles east of the place the Duke had pre-selected early on the 16th as the probable decisive battle-ground. From midday on the 17th, the Allied army began progressively to thin out as unit followed unit northwards along the highway towards Brussels. Still anxious for his line of communication with Ostend, the Duke ordered General Hill to take two divisions' worth of troops to Hal.

That this manoeuvre was permitted to take place at all was partly the fault of Napoleon and partly that of Marshal Ney. The Emperor had learnt by 7 a.m. that streams of Prussians were moving down the Namur road as expected (in fact his patrols had spotted only ambulances and a mass of deserters) and also that Ney was still faced by an opponent at Quatre Bras. Napoleon, not realizing that Wellington was still in the dark about the precise fate of the Prussians the previous day, could not conceive that the Duke would be so foolhardy as to be holding his position and still doubted that he was there in strength. He therefore sent Ney a rather indeterminate order, declaring that 'it is necessary to end this operation today . . .'—requiring him to secure Quatre Bras in due course. But all the Emperor's actions that fateful morning were lethargic in the extreme. He appeared unwell and indecisive after the hectic activity of the previous days. He refused to unleash a proper pursuit of Blücher until almost 11 a.m., when Grouchy was at last authorized to move off towards Namur. Most of the morning the Emperor spent inspecting the battlefield of Ligny. A half-hearted cavalry probe was sent out to reconnoitre the ground towards Quatre Bras, but that was all. Grouchy's requests for leave to follow Blücher were ignored or snubbed.

As the master—so the man. Ney made no attempt to resume the attack on Wellington throughout that morning. His troops sat along the roadside around their bivouac fires awaiting orders that never came, hour after hour. Had Ney but attacked as late as midday, this could have rendered Wellington's disengagement all but impossible—but nothing was done, and the Duke was provided with several invaluable hours' start in what would soon become the critical race for Mont-St. Jean.

Some time after eleven the Emperor suddenly awoke from his lethargy. At long last he ordered Grouchy to set off after the Prussians. The tardy arrival of Ney's full report on the previous day's fighting convinced the Emperor for the first time that

Wellington had been present there in full array; then his cavalry patrols returned with the incredible news that not only was there no indication of fighting near Quatre Bras but that the enemy was still there in strength. Napoleon now realized how great an opportunity was being missed. If only he had headed towards Ney up the lateral road earlier in the day he might well have trapped Wellington in a hopeless situation. Even now, it might still not be too late if Ney bestirred himself. Soon the Emperor and his staff were galloping towards Marbais, with the Guard and Lobau's Corps moving up behind them.

The village of Marbais was reached by 1 p.m., but there were still no sounds of firing ahead. Spurring cross-country, the Emperor came upon Ney's troops taking their ease along the roadside, and not even Napoleon's fiery remonstrances could get them ready for movement before 2 p.m. It was now clear that Wellington had abandoned Quatre Bras, and was retreating northwards. D'Erlon was sent off in hot pursuit towards Genappe to try and catch the Allied rearguard, but even Napoleon was moved to remark to him that 'France has been ruined'.

Now the race was on—but Wellington had gained a good start on his pursuers. Nevertheless, the reputation of the French for out-marching any opponent was indeed redoubtable, and it was still possible that they might have caught up with the Allies. However fate now intervened in the form of a violent storm accompanied by pouring rain, and the French columns that were pressing along narrow lanes and over the countryside itself in their attempt to outflank and cut off Wellington soon found themselves struggling through thick mud which materially hampered their progress. Wellington's rearguard—Lord Uxbridge's cavalry and the horse artillery—fought a model ridge-by-ridge withdrawal action, continually turning at bay to check the foremost French pursuers.

Owing to this circumstance, it was soon evident that Wellington was not going to be caught. His troops had begun to send back their wounded and transport as early as 10 a.m., and when the main withdrawal began about midday—without the least hindrance from Ney, as we have seen—Lord Hill had led his divisions back towards Hal and Braine l'Alleud whilst the Prince of Orange led his command directly through Genappe, both having received orders to occupy a position stretching from the tiny hamlet of Papelotte in the east to Braine l'Alleud in the west, with a further detachment under Prince Frederick of Holland at Hal to guard the outer flank against any French attempt to outflank the position from that direction. For Wellington had determined to stand and fight around Mont-St. Jean provided he received assurances from Blücher that he would come up to his aid from the east during the morrow. This was a vital consideration in the Duke's strategy; left to itself, the hybrid Allied army, now barely 68,000 strong in combat terms, was unlikely to withstand a determined attack by 72,000 French troops led by Napoleon in person. The Allies had fought well enough at Quatre Bras, it is true, but as we have seen Ney had badly mishandled the situation at the command level; to face Napoleon in person would prove quite a different matter.

By 6.30 p.m. it was evident that Wellington had indeed evaded the clutches of the French. At about that hour Napoleon reached the inn of La Belle Alliance. He was now less than a mile from the ridge of Mont-St. Jean, but there was precious little sign of the Allied army ahead. He therefore ordered General Milhaud to probe ahead up the road with his division of *cuirassiers*. A sudden roar of shot and shell from over sixty Allied guns greeted the horsemen amidst the pelting rain; having performed their intended function, they fell back. Wellington was clearly present in strength; he was not for the moment trying to retire further towards Brussels. It was clearly too late for the exhausted French to try anything further that day. 'Have all the troops take up positions and we will see what happens tomorrow,' remarked Napoleon to d'Erlon, before returning down the road for a mile and a half to the farmstead of Le Caillou, where his headquarters had been established for the night.

In the darkening gloom the foot-sore and rain-sodden French army slowly closed up around their leader. There was much weariness and despondency in evidence; everybody seemed to be blaming the generals for the discomforts of the evening and night, and the word 'treason' was already being muttered. The Imperial Guard arrived '. . . our greatcoats and our trousers . . . caked with several pounds of mud. A great many of the soldiers had lost their shoes and reached the bivouac barefoot,' as Sergeant Hippolyte de Maudit recalled. It was fully midnight before the bulk of his regiment arrived to seek what shelter could be found amidst an orchard.

It was a wild night. 'Rain poured down', noted d'Erlon, 'and soaked the ground so badly that the deployment of the artillery was seriously impeded. Our soldiers spent the night without shelter, and no musket would fire.' It was equally miserable

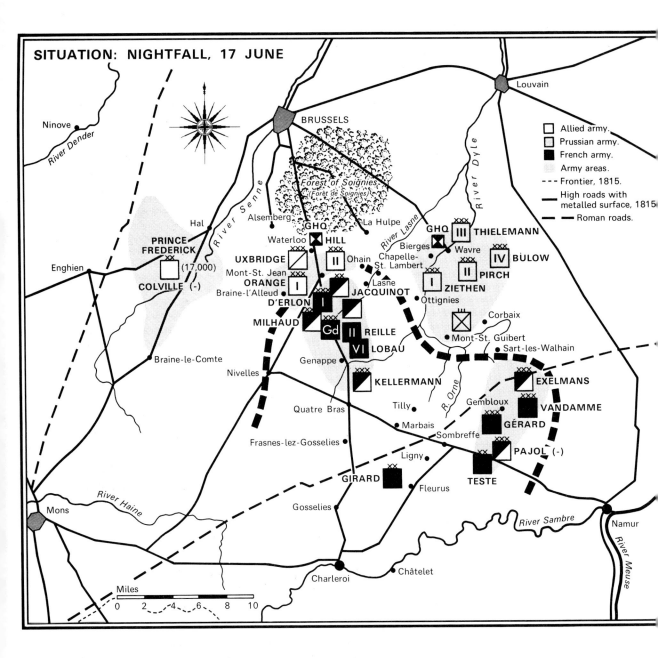

SITUATION: NIGHTFALL, 17 JUNE

for Wellington's men hunched over their inadequate and smoking fires on the other side of no-man's-land. Yet, as one young British cavalry surgeon recalled, '... notwithstanding rain, mud, and water, cold and the proximity of the enemy, most of us managed to sleep.' Wellington spent the night in his head-quarters in the village of Waterloo, some two miles behind the front; Napoleon, as we have said, was quartered at Le Caillou.

But as was his wont he proved more restless than his British adversary. Ever anxious lest Wellington might try to slip away during the hours of darkness, the Emperor was continually calling for evidence of his foe's continued presence, and the early hours of the 18th found him, accompanied only by Bertrand, pacing the outpost line and staring towards the mass of camp-fires twinkling uncertainly through the rain which marked the Allied bivouacs in front of the Forest of Soignies. Not until first light was his mind finally put at rest on this matter.

When he returned to his quarters about 4 a.m. he found a despatch from Grouchy awaiting him. This reported that it seemed that at least part of Blücher's army might in fact be falling back towards Wavre. Grouchy declared that if this suspicion was confirmed he would manoeuvre with his wing to ensure that the Prussians were headed off from both Wellington and Brussels. But by an oversight the Emperor did not reply to this key communication for almost six hours; had he responded at once, and ordered Grouchy to head for Walhain without delay, Wellington would have been fortunate to see even a single corps of Prussians at Mont-St. Jean later that crucial day. Possibly Napoleon considered the Prussians a spent force after Ligny, unworthy of serious attention. If so he was underestimating Blücher's loyalty and pugnacity as much as he tended to discount Wellington's tactical sense and staying-power.

In fact, the Prussian army was fast recovering from its heavy defeat as it trudged northwards over the eighteen miles separating Ligny from Wavre during the 17th. This was not only caused by meeting Bülow's fresh corps, which had not been engaged at Ligny, but was also very much due to their commander's example and inspiring leadership. 'The firm bearing of the army', recorded a *Landwehr* captain, 'owed not a little to the cheerful spirit and freshness of our seventy-four-year-old Field Marshal. He had had his bruised limbs bathed in brandy, and had helped himself to a large schnapps: and now, although riding must have been very painful, he rode alongside the troops, exchanging jokes and banter with many of them and his humour spread like wildfire down the columns.'

All the components of the great battle of Waterloo were now fast assembling.

Chapter Six

Waterloo and Wavre-
Preparations and Plans

It is important to recognize that the climacteric moment of the Napoleonic wars was a double-battle. Waterloo has always received most of the attention, but events ten miles away to the east were also important, if on a smaller scale, and had a considerable effect on the outcome of the main battle.

First it is necessary to describe the ground of the two scenes of action—and of the terrain between them. Waterloo battlefield is remarkable for its compactness. The area of conflict measured just under three miles from east to west, and barely a mile and a half from north to south; a mere half-mile divided the two armies at the opening of the conflict. Within these narrow bounds—barely four square miles in area—would be massed 140,000 men and more than 400 guns, and these combatants would be joined by the greater part of a further 72,000 Prussians before the day was over. Yet the whole area can today be surveyed with ease from the summit of the Lion Mound—the massive memorial raised to commemorate the place where the Prince of Orange fell wounded in the battle. Wellington's position, backed by the Forest of Soignies, occupied the length of a low ridge set slightly south of the village of Mont-St. Jean. A small road—the Chemin d'Ohain—ran along the crest, which was lined by a thick hedge and sundry thickets along its eastern sector. In 1815 the central area was more pronounced, but the raising of the Mound has changed the lie of the land. Behind this line—destined to form the main Allied position—were a number of useful rear slopes. To the fore of it, the ground was broken to the east of the Brussels high road by a number of small rises and depressions, but the western sector was a relatively flat and unbroken area. Three key points were occupied by the

Centre of the British Army by T. Sutherland. A contemporary portrayal of the fighting in the vicinity of the farmhouse of La Haie Sainte to the immediate front of Wellington's centre

OVERLEAF An example of contemporary cartography, published within a year of the battle

Allies to the south of the main ridge. In the west, set some 400 yards before Wellington's operational right wing, was the Château of Hougoumont (or Goumont), a more extensive building in 1815 than today, with a walled garden and orchard to its east, and an adjoining area of woodland (now gone) to its south. Close to the centre of the Allied position still stands the farmstead of La Haie Sainte in a dip to the west of the Brussels highway: a little closer to Mont-St. Jean ridge, on the eastern side of the road, was a gravel-pit, also destined to be the scene of much fighting. Finally, away to the east was a group of three hamlets set amidst woodland, namely Papelotte, La Haie and Frischermont. These three groups of buildings would serve as breakwaters which would attract and divert much of the fury of the coming French attacks.

The *pavé* Brussels–Charleroi highway formed the central

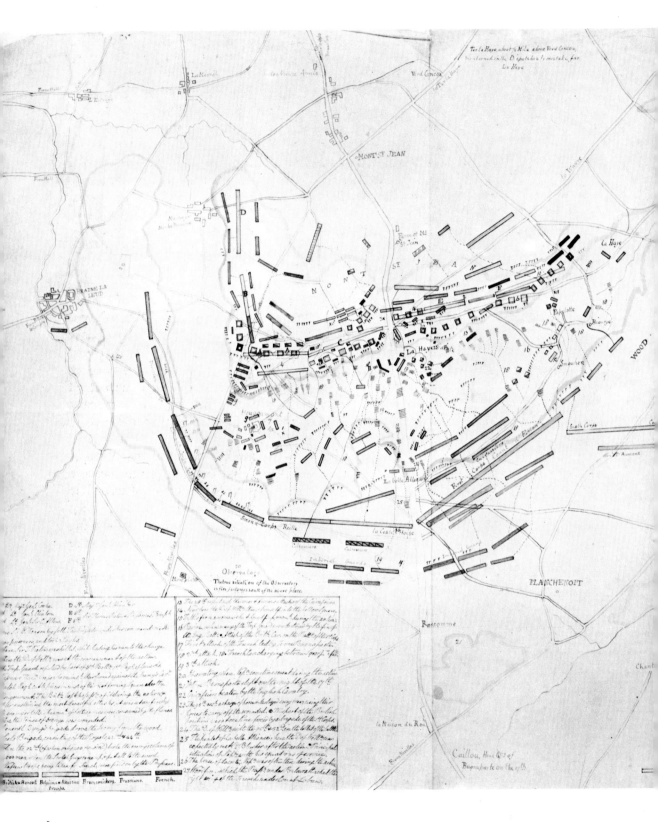

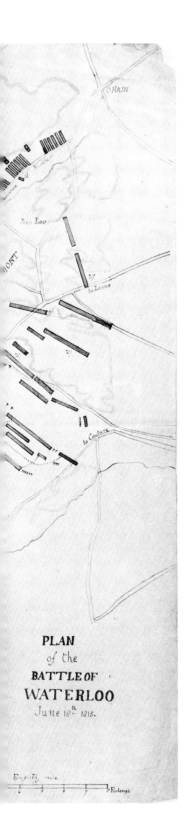

PLAN
of the
BATTLE OF
WATERLOO
June 18ᵗʰ 1815.

axis linking the two rival armies. The road dips south of La Haie Sainte and then runs straight and almost flat to the second ridge near the hostelry of La Belle Alliance. This had, in fact, been Wellington's first choice for a position, but de Lancey had opted for the shorter line at Mont-St. Jean on the 17th. Here, to the east, the ground rises slightly—destined to be the site of the Great Battery; behind this, on a slight eminence, Napoleon's second command post would eventually be established. To the west of the Brussels road, which for much of its length was lined with poplars in 1815 (but not today), the ground is somewhat lower but undulating, facing towards Hougoumont. Two narrow roads linked the highway with the distant Nivelles road, one passing to the rear of the Château, the second running from Rossomme Farm (near the site of Napoleon's first observation post), almost parallel but 1,000 yards further south. Finally, the Brussels highway ran away south past the farms of Maison du Roi and Le Caillou towards Genappe and distant Quatre Bras. The village of Plancenoit lies in a dip near the Lasne stream some 1,500 yards north-east of Maison du Roi. Several areas of the position described were beneath high-standing corn, interspersed with pastureland but largely devoid of hedgerows or other obstacles, but it is important to remember that much of the ground had been made very sodden by the recent heavy rain.

To the east of the whole battle area stretched the Wood of Paris—now much thinned—which formed in large measure the link between the field of Waterloo and that of Wavre. The ground in this considerable region was very broken, steep ravines and many streams interspersed with thick woods making it very difficult for military manoeuvre. The roads were little more than rough tracks, turned almost into quagmires by the downpour of the 17th. A number of small villages and hamlets are scattered over this area, of which the most important for our story are Chapelle-St. Lambert, Ohain and Limale.

The town of Wavre itself stood mainly on the north bank of the river Dyle in 1815, with two stone bridges linking it with its southern suburb. Through the town ran the Namur to Brussels highway. The Dyle itself was not very deep but was swollen by the recent rain. Two long but low heights line the valley, both being covered in places by thick woodland, the spur on the right bank being slightly the higher, that on the left bank somewhat steeper—and thus more suited for the defence of the river and its crossing places. It was soon to be the scene of a staunch action by part of the Prussian army, covering the march of the

remainder towards Waterloo in fulfilment of Blücher's promise to Wellington.

Such were the two battle areas. How did the armies deploy? As might be expected of Wellington, the Allied dispositions made the most of every advantage available—both natural and man-made. The mass of the Allied army—which totalled on the field 49,608 infantry, 12,408 cavalry and 156 cannon served by 5,645 gunners, or 67,661 men in all—was deployed on the reverse slopes adjacent to the Chemin d'Ohain running along the crest of Mont-St. Jean. Here they were protected from both the view and the fire of the French. A substantial part of II Corps (Lord Hill's command) was drawn up on Wellington's right, between the village of Merbraine and the Nivelles road, with General Chassé's Division of I Corps (placed under Hill's command for the day) a mile further to the west, holding Braine l'Alleud and its area (d'Aubremé's and Ditmers's brigades). To their forward left was Mitchell's Brigade of Colville's Division, with the three brigades of Clinton's Division (under Adam, du Plat and Hew Halkett) in a second-line posi-

The Exterior of Hougoumont at the commencement of the Battle of Waterloo by T. Sutherland. A somewhat fanciful idea of the fighting for Hougoumont, the British-held position to the fore of Wellington's right wing. Despite the caption, the Château did not present so ruinous an appearance until the late evening

OVERLEAF LEFT *Major-General Sir Colin Halkett* (1774–1856) by Salter. A commander who had led part of the King's German Legion in Spain, in 1815 he was in command of a brigade of British troops at both Quatre Bras and Waterloo. In later years he rose to high command in India, and he ended his career as Governor of Chelsea Hospital

OVERLEAF RIGHT *Major-General Sir Peregrine Maitland* (1774–1854) by Salter. First commissioned in 1792, he served in Flanders and Spain in many campaigns, and was promoted major-general in 1814. At Waterloo he commanded a brigade comprising the 2nd and 3rd Battalions of the First Foot Guards, just under 2,000 men, which played a large role in the repulse of the attack by the Imperial Guard. In recognition of this feat of arms, the regimental title was changed to the Grenadier Guards

tion. Such was Wellington's right wing, a very powerful force drawn up in some depth for reasons that will become clear later.

Wellington's centre comprised the Prince of Orange's I Corps together with part of the General Reserve. Along the ridge to the west of the Brussels to Charleroi highway were deployed General Cooke's Guards Division (Byng's and Maitland's brigades) stationed along the ridge to the north of Hougoumont with the three brigades of Alten's Division (commanded by Colin Halkett, Kielmansegge and Ompteda) drawn up on their left. Kruse's Nassau detachment formed a local reserve. To the east of the high road stretched Wellington's left centre, made up of the three brigades of Picton's Division (led by Kempt, Pack and Vincke), interleaved with Best's Brigade of Cole's Division (although General Sir Lowry Cole in fact missed the battle, being on leave of absence to get married), and with Bylandt's Brigade of Perponcher's Division (part of I Corps) set on the forward slope of the ridge—whether intentionally or by oversight is still subject to debate—to the east of the gravel-pit. The Allied left wing comprised mainly the cavalry brigades of Vivian and Vandeleur.

Manning the important positions ahead of the main line were the following the Château of Hougoumont and the adjoining woodland were garrisoned at first by four light companies from the Guards Division, some Nassauers, some Lüneburgers and some Hanoverians, but they would be reinforced in due course by more detachments of Guards. In front of the centre, a detachment of the King's German Legion occupied La Haie Sainte, whilst part of the 95th Regiment (later the Rifle Brigade) manned the gravel-pit. Finally, to hold Papelotte, La Haie and Frischermont on the extreme left, the Nassau Brigade commanded by the Prince of Saxe-Weimar (part of Perponcher's command) was deployed well to the fore. These forces, together with a screen of light cavalry on the flanks and a series of infantry pickets, completed the Allied forward dispositions.

In reserve, massed behind the centre, Wellington stationed most of his cavalry. East of the high road were the brigades of Ponsonby (part of Uxbridge's heavy cavalry) and Ghigny (part of I Corps' divisional cavalry). To the west were Somerset's heavy brigade, backed by the remaining two brigades (under Trip and Merlen) of I Corps' cavalry and the greater part of the artillery reserve, with Lambert's infantry brigade in rear of all. Further to the right, nearer to the Nivelles road, stood the massed squadrons of Grant's, Dornberg's and Arentschildt's brigades of Uxbridge's light cavalry, with the battalions and

squadrons of Brunswickers in the rear. For the approximate placing of the twenty-six artillery batteries, the reader's attention is directed to the map. This completed Wellington's battle array, but mention must be made of a further 17,000 men and thirty guns, commanded by Prince Frederick of the Netherlands, who were stationed ten miles to the west at Hal and Tubize in order to guard the extreme flank against any French attempt at an envelopment. These troops included two-thirds of Sir Charles Colville's Division (namely Johnstone's and Lyon's brigades), the whole of Stedman's Dutch–Belgian Division (Hauw's and Eerens's brigades), Anthing's Indonesian Brigade and some Hanoverian cavalry under Estorff, and were destined to take scant part in the fighting on the 18th.

The general disposition of Wellington's army gives rise to three comments. First, it was a carefully chosen position, selected some time previously after full examination by his staff. Second, the fact that it was backed by the Forest of Soignies (although this attracted considerable criticism from Napoleon) was not a dangerous feature as the Duke calculated that it would aid, rather than hinder, any further retreat should this become necessary, as it would only hamper cavalry. And thirdly, the shape of the Allied position—a large triangular wedge with the greater part of the troops drawn up on Wellington's right (or western) wing, reveals that the Duke was relying on the arrival of at least two Prussian corps (as requested from, and promised by, Blücher) to complete his battle array. Space had accordingly been left for these formations on the Allied left.

Passing on to consider Napoleon's disposition of l'Armée du Nord, we find a simpler layout on the ground than that adopted by Wellington. To the west of the Brussels high road, its right flank a little short of La Belle Alliance, was drawn up the II Corps of General Reille, which described a long concave arc around the Château and Wood of Hougoumont to just beyond the Nivelles road westwards. On the extreme left flank was the cavalry division of Piré. Next, running in order from west to east, came three of Reille's infantry divisions commanded by Jérôme Bonaparte, Foy and Bachelu—Girard's bereaved division had been left to garrison the Ligny area. From the front of La Belle Alliance to the eastwards stood the four infantry divisions of d'Erlon's I Corps—under Quiot, Donzelot, Marcognet and Durutte respectively, with Jacquinot's eleven squadrons (the Corps cavalry) on the extreme right opposite La Haie and Frischermont. These two corps d'armée formed the front line

Duke of Wellington visiting the Outposts at Soignies by Hippolyte Lecomte. Before the campaign opened, the Duke of Wellington was everywhere inspecting his troops. Here, accompanied by his staff, he rides through an encampment of the Reserve near Brussels.

of the French army. Before them extended a thick screen of light infantry, and, directly in front of Quiot's Division would eventually be massed the grand battery of eighty-four guns, ready to blast a gap through the Allied centre on the facing ridge, barely 700 yards away.

In the second line, the French deployed the mass of their cavalry reserve. Behind Reille, General Kellermann drew up the two divisions (under L'Heretier and d'Urbal) of his III Cavalry Corps, and to their rear stood Guyot's Division of Guard cavalry. Similarly, behind d'Erlon were the pair of divisions (under Walther and Delort) of Milhaud's IV Cavalry Corps, containing many *cuirassiers*, and once more to the rear was deployed Lefebvre-Desnouëtte's Division of Guard cavalry. Finally, in central reserve on each side of the Brussels road, Napoleon deployed his reserves. To the east of Maison du Roi

were placed the long cavalry columns of Domont's and Subervie's divisions, the former having been switched from the role
of Corps cavalry division to Vandamme's III Corps (presently
with Grouchy near Wavre) and the latter being half of Pajol's I
Cavalry Corps. On the opposite side of the road were the infantry columns of Simmer's and Jeannin's divisions of Count
Lobau's VI Corps. Last, but by no means least, stood the
serried ranks of the Imperial Guard, flanked by the guns of the
artillery reserve, on either side of the farm of Rossomme.

Taken together, this represented a force of 71,947 men—
48,950 infantry, 15,765 cavalry and 7,232 gunners serving a
total of 246 cannon. In the first line were seven infantry divisions
and two of cavalry; in the second (including Lobau's centrally
placed reserve corps) were six cavalry divisions and two of
infantry; and in the third echelon (including Guyot's and
Lefebvre-Desnouëttes' Guard squadrons) were the effective
strength of three Imperial Guard divisions and two divisions of
élite cavalry. Such were the general dispositions of the two main
armies at approximately midday on 18 June, shortly before the
opening of the main battle.

Meanwhile, over by Wavre, the remaining forces involved in
this drama were also drawing up. Grouchy's pursuit of Blücher
on the 17th had been late starting, and then took the wrong
direction, as we have remarked earlier. He had only appreciated
his mistake at Gembloux at 10 p.m. on the 17th, when his
cavalry revealed that the mass of the Prussians was in fact
retiring on Wavre and not, after all, towards Namur. Even then,
Grouchy contented himself with passing this news on to
Napoleon's headquarters as we have related, and ordered
Vandamme to be ready to march after the enemy towards
Sart-les-Walhain at 6 a.m. on the 18th, with Gérard following
him two hours later. In fact the general lethargy that afflicted
Ney's wing of the army on the 17th seems to have spread to the
right wing as well. The troops were understandably weary after
the fighting on the 16th, but this would never have affected the
pursuit capacity of the French army in the great years. As a
result it was not in fact until 8 a.m.—two hours behind schedule
—that Vandamme was at last on the road, and because of this
delay it was 9 a.m. before Gérard set out. Just over an hour later,
however, Grouchy was able to confirm, from near Walhain,
that the mass of the Prussians were indeed around Wavre; he
wrote of his intention of interposing his corps between Wavre
and Mont-St. Jean to preclude any attempt at an Allied link-up.
In fact, however, by that time substantial Prussian forces were

already on the march towards the west, and not a shot had yet been fired at Wavre.

Overnight Blücher had undertaken, as we have mentioned, to move to Wellington's aid with at least two corps—and he was to prove as good as his word, although confirmation of his intention only reached Wellington at 6 a.m. on the 18th. By 11 a.m., the staunch old soldier was riding to the head of his columns as they floundered and staggered through the mud in the narrow defiles. 'Lads,' he cried to the soldiers of Bülow's IV Corps, 'you will not let me break my word!' Gneisenau had been left at Wavre with orders to watch the French, and determine whether or not it would be safe to send further troops off to the westwards. French inaction soon convinced him that there was no need to retain more than a single corps at Wavre, and Pirch's II Corps, at about noon, and then Ziethen's I Corps at much the same time, were sent on their way to follow Bülow.

In all, no less than 72,000 Prussian troops marched to Wellington's aid. Thielemann and some 15,000 men of his III Corps were given the task of covering this important movement. His orders were largely discretionary: if the French to his front made no aggressive move, he, in his turn, was to follow the rest of the army, leaving merely two fusilier battalions to hold Wavre and the two Dyle bridges. This, we shall see, he was not destined to do. Nor was the movement of the main Prussian forces without its problems. Bülow's advanced brigade was hardly clear of Wavre before a major fire broke out in the town which held up the rest of his corps for some time before it was extinguished. His advance guard reached the Wood of Paris through Chapelle-St. Lambert before it halted to await the rear elements. Fortunately the French were in utter ignorance of this disjointed advance. A little later Ziethen's strong Corps was setting out towards the left bank of the River Lasne, routed towards Ohain, a little to the north of Bülow's line of march. Pirch, however, followed on the heels of Bülow by the more southerly route. Shortly after, the Prussian rearguard closed up about Wavre.

But this is to anticipate important developments on the main battlefield. If there was still no sign of a big action developing at Wavre, the situation was different to the south of Mont-St. Jean, where the guns spoke abruptly forth at 11.25 a.m. In fact, however, the main body of the French army was also decidedly late in opening the battle, and this circumstance requires some explanation, for we have already seen enough to

OVERLEAF *Dawn at Waterloo* after Lady Butler. Both armies spent a miserable night in pouring rain over the 17–18 June. At Reveille (shown here being sounded by the buglers of the North British Dragoons), the clouds began to dissipate and there was every prospect of a fine early summer's day. For many, it would be their last

appreciate that Wellington's strategy was to play a 'waiting game' in the hope that Blücher might join him, and every hour the French dallied before launching their attack was an hour gained for the Allies.

At nine o'clock Napoleon had called a staff meeting at Le Caillou to give his orders. Marshal Soult, anxiously aware that no reply had yet been vouchsafed to Grouchy's message of the previous evening, suggested that the right wing should be ordered to march towards the main body without delay. Napoleon scornfully discarded the suggestion, and expressed his low opinion of both Wellington and his army. He was clearly convinced that the troops already available would more than suffice to deal with the 'Sepoy General', and was not for an instant anticipating a significant Prussian intervention in the struggle despite evidence brought forward by Prince Jérôme of an overheard conversation between two Allied officers at Genappe the previous day. In this overconfidence lies one reason for his delay in opening the battle. A second, and even more significant, one related to the state of the ground. The Emperor agreed with General Drouot that the ground was still too wet to allow the cannon to be moved with ease, or to employ richochet fire. He therefore decreed that time should be allowed to give the ground a chance to dry out, and that the main battle should not open before 1 p.m. This was to prove one of the most fateful decisions of the day. 'We have ninety chances in our favour,' boasted Napoleon, 'and not ten against us.'

An hour later the Emperor moved up with his entourage to the farm of Rossomme. Here at last he bethought himself of the need to send a reply to Grouchy—fully six hours later than might have been the case. Even now, it was a vague order that emerged—neither recalling Grouchy, nor authorizing him to continue in his independent role. He was merely enjoined to head towards Wavre and keep in touch with the main French army—largely contradictory orders in fact. Napoleon then set out to inspect his army, riding along the forming battle lines and receiving his usual rapturous salutation from his troops. At last, shortly after 11 a.m., Napoleon dictated his plan of battle. It was hardly one of his most subtle schemes: no time was to be wasted on manoeuvre—success was to be won by a series of massive frontal attacks. Perhaps this was further evidence of his low opinion of his opponents; perhaps it was all he felt he could entrust to Marshal Ney, who had now been appointed in practical terms the battlefield commander, Napoleon himself only assuming an overall supervisory role. This decision is

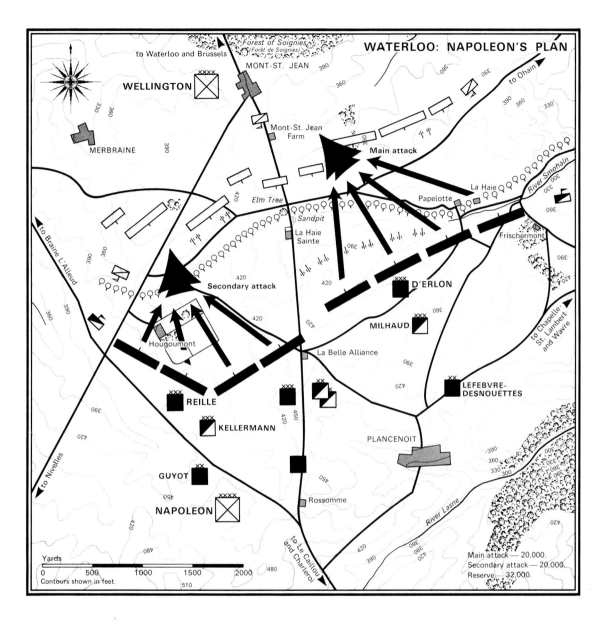

Waterloo: Napoleon's Plan

barely credible, given the mistakes Ney had perpetrated during the past few days. His conduct at the battle of Jena-Auerstädt in 1806, and at Bautzen in 1813, had shown up his deficiencies in battle—he was either far too impetuous or else far too slow by turns, and to entrust the general direction of the battle of Waterloo to this officer was to take an enormous risk.

But Napoleon was always a gambler—the master, in previous campaigns, of the calculated risk. He was fully aware of Ney's impaired, fluctuating intelligence and other short-comings, but against these he balanced his impeccable reputation for dash and personal gallantry in action, his excellent *rapport* with the rank and file of the French army, and his desire to make up for the mistakes committed near Quatre Bras over the past three days. To refurbish his somewhat tarnished reputation, the 'bravest of the brave' might be expected to produce a virtuoso performance, particularly as the plan Napoleon laid down at the grand tactical level was basically a simple one, calling for little originality on the part of the battle commander. Little more than a frontal battle of attrition was envisaged.

'Directly the army has formed up,' ran Napoleon's written order, 'and soon after 1 p.m., the Emperor will give the order to Marshal Ney and the attack will be delivered on Mont-St. Jean village in order to seize the cross-roads at that place. To this end the 12-pounder batteries of II and VI Corps will mass with those of I Corps. These twenty-four guns will bombard the troops holding Mont-St. Jean, and Count d'Erlon will begin the attack by first launching the left-hand division, and, when necessary, supporting it by other divisions of I Corps. II Corps will also advance, keeping abreast of I Corps. The company of engineers belonging to I Corps will hold themselves in readiness to barricade and fortify Mont-St. Jean directly it is taken.'

Some time later, Marshal Ney added an amendment on the back in pencil: 'Count d'Erlon will note that the attack will be delivered first by the left instead of beginning from the right. Inform General Reille of this change.'

This order makes no mention of an attack upon Hougoumont as a preliminary, nor provision for any possible Prussian intervention—clearly Napoleon did not even regard this as a remote possibility at this time. It is clear that he expected to blast his way through to Brussels, scattering Wellington's hybrid army in the process. The Emperor was seeking a quick victory of an unsophisticated type; the sodden nature of the ground would have hampered any more imaginative scheme based upon manoeuvre, but he did not believe that an outflanking attack would be necessary even if it had been practicable. As was his wont, all matters of tactical co-ordination were left to his designated battle-commander—a decision that would be regretted by the end of the day. His orders given, Napoleon sat on his horse watching movements on the opposite side of the valley. 'How steadily those troops take the ground. How beautifully those cavalry form! Look at those grey horses! Who are those fine horsemen? These are fine troops, but in half an hour I shall cut them to pieces.' Such were the comments

OVERLEAF *Napoleon's last Inspection before Waterloo* after J. P. Beadle. Napoleon acknowledges the cheers of the Horse Grenadiers of the Imperial Guard and a detachment of *cuirassiers* at about 11 a.m. on 18 June as French gunners toil to position a battery of guns. It was the need to allow the sodden ground to dry out that decided Napoleon, on the advice of General Drouot, to delay the opening of the battle by two hours. This respite was a gift to the Allies, who were anxiously awaiting the arrival of Blücher's Prussians from the direction of Wavre

recorded by a local peasant, Decoster, who had been pressed into service as a guide and spent much of the day near Napoleon as an unwilling spectator of events.

Around Mont-St. Jean the Allies also prepared for battle after the wretched night. Muskets were fired to ensure that damp had not attacked the powder, and then reloaded and reprimed. A thousand camp-fires were blazing now that the weather had improved, and the troops ate what rations they could procure. Captain Mercer's troop of horse artillery was

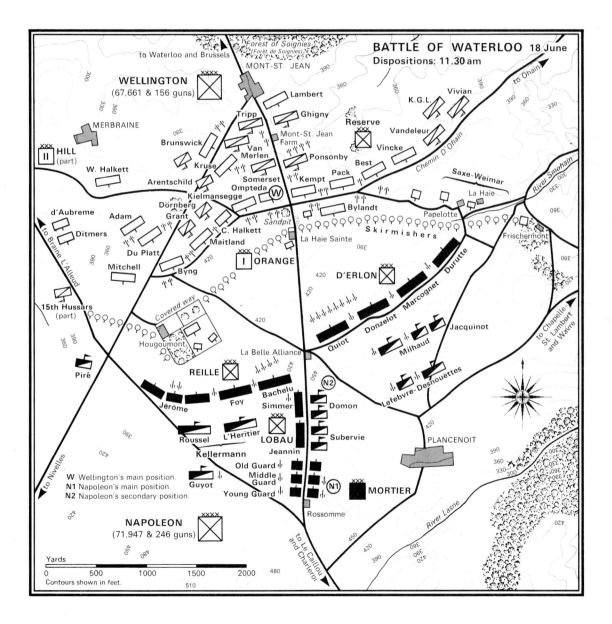

more fortunate than most: a driver of an ammunition wagon coming up from the rear '. . . had picked up and brought on a considerable quantity of beef, biscuit and oatmeal, of which there was abundance scattered about everywhere. . . . The rum was divided on the spot.' Meanwhile the riflemen of the 95th, close by La Haie Sainte, boiled a huge brew of tea in a cauldron at the roadside, '. . . where all the bigwigs of the army had occasion to pass. . . . I believe almost every one of them, from the Duke downward, claimed a cupful,' as Captain John Kincaid recalled later.

Wellington himself had been astir since before 6 a.m. Mounted on his horse, Copenhagen, he was accompanied by a staff of almost forty officers and escort-troopers. 'Now Bonaparte will see how a sepoy general can defend a position,' he remarked to the Prussian liaison officer, Baron Müffling. He rode along the line, inspecting every sector with his habitual care. Despite the indications that the French were preparing for a frontal attack, the Duke took no steps to recall Prince Frederick of the Netherlands' 17,000 men from Hal. Perhaps he wished to ensure that a line of retreat would remain open to the west; perhaps he believed that the promised Prussian aid would provide all the help he required, now that he knew that more than one corps was promised. Wearing his cocked hat with four small cockades, and wearing a dark blue overcoat and cape, white buck-skin breeches, and tasselled boots, he made an impressive if soberly dressed figure, and put fresh heart into his men.

Shortly after 11 a.m. Wellington took up his position beneath a solitary elm-tree at the south-west corner of the cross-roads atop Mont-St. Jean ridge, destined to serve as his command-post. Seven miles to the east, *Alte Vorwärts* was cheering on his mud-bound columns approaching Chapelle-St. Lambert. At the same time Napoleon moved forward to mount a low mound close to Rossomme, and strode back and forth deep in thought. Opposite Wavre away to the east, Marshal Grouchy complacently settled down to a late breakfast.

After a final survey of the still-quiet field through his telescope, Napoleon gave a slight nod. At once an aide galloped off to pass the word to Marshal Ney. At 11.25 a.m. the silence was shattered by a thunderous salvo from the French artillery: it was heard as far away as Wavre, where Grouchy promptly rose from table and abandoned his breakfast. The battle of Waterloo had at last begun.

Chapter Seven

Waterloo and Wavre-
The Early Stages

The opening of the battle has been ascribed to various times of day. In the Waterloo Despatch, Wellington claimed that it was 'about ten o'clock', but over the years a consensus has grown that the first major exchange of fire occurred an hour and a half later. Captain F. Powell of the 1st Guards informed the famous historian Siborne in 1834 that 'the first cannon shot was fired at 10.45 a.m. (by my watch)', but most historians put it at three-quarters of an hour later, or thereabouts.

The first blast of fire that Grouchy and his staff heard over ten miles away signalled the start of an attack by part of Reille's II Corps against the Château of Hougoumont to the front of Wellington's right wing. This was intended to be a preliminary and diversionary affair, but it was to prove very different. The Emperor—or more probably his battle-commander, Marshal Ney—may have calculated that Hougoumont was too close to the main French position for comfort, and may also have hoped that an onslaught against it might induce Wellington to move reserves from the centre of his line, thus weakening the sector destined to receive the main French effort.

Prince Jérôme Bonaparte, commanding the strong left-hand division of Reille's Corps, was entrusted with the task. His determination to succeed was going to lead to difficulties. With Piré's cavalry in support, he launched four regiments forward to clear the wood leading to the Château. Twice the Nassauers and Hanoverians defending the area drove back the French, killing the leading brigade-commander. Gradually however, the French made ground, and in the end the Allied troops were driven back to the main position—the Château and its orchard —which were already garrisoned by certain detachments of the

British Guards, ready and waiting for the onslaught to begin.

'The farm is well calculated for defence,' wrote Colonel Woodford of the Coldstream Guards. 'The dwelling-house in the centre was a strong square building, with small doors and windows. The barns and granaries formed nearly a square.' Today many of these features have disappeared, but the famous garden wall, with signs of loopholes driven through, still stands, as does the chapel. The French came on under a hail of fire, both musketry and howitzer shells, and the main struggle began. By this time Jérôme's blood was thoroughly aroused, and despite repeated orders to consolidate his position, he insisted on drawing in regiment after regiment of his 6th Division, until practically the whole formation was involved. Losses soared, but still the French surged forward, wave after wave, in attempts to penetrate the defences. They would have been better advised

The First Shot At the Battle of Waterloo by W. Wollen. An imaginative picture showing the treatment meted out to an over-bold French *cuirassier* on picket-duty by Light Infantry holding the edge of the Wood of Hougoumont

to leave the task to artillery, but fortunately for the defenders this thought only came to them later in the day. True, Jérôme's men did achieve a hold over part of the orchard, but they never penetrated the garden, or, for long, into the Château courtyard. The six-foot garden wall proved an unscalable obstacle, though many were shot down or bayonetted in the attempt.

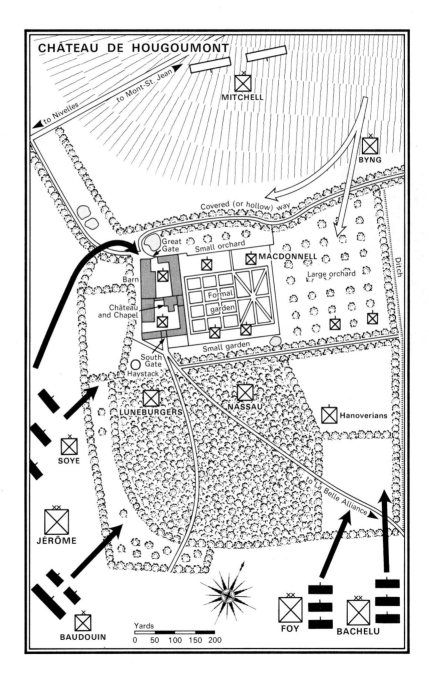

More critical were events to the north of the position, whither
the French had penetrated by lapping around the building. The
1st Light Regiment of General Soye's Brigade, led by the
gigantic *sous-lieutenant* Legros (nicknamed '*l'Enfonceur*' or 'the
Smasher') wielding an axe, drove back the outlying defenders
towards the Château and succeeded in bursting into the courtyard through the Great Gate in the northern wall. After a titanic
hand-to-hand struggle, the doors were reclosed, and the French
within cut down to a man. A single French drummer-boy, less
his lost drum, was taken prisoner.

At this juncture Colonel Woodford arrived from the ridge
with four companies of reinforcements, and repulsed the
French from the northern side of the position. The Cold-
streamers then joined the garrison. Thus the battle was developing very differently from the way the French had intended. The
whole of Jérôme's Division became inextricably involved for
the whole of the battle, and his furious and often ill-considered
attacks eventually drew in half the neighbouring division of
General Foy as well. As for Wellington, he only reinforced
Hougoumont with thirteen companies of Guardsmen in all
(although the Scots Guards and part of the 1st Guards were
also involved in the struggle for the orchard, so practically the
whole of Byng's 2nd Guards Brigade was eventually involved),
and the Allies therefore were not induced to redeploy in a major
way at all. The defenders were able to draw reinforcements
along a sheltered dip in the ground running back to the main
position, and this in no small measure contributed to the
success of the defence.

Only later in the afternoon—at about 3.30 p.m.—did the
French, at Napoleon's direction, subject the buildings to heavy
howitzer fire, which set some of the buildings ablaze. This
added complication was tackled effectively, and the watchful
Duke sent down a message to Lieut.-Colonel Macdonnell: 'I
see that the fire has communicated from the hay stack to the
roof of the Château. You must however keep your men in those
parts to which the fire does not reach. Take care that no men are
lost by the falling in of the roof or floors. After they have fallen
in occupy the ruined walls inside of the garden, particularly if
it should be possible for the enemy to pass through the embers
in the inside of the house.' Much of the original set of buildings
perished amidst the conflagration, and many wounded of both
sides died in the flames despite the efforts of their comrades to
save them. But Hougoumont never changed hands, and fighting
was still continuing in the neighbouring woodland at 8 p.m.

that evening—*after* the repulse of Napoleon's Guard from the ridge.

Wellington paid just tribute to the feat performed by Byng's 2,000 Guardsmen and a few hundred Nassauers and Germans, in holding at bay at least 13,000 French troops. As Creevey recorded, the Duke '. . . praised greatly those Guards who kept the farm against the repeated attacks of the French.' On another occasion, he mentioned the reclosing of the courtyard gates as the critical moment of the entire battle. The retention of Hougoumont not only tied down French troops and secured Wellington's right flank but, as we shall see, gravely hampered the employment of the massed French cavalry later in the battle. The staunch resistance must also have inspired those Allies on the ridge behind, when the smoke cleared enough to permit it to be seen. But all this was only achieved at grave cost. The Coldstream Guards lost 304 killed and wounded in and around Hougoumont; the 3rd (or Scots) Guards lost 239 casualties. Today, the chapel forms a touching memorial to the fallen.

For an hour and a half after the first salvos, the fighting around Hougoumont constituted the only major activity on the field of Waterloo. There was skirmishing at other points, and some exchange of cannon-fire, but little more. Ten miles away, south of Wavre, there was still singularly little action, but in fact a decision, critical to the whole outcome of the whole double-battle, had been taken at about 11.45 a.m. For if Jérôme's rash attacks and unauthorized initiatives constitute the first major French tactical error of the day's fighting, Marshal Grouchy's caution and lack of imagination would prove another vital factor affecting the eventual outcome.

We have already described how the Marshal's breakfast was disturbed by the sound of gunfire away to the west. He was at once approached by General Gérard, commander of IV Corps, who demanded—no lesser word will suffice—that the right wing of *l'Armée du Nord* should forthwith 'march on the sound of the guns'. This suggestion had ample precedent to back it, but Gérard was so tactless and obviously disapproving that he instantly offended his superior. Grouchy accordingly referred to the last order received from the Emperor (he had not yet, of course, received any reply to his message of the previous night) which spoke of the need to secure possession of Wavre. Until ordered otherwise, that was the course he would pursue. The troops would accordingly march on Corbaix as a preliminary to assaulting the Prussians holding Wavre. Thus a great oppor-

The North Gate of Hougoumont, as it appeared the day after the battle of Waterloo, from a painting by D. Dighton

tunity was let slip. Even if Grouchy had moved westwards as late as midday—as Napoleon's 10 a.m. order required—he would have been able to intercept Blücher's main body before it could reach Waterloo. Instead, Grouchy chose to interpret his last-received orders literally, for Napoleon's subsequent message only arrived after 5 p.m., by which time it was too late to implement its contents. The ultimate error which was going to doom Napoleon to catastrophic defeat had thus been committed, but in the last analysis responsibility for this must lie in the Emperor's oversight in not replying to Grouchy's overnight report before 10 a.m. As it was, not until about 4 p.m. would the French right wing be seriously in action against Thielemann near Wavre. By that hour, both Pirch and Bülow would be fighting between Frischermont and Plancenoit against Napoleon's exposed flank.

But this is to anticipate events. Back at Waterloo, as the struggle around Hougoumont raged on, Napoleon and Ney were supervising the massing of eighty-four guns slightly to the fore of Quiot's Division of I Corps on a low rise to the east of the Brussels highway. To the two dozen 12-pounders originally designated for the task of blasting a gap through Wellington's left centre had been added the twenty-four 'beautiful daughters' (also 12-pounders) of the Guard artillery and all forty 8-pounders belonging to the divisional artillery of d'Erlon's Corps, together with some horse artillery batteries. At about 1 p.m. this impressive battery opened a thunderous barrage against Wellington's line at 700 yards' range. In fact they had precious little to fire against—for apart from Wellington's artillery, his forward pickets, and of course Bylandt's exposed Brigade, the bulk of his army was concealed on the reverse slopes. The French might have hoped under normal conditions that many of their shots would ricochet and plunge over the crest to harm the lines of men sheltering beyond, but the wetness of the ground prevented this effect, and most cannon-balls were swallowed up in the mud on the forward slopes. Of course the unfortunate Dutch and Belgian troops of Bylandt, in their blue uniforms with orange facings, suffered grievously from the fire of the massed guns. As the salvos thundered on, the four divisions of d'Erlon's Corps prepared to advance to execute the first main attack called for in Napoleon's plan of battle.

The North Gate of Hougoumont as it is today. The main Château building used to stand to the left—but only the chapel, now a monument to the Guards Division, remains

Before this could be launched, however, the Imperial staff around Napoleon were noticed to be anxiously scanning the horizon to the north-east. Signs of movement could be detected amongst the trees in the direction of Chapelle-St. Lambert.

Could it be the arrival of Grouchy's advance guard? Any such hopes were dashed by the arrival of a patrol of the 7th Hussars, escorting a captured Prussian courier whom they had taken not far from Frischermont. He revealed under questioning that all of 30,000 Prussians, under Blücher in person, were well on their way to attack the French right. Napoleon took the news calmly. 'This morning we had ninety chances in our favour. Even now we have sixty chances, and only forty against us.' The battle was to continue—Wellington and Bülow (the Emperor had no conception that all of three Prussian corps were bearing down on his position) were to be defeated together. But Soult added a postscript to his reply to Grouchy's newly received second message mentioning his advance on Corbaix and Wavre. 'A letter which has just been intercepted states that General Bülow is about to attack our flank. We believe we can see this corps on the heights of St. Lambert; therefore lose not an instant in drawing nearer to us and joining us, in order to crush Bülow whom you will take in the very act [of concentrating]'. As already noted, this message was not destined to reach its addressee until after 5 p.m. If only Grouchy had drawn closer earlier with the main army, the outcome might have been very different. To guard against the newly revealed threat, the French command ordered Domont and **Subervie** to move their cavalry to the north-east, and soon they were followed by the 10,000 men of Lobau's VI Corps. This meant that fully half of Napoleon's central reserves had been committed before the main fighting of the day had got under way: only the Imperial Guard now remained in reserve. The need to extemporize a defensive flank to the east, facing the Wood of Paris, thus tied down valuable formations—in fact, all of four divisions. In many an earlier battle Napoleon had used a similar manoeuvre to the one now being used against him to disconcert his adversaries. It was a fair case of 'the biter bit'.

But now all attention was turned to the French right centre, as d'Erlon's four divisions, supported by skirmishers and two brigades of heavy cavalry—Dubois's *cuirassiers* of Wathier's Division abreast the Brussels highway and part of Travers's *cuirassier* Brigade to the left of Donzelot's Division—prepared to move forward. At 1.30 p.m. this mass of men, perhaps 17,000 strong, began to advance, preceded by a hurricane of shot and shell before the guns fell silent as the masses obscured the line of fire. However, another bad mistake was being committed. For some unknown reason—possibly a garbled or misread order— two of the infantry divisions had been drawn up in vast, im-

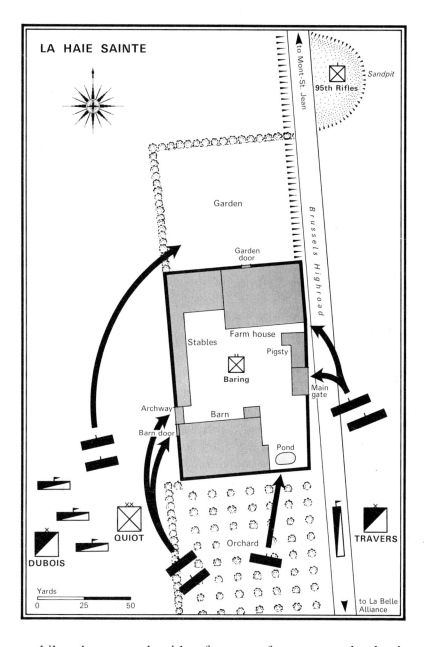

LA HAIE SAINTE

mobile columns, each with a frontage of 200 men and a depth of eight or nine battalions—or twenty-seven ranks. These massive *colonnes de bataillon par division* were an outdated formation which severely restricted their tactical flexibility; the normal, far handier, *colonnes de division par bataillon*—a chequer-board of battalion columns, each with a two-company frontage of some seventy men and a total depth of nine ranks, and with sufficient room between each column for the formations to deploy into line if necessary—would have proved far more suitable. As it was, the huge columns made marvellous targets for the Allied gunners as they surged ponderously forward over no-man's-land.

Nevertheless, the advance made a daunting sight to the waiting Allies atop the ridge. Quiot's Division, on the left of d'Erlon's line, lapped around the farm of La Haie Sainte (defended by Major Baring and a battalion of the King's German Legion) and eventually cleared its orchard and garden. When Wellington sent a battalion of Lüneburgers from Kiel-mansegge's Brigade to Baring's aid, they were caught by a regiment of Dubois's *cuirassiers* and butchered. To the east of the road the French occupied the gravel-pit for the time being, and some Netherlanders broke and fled at the prospect facing them. Fortunately Picton was at hand to fill the gap with part of Kempt's Brigade, whose charge repulsed the French on their sector for the moment. Meantime Donzelot's and Marcognet's massive columns were breasting the slope, only to be met by the blazing volleys of Pack's and Best's brigades lining the thick hedgerows with extemporized embrasures hacked through them for the guns, which caused them to shrink back. At this moment—about 2 p.m.—an unfortunate shot struck General Picton (still wearing the civilian clothes and top-hat he had sported since the 16th) through the forehead, and he fell dead.

It was a critical moment for Wellington's centre. Kempt and Pack mustered barely 3,000 infantrymen between them, with no infantry second-line reserves behind them, and were now facing all of 10,000 men of two of d'Erlon's divisions. But Lord Uxbridge had his two heavy cavalry brigades in readiness, namely Somerset's Household Brigade, nine squadrons strong, to the west of the Brussels road, and Ponsonby's Union Brigade, also nine squadrons strong, to the east. The charge was sounded; and through the intervals between the Hanoverians and King's German Legionaries of Ompteda's Brigade manning the crest to the north and north-west of La Haie Sainte, spurred the British 'heavies'. Favoured by the slope, Somerset's seven leading squadrons—led by Uxbridge in person—swept irre-sistibly into the ranks of General Dubois's cavalry brigade. The two lines met with a resounding crash near the farm. The French *cuirassiers*, although their swords were longer than the British sabres, were less well mounted, and they turned and fled, accompanied by part of the infantry of d'Erlon's left-hand division from around La Haie Sainte. Many French were cut down and two horse artillery batteries overrun before Somerset's

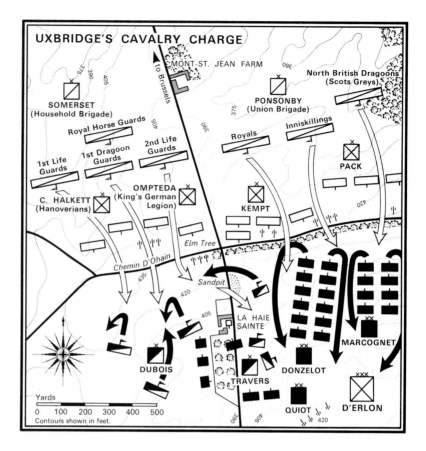

Brigade rallied under cover of the two fresh squadrons of the Royal Horse Guards, which had been held in reserve. Some parties of his Dragoon Guards and Life Guards, however, pushed too far south in their excitement and even reached part of Napoleon's great battery before they were repulsed with loss by French infantry and more *cuirassiers*.

Meanwhile, east of the Brussels road, Ponsonby's Union Brigade had also gone into action, with six squadrons of the Royals and Innerskillings in the first line and three more of Scots Greys (or 2nd Royal North British Dragoons) in reserve to their left rear. To the amazement and consternation of the French infantry, who had anticipated only infantry opposition, the abrupt appearance of these horsemen over the ridge through intervals in Kempt's and Pack's brigades, signalled defeat. One officer noted: '. . . English cavalry from every side, forcing their way into our midst and hacking us to pieces.' Donzelot's and Marcognet's divisions, which shortly before had been scenting victory, began to dissolve into a horde of fugitives. Some 'fought

Vernet 1816.

like tigers', however, before retreating. These events proved too much for the Scots Greys, who forgot their supporting role and rode forward to join the battle at increasing speed. On their way, still moving at the walk or slow trot, they passed through the 92nd Highlanders, many of whom grabbed hold of their stirrups to be borne forward into the fray. 'Hurrah, 92nd! Scotland for ever' went up the cry. Then, gathering speed, the bearskinned Greys crashed through Marcognet's columns. Sgt. Ewart captured the eagle standard of the French 45th Regiment; Capt. Kennedy Clark and a corporal of the Royal Regiment of Dragoons took another. D'Erlon's attack rolled back in ruin, losing possibly 5,000 men, including 3,000 prisoners. Only on the far right, where General Durutte had wisely adopted a more flexible formation for his division, did the troops of I Corps make any ground, capturing parts of both Papelotte and Frischermont from the Nassauers after hard fighting. But these limited successes could not disguise the fact that Napoleon's first major attack of the day had foundered.

However, there was a postscript to be fought out. The Scots

Waterloo, 18th June 1815 by C. Warren. The Union Brigade, led by Major-General Ponsonby, followed Uxbridge's Heavy Brigade into action against d'Erlon's reeling infantry divisions. Part of the Union Brigade comprised the Second North British Dragoons (later the Royal Scots Greys and today the Royal Scots Dragoon Guards). Sergeant William Ewart of the regiment distinguished himself by capturing, and bearing safely to the rear, the eagle standard of the French 45th Regiment of the Line

Greys, carried away by their success, failed to rally, but charged on over the valley to plunge amongst the French gunners beyond, silencing thirty French guns. This rash feat earned speedy retribution. As the blown and scattered horsemen strove to rally, far too late, they were attacked by fresh *cuirassiers* and a regiment of Jacquinot's lancers, and suffered heavy losses. Sir William Ponsonby himself was captured and then killed. Meanwhile, Vandeleur's three dragoon regiments, accompanied by some Dutch dragoons and Belgian lancers, all from the extreme left of Wellington's line, spurred forward to recapture Papelotte, and then did their best to cover the retreat of what was left of the Scots Greys and other parts of the Union Brigade. Colonel Frederick Ponsonby of the 12th Light Dragoons was severely wounded in this task, but survived the day to recover. Many another cavalryman was not so fortunate. It is estimated that of some 2,500 British cavalry involved in the twin charges by the two heavy brigades of Lord Uxbridge, fully a thousand became casualties. Thus Wellington had survived the first great crisis, but at a great cost to his cavalry, the heavy components of which were virtually out of action by the day's close. This was partly due to the old failing—often noted in the Peninsula—of failing to re-form after a charge; perhaps the traditions of the fox hunt were too deeply engrained to be denied, and indiscipline resulted. Furthermore, Uxbridge's failure to organize his brigades into cavalry divisions hindered the passage of orders and the maintenance of control. This notwithstanding, the eighteen squadrons had given sterling service. By 3 p.m. fighting had temporarily died away except near Hougoumont and La Haie Sainte, and more time had been won for Blücher's men to arrive and intervene in the struggle. Wellington used the respite to bring up Lambert's Brigade and Ghigny's horsemen from reserve to strengthen his left centre, to appoint Kempt to command Picton's bereaved Division, and to re-occupy the gravel-pit. He also ordered the Brunswick Corps to move forward to occupy the area formerly held by Byng's Guardsmen, and placed Hew Halkett's Hanovarians in their support.

Marshal Ney was enraged by the rout of d'Erlon's Corps. Napoleon too, had just received Grouchy's 11.30 a.m. message, which disposed once and for all of any hopes that the French right wing could join the battle that afternoon. The Emperor decided that La Haie Sainte must be taken without further delay, and sent a categorical order to Ney to that effect. The Guard closed up, ready to exploit Ney's anticipated break-

OVERLEAF *Capture of the French Guns* after W. Wollen. The success and momentum of the Union Brigade's charge carried it right over the intervening valley and into part of the French gun-line beyond. Only then did the North British Dragoons and the Royals and the Innerskillings attempt to rally and re-form. But their horses were blown, they were counter-attacked on their way back to the Allied lines by Jacquinot's lancers and other French cavalry, and suffered heavy losses

through. Ney gathered two serviceable brigades of I Corps, and flung them back up the road against the farm. Major Baring, however, received timely aid from a Hanoverian battalion, and the attack was repulsed. At this juncture Ney, well to the fore as usual, noticed what he chose to interpret as signs of Allied weakness in the centre. What he probably saw were the British battalions returning to the cover of the reverse slopes during a lull, together with parties of wounded, French captives and ammunition wagons moving to the rear. What he thought he saw was the beginning of an attempt by Wellington to retreat on Brussels. In an excess of ardour, he at once ordered a brigade of Milhaud's *cuirassiers* to cross over to the west of the high road and charge forthwith, hoping to rout the Allies with no more ado. The time was approximately 4 p.m., and the next great act of the battle-drama was about to open.

What started as a relatively small cavalry charge rapidly escalated into a major mounted attack. Division after division of French cavalry were drawn into the battle, many without orders. Lefebvre-Desnouëttes followed Milhaud's *cuirassier* Corps, and by 4 p.m. all of 5,000 French cavalry—both heavy and light—were pounding towards the crest, towards the Allied right centre. This was a mistake for several reasons. First, it obscured the fire of part of the main French battery, in the process of being resited to the west of the Brussels highway. Second, the need to give both Hougoumont and La Haie Sainte a wide berth forced the French cavalry to operate on only an 800-yard front in a long column of squadrons; and thirdly, the very soggy nature of the ground in the area prevented them working up to more than a trot. Fourth, and worst of all, no measures were taken to support the cavalry with sufficient infantry or horse artillery units. In his haste to seize what he considered to be the great opportunity of the day, Ney had quite overlooked to lay on a properly co-ordinated attack.

The serried ranks of horsemen made an unforgettable target for the Allied gunners. The infantry battalions transformed themselves into twenty fire-fringed squares and rectangles, and the first French horsemen began to crash to the ground. The British gunners manned their pieces to the last moment, and then either took shelter between the wheels or ran for the nearest square. For a full hour surge after surge of French cavalry beat like twelve waves against the lines of squares—unavailingly, for, despite mounting losses, they stood firm. Conditions within the squares became appalling—suffocating smoke, piles of wounded and dying, desperate thirst—but the

Ney's ill-coordinated mass cavalry attacks surged twelve times around the British squares atop the western part of the ridge of Mont-St. Jean. Their *cuirassiers* made no lasting impression, however, as they came on without infantry or close-range horse artillery support, and the squares retained their cohesion, although they sustained heavy casualties in the process

French cavalry could not break them. As each successive wave of horsemen recoiled the Allied gunners remanned their pieces and sent several rounds after the retiring foe. Judging his moment with great nicety, Lord Uxbridge launched a counter-attack with his massed light cavalry brigades of the right wing and centre. This cleared the French horsemen from the ridge area, but at the foot of the slope they lost no time in re-forming and coming on again—only to be flung back once more.

Napoleon had viewed these events with growing alarm from his new command post on a bank a little to the east of La Belle Alliance, to which he had now moved forward. 'This is a premature movement that may lead to fatal results. He [Ney] is compromising us as he did at Jena.' The only way to redeem the position and extricate the forty or so squadrons already in action was to use the remaining French cavalry—the squadrons of Kellermann and Guyot from behind the left wing. By 5 p.m. no less than 10,000 horsemen were mounting a third series of heroic charges—along an encumbered front that only really justified the use of 1,000 cavalrymen at a time. Wellington's squares were now under very heavy pressure, for a French horse artillery battery was causing terrible damage at a range of 400 yards; fortunately it was only very belatedly that Ney—who had lost four horses killed under him—bethought him of the 8,000 unemployed men of Reille's II Corps (the one and a half divisions not tied down around the blazing ruins of Hougou-mont), but it was 5.30 p.m. before they could come up, only to lose 1,500 men in ten minutes from the hurricane of fire launched

at them by the Allied artillery and infantry. The French understandably fell back. One Allied cavalry unit—the Cumberland Hussars—disgraced itself by flccing thc ficld, but for the rest Wellington's line stood firm. Thus the second attempt to dislodge Wellington from the Mont-St. Jean ridge had failed.

For some little time, moreover, Napoleon's attention had been increasingly taken up by events on his right flank, for at last the Prussians had arrived. After pausing at Chapelle-St. Lambert at midday to allow his column to close up, Bülow had pressed on for the battlefield. At 4 p.m., he at last began to emerge from the Wood of Paris in strength. Wellington had hoped for reinforcement by the late morning, but the combina-

The Ravine at Waterloo by U. Checa; Popular Myth versus Historical Fact. One short portion of the Chemin d'Ohain to the west of the cross-roads was in 1815 a sunken lane. This fact was siezed upon by the great French novelist, Victor Hugo, and elaborated in *Les Miserables* into a hidden ravine which he used to explain the failure of the massed French cavalry attacks

tion of the fire in Wavre, some confusion on the march (through faulty staff-work two large columns had crossed each other's paths), and the mud, had between them ruled out all hope of a speedier intervention. Now, however, Napoleon faced a real crisis. Domont's cavalry and Lobau's VI Corps were forming a new line at right angles to the main front, Lobau's left-hand division eventually linking up with Durutte of d'Erlon's I Corps, and the French attacked before Bülow could deploy all his 30,000 men—but soon expended their energy. Bülow gave a little before the French, but then shifted his line of attack towards the village of Plancenoit, threatening to turn Lobau's right flank. The French could only fall back, and by 5 p.m. the village was in danger as the Prussians swept towards it from three sides at once, for now Pirch's II Corps was coming into action to the south of Bülow. Prussian cannon-balls began to howl over the main Brussels–Charleroi high road—a reminder to the Emperor that his line of communication, and possibly of retreat—was becoming vulnerable. To stop the rot, a division of the Young Guard was sent off under General Duhesme to recapture the lost parts of Plancenoit and ease the pressure on Lobau's tiring troops, thus enabling them to occupy a better position north-east of the village.

The Young Guard managed to become masters of Plancenoit, but only briefly, for they were repulsed again by a new surge of Prussian attackers. There was nothing for it but to send in two battalions of the Old Guard under Generals Morand and Pelet, to retake the village. The remainder of the Guard—eleven battalions—were meanwhile formed up in a long line to the east of the main road facing towards the Wood of Paris, as a buttress for the eastern flank, just in case the Prussians broke through. In fact this proved an unnecessary precaution (and one that lost Ney a possible chance of victory against Wellington's centre, as we shall describe in the next chapter) for the 'oldest of the old', the 1st/2nd Grenadiers and the 1st/2nd *Chasseurs* of the Old Guard swept into Plancenoit with the bayonet amidst a storm of rain and expelled all of fourteen Prussian battalions in very short order. The Young Guard then regarrisoned the village, but the victors pressed a little too far beyond in pursuit of the discomfited Prussians, and were tellingly counter-attacked by Bülow and forced to withdraw. Nevertheless, within an hour the situation on Napoleon's right flank had been stabilized, and by 6.45 p.m. it proved possible to recall most of the Guard battalions into central reserve. The battle had still to be won—and lost.

Chapter Eight

Waterloo and Wavre-
The Final Crises

Blücher had been a witness to some of the later events around Plancenoit. He and Gneisenau were meanwhile receiving a series of reports and appeals from Thielemann at Wavre, for 4 p.m. had at last seen the launching of Grouchy's attack against the Prussian rearguard.

The main onslaught was entrusted to Vandamme's III Corps, which fought its way forward to the Dyle, pressing back outlying Prussian formations before it. With 33,765 men at his disposal, facing only 15,200 Prussian, Grouchy had a daunting numerical advantage, but was not of course fully aware of it, so broken and obscure was the ground in the area of operations. Therefore he did not feel justified in sending part of his force towards the westwards to open and maintain closer links with Napoleon, but decided to implement his earlier instructions to become master of Wavre. Accordingly he ordered Gérard to send Hulot's Division to take the Mill of Bierge a little south of Wavre and to effect a passage over the Dyle at that point. Thanks to the heavy Prussian artillery fire and the activities of Thielemann's skirmishers, Hulot failed to make much progress, whilst Vandamme's main attack against the bridges at Wavre itself was also frustrated. Several French formations—including Pajol's Cavalry—had still to make their appearance on the field.

Growing increasingly impatient, Grouchy decided to change his grand tactics. Riding back with Gérard, he diverted the formations of his corps towards Limale, two miles south-west of Wavre, in the hope of outflanking the Prussian position. A little earlier, he had received Napoleon's 1 p.m. order mentioning Bülow's presence at Chapelle-St. Lambert, so this move might also help to open closer links with Napoleon and hinder

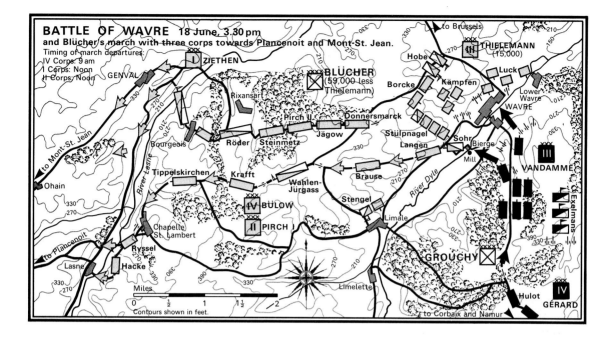

BATTLE OF WAVRE 18 June, 3.30 pm
and Blücher's march with three corps towards Plancenoit and Mont-St. Jean.
Timing of march departures:
IV Corps: 9 am
I Corps: Noon
II Corps: Noon

the Prussian march. But as the time was already approaching 5 p.m. there was no chance of marching to Mont-St. Jean that day. Returning to Wavre, the gallant Marshal led a new onslaught on the Mill of Bierge in person—but again to no purpose as the Prussians were too stubborn. Indeed, General Gérard was severely wounded in the chest during the same attack. Grouchy, who was nothing if not personally active once the battle at Wavre had at last opened, decided to leave Vandamme and Exelman's cavalry to maintain frontal pressure on the town, and took himself off to lead the attack at Limale. Arriving there, he found that Pajol's cavalry had at last joined the battle. The bridge was defended by a flank guard of Ziethen's Corps under Stengel, but Pajol was soon its master, and the French poured over to occupy a position on the heights beyond. This new danger induced Thielemann to move his 12th Brigade from Bierge to the Limale area, where Colonel Stulpnagel decided to launch it—unwisely as it proved—in a night attack against the French which became badly confused in the darkness and failed to dislodge them. By the end of the day, therefore, the situation was one of stalemate before Wavre itself, but of considerable French advantage at Limale. No word of the outcome of Waterloo had reached Grouchy at this time.

At the height of the late afternoon's fighting, a desperate Thielemann had sent an urgent plea for assistance to Gneisenau.

That officer, originally opposed to sending aid to Wellington as we have seen, had by now changed his tune. 'It doesn't matter if he [Thielemann] is crushed,' was his chilling response, 'providing we gain the victory here.'

We must now retrace our steps and recount what was happening at Waterloo. We left the main field when the French had stabilized their extemporized right flank against the Prussians after a long struggle around Plancenoit. It is necessary to return our attention to events on the northern battle sector, for there Wellington's greatest crisis of the day was now impending. Although the great cavalry attacks had been repulsed, Wellington's line was both battered and tiring, and new stresses and strains were about to be experienced. Fortunately, thanks in large measure to Baron Müffling, aid would eventually materialize on the northern as well as the eastern flank of the battlefield. It will be recalled that Wellington's disposition of his troops had left a large area on his left wing for occupation by Prussian

Death of General Picton by J. Atkinson. The veteran infantry commander, Sir Thomas Picton, was seriously wounded at Quatre Bras, but refused to be treated. Two days later, at the height of the onslaught by d'Erlon's I Corps, he was shot through the top hat he had been wearing since the 16th. He died amongst the ranks of his beloved Fifth Division

reinforcements. This was the intended role for Ziethen's Corps, moving through Genval and Ohain. But as these troops approached news reached the corps commander that Wellington was in fact retreating. This was not true, but Ziethen decided to turn south to join the Plancenoit battle. Fortunately for the Duke, Müffling encountered the column as he rode on a mission, and persuaded its commander to keep to his original orders and head for Frischermont once more.

It was just as well that Ziethen returned to his correct line of advance, for since 6 p.m. Wellington's army had abruptly come under its worst strains of the day. For, on the Emperor's order, Ney had renewed his attack on La Haie Sainte for the third time that afternoon, at the head of part of Bachelu's and Donzelot's divisions, some cavalry, and a few guns. At last Ney arranged a properly co-ordinated attack—involving horse, foot and guns fighting as a combined team—and this fact, together with Baring's men of the King's German Legion running out of ammunition at an untimely moment, resulted in the stalwart defenders of the farm being driven out of their staunchly held position. Ompteda's attempt at a counter-attack was crushed by French *cuirassiers* and the brigade commander killed. Of Baring's original 400 defenders, barely forty-two were still on their feet and able to fight their way out. Thus the French suddenly found themselves in possession of the prize that had eluded their grasp all day. The neighbouring buildings, sand-pit and garden also fell into French hands. This time Ney did not hesitate. Using all his drive and leadership, he soon had a battery sited beside the Brussels road above the farm pointing straight at Wellington's centre at a range of only 200 yards. Further troops—remnants of d'Erlon's Corps—also appeared through the smoke, and soon salvos and volleys were tearing into Wellington's formations at point-blank range. One whole side of a Hanoverian square was destroyed by artillery fire; under this new pounding, there were unmistakable signs that the tired centre was wavering. Lambert's 10th Brigade was decimated, and Colin Halkett's formations, closing in from the west, were also badly mauled, as desperate attempts were made to fill the gap left by Ompteda's destruction.

Scenting another chance of victory, this time with some reason, Ney sent Colonel Heymes galloping south to find the Emperor and to request him to send up the Guard immediately to clinch the victory. 'Troops? Where do you expect me to get them from? Do you expect me to make some?' snapped back Napoleon. At this moment, of course, the fight for Plancenoit was at its height as already described, and all the Guard were deployed, or about to be, in support of that crisis. As a result, the best chance of victory was allowed to slip by on the northern front. Ney clung on to his gains, but the loss of impetus in his exploitation enabled Wellington to take emergency measures to reinforce his centre.

The gravity of the Allied situation was plain. Ompteda's and Kielmansegge's brigades were in ruins, and thus Alten's Division was almost a spent force. Ney's battery was indeed causing frightful havoc. The Prince of Orange fell wounded at the head of Kruse's Brigade of Nassauers, so Wellington in

The Prince of Orange (nicknamed 'the little frog') was given command of the I Allied Corps. He bore himself gallantly, and was struck by a spent ball in the left shoulder and slightly wounded. On the left of this engraving by W. Van Senus, a corporal of the Royal Regiment of Dragoons carries away another captured eagle standard

person led up the Brunswick Infantry and summoned Chassé's Division from the far right, almost his last reserve, to plug the growing gap in his centre. Newly reassured concerning the imminent arrival of Ziethen on his left flank, he would a little later also be able to order Vivian and Vandeleur to bring over their cavalry brigades from the far left. Every available gun was summoned, and a Belgo–Dutch cavalry division was also redeployed, and these troops, together with the remnants of Somerset and Ponsonby (barely two squadrons strong between them), who were drawn up in a single rank to present at least a show of strength to the French and to help the morale of the Allied troops in their vicinity, proved just sufficient for the task. But it was indeed fortunate that Napoleon had not been able to support Ney as requested at 6.30 p.m., for a determined thrust by *élite* troops at that moment must have proved fatal. Wellington, at about 7 p.m., sent Lord Uxbridge to summon Vivian and Vandeleur to the centre. The cavalry commander found Vivian already executing this move on his own initiative, and the arrival of these relatively fresh squadrons in support of the centre did a great deal to improve morale, particularly among the Brunswickers, who had begun to waver. The French attack was thus checked.

Napoleon carefully examined the field of battle. The Plancenoit flank was relatively secure for the time being, and nine battalions of the Imperial Guard had now returned into central reserve, but elsewhere the situation was far from his liking. He was well aware that the dark masses of troops to be seen on the north-east horizon were Prussians, and that if the battle was to be won the supreme effort must be delayed no longer. In fact, as we have noted, the best chance of victory was already past. But the long-awaited order was issued: '*La Garde au Feu*': 'Send up the Guard.' Generals Drouot and Friant at 7 p.m. placed themselves at the head of the available battalions, eight of them belonging to the Middle Guard, and the Emperor himself led them forward to within 600 yards of the battle line before handing command to Marshal Ney. It was vital that the tired troops of Reille and d'Erlon should re-engage on all sectors in support of the Guard's impending attack. To achieve this, Napoleon had recourse to a desperate gamble. Noticing Ziethen's columns coming into sight, he ordered Ney to send aides up and down the line announcing that in fact it was Grouchy who was arriving. 'I set off at a gallop,' recalled Colonel Levavasseur, 'with my hat raised on the point of my sabre, and rode down the line shouting "*Vive l'Empereur!*

OVERLEAF *Napoleon and the Old Guard before Waterloo* by E. Crofts. At 7.30 p.m. on the 18th Napoleon plays his last card—sending in the battalions of the Middle Guard in a desperate attempt to snatch victory from the jaws of defeat as the Prussians poured on to the battlefield from the north and east. The Emperor personally led the veterans of many campaigns and battles to within 500 yards of the ridge of Mont-St. Jean before handing them over to Marshal Ney's command. The captive peasant in charge of the *cuirassier* (right foreground) was Decoster, a local Belgian pressed into Napoleon's service for the day as a guide

Soldats, voila Grouchy!" The shout was taken up by a thousand voices. The exaltation of the troops reached fever pitch. . . .' But it was to prove short-lived: the bubble of false hope would soon burst.

Wellington, meanwhile, had been warned by a deserter that he could soon expect an attack by the Guard. He continued to take all possible steps to strengthen his line. Hougoumont—still smouldering—was sent du Plat's Brigade of the King's German Legion, supported by Hew Halkett's Hanoverians.

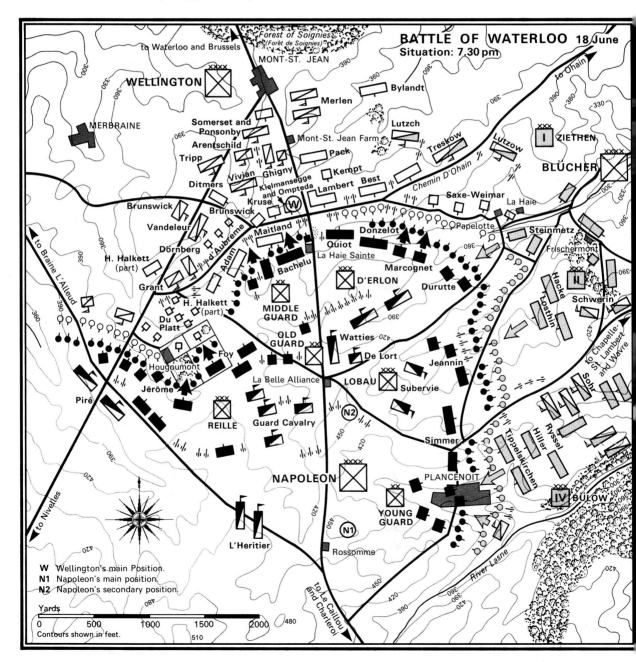

The steps taken to contain La Haie Sainte have already been described. To reinforce the main ridge, he completed the transfer of Chassé's Belgo–Dutch Division from the right, together with Mitchell's Brigade. As Ziethen was now close at hand, he had no great anxiety for the security of his left. These dispositions complete, he ordered his men to take cover from the fire of the French artillery, and waited upon events.

One of the most celebrated engagements of military history was now about to take place, but its details in some respects remain obscure. The time was 7.30 p.m. The Guard was approaching. One battalion had been left at Le Caillou as the Emperor's bodyguard. Two battalions faced west towards Hougoumont to create a defensive flank, while the remaining battalions in the attack—various accounts say four, five or six—marched impressively on in a single 'close column of grand divisions' (on a two-company frontage) to the beat of their drums interspersed by occasional concerted cries of '*Vive l'Empereur*'. Leaving the 2nd/3rd Grenadiers in square near Rossomme Farm to provide a firm base, the column eventually opened out, each battalion swinging away to the left in turn to adopt an echelon formation, the leading battalion column being formed by the 1st/3rd Grenadiers on the right, whilst the guns of the two batteries of horse artillery accompanying the attack took station in the intervals between the battalions. Why Ney veered to the west from the line of the high road has been much debated, for it led straight towards the most battered part of Wellington's line, but perhaps the way past La Haie Sainte was blocked by the French guns and the intermixture of Quiot's and Donzelot's survivors. Be that as it may, the Middle Guard attack moved inexorably towards Wellington's right centre, passing La Haie Sainte on their right. 'As the attacking force moved forward, the *chasseurs* inclined to their left,' recalled General Maitland of the British Guards. 'The grenadiers ascended the acclivity toward our position in a more direct course . . . moving towards that part of the eminence occupied by the Brigade of Guards.'

As each part of the attack breasted the slope in turn, it came in for a hot reception. Nearest to La Haie Sainte, the 1st/3rd Grenadiers defeated some Brunswick troops, but Sir Colin Halkett rallied his brigade, and stood his ground. Halkett then fell seriously wounded, but he had won time for General Chassé to deploy Ditmers's Belgo–Dutch Brigade on his left and place a battery of guns on his right. The tide of fortune soon swung against the French. A little further west, the French

4th Grenadiers and 1st/3rd *Chasseurs* meanwhile penetrated to within sixty yards of the Ohain road. Waiting for them, lying behind a low bank, was Maitland's Guards Brigade. 'Now Maitland, now's your time', shouted Wellington (he did *not* use the phrase—*pace* the long-established tradition—'Up, Guards and at 'em') and the redcoats rose in their long ranks only twenty yards from the startled French, who 'suddenly stopped'. Volley after volley at point-blank range tore into their undeployed ranks, and very shortly they, too, were forced to fall back, hastened upon their way by a well-timed British bayonet charge by the 2nd and 3rd Battalions of the First Foot Guards, who, confident now of success, attacked vigorously.

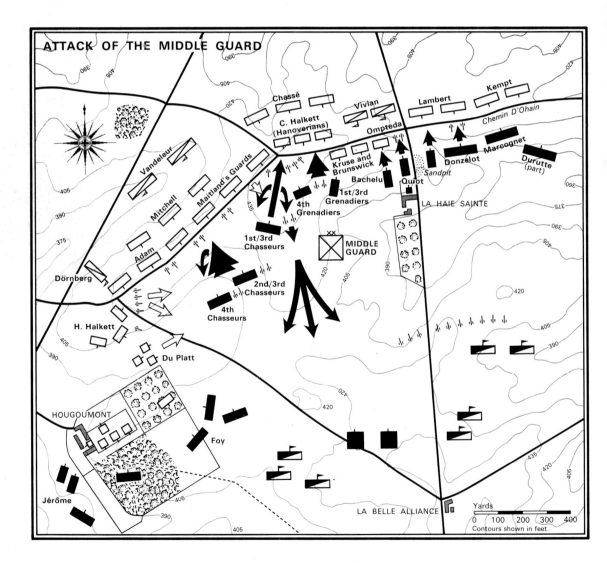

'*Now Maitland! Now's Your Time!*' by T. Jones Barker. The timing of the clinching advance by the Allied Army to convert the repulse of the Middle Guard into a full-scale rout of the entire *Armée du Nord* was a matter for neat calculation. With customary skill, Wellington judged the moment well, and taking off his hat he waved it three times to launch the whole army forwards with a grim cheer. Faced by such a daunting spectacle, the French cried '*Sauve qui peut*' and began to melt away

There still remained the 2nd/3rd *Chasseurs* and the 4th *Chasseurs* to deal with. The discomfited French Guardsmen of the central attack rallied behind them, and advanced once again towards the crest. But once again, the British troops were ready. As the French breasted the slope, they found Adam's light brigade drawn up behind a screen of high-standing corn. As the firing flared up, Colonel Colborne swung his 52nd Regiment to its left, parallel to the line of the French advance. Then a company was sent forward in extended line to snipe at the column's flank. Stung into retaliation, the *chasseurs* halted and partially turned to face the new challenge. In so doing they lost their momentum, and fell into some disorder. Another hail of British fire, and another bayonet charge, and this attack in its turn was routed, sweeping back with it the rallying battalions to the right. Both sides lost heavily in the ensuing mêlée, but there was no disguising the outcome—the attack by the Imperial Guard had failed, and with it Napoleon had lost his last chance of winning the battle.

'*La Garde recule.*' The incredible words spread through the ranks of the French army like wild-fire. Even before the Guard attack had gone in French morale had begun to crumble, especially on the right, where the troops supposed to be Grouchy's wing of the army had quickly revealed their true colours. '*Voyez! Ces sont les Prussiens!*' Astounded, the French had hesitated, pinning every remaining hope on the Imperial Guard. Now it, too, for the first time in its distinguished history, had tasted heavy defeat. By 8 p.m., as new Prussian attacks swept in to regain La Haie and Papelotte, and to re-occupy part of Plancenoit yet again, the French resistance suddenly cracked. '*Sauve qui peut*' was to be heard on every side; also the feared cry of '*Trahison!*' For those who still thought the newly arrived troops on their right front were Grouchy's men, as Napoleon had announced, the heavy firing could mean only one thing to their bewildered minds—treachery. From the start of this campaign, as we have seen, this fear had lurked within *L'Armée du Nord*, and now the calling of Napoleon's deliberate bluff led to terrible results. The morale of his army shattered, and its cohesion snapped as unit after unit dissolved into a mass of fugitives.

Such a moment was not to be missed by so experienced a commander as Wellington. Vivian and Vandeleur's brigades of light horse swept down amongst the remnants of the Middle Guard, and at a word from the Duke the whole line swept forwards with a great cheer as more and more Prussians poured on to the field. The victory had been won.

Vainly Napoleon tried to check the flight of his army, but nothing could be done except attempt to cover the panic-stricken fugitives and hold up the pursuit. This became the task of the Old Guard, which formed a line of squares, whilst the Emperor's escort squadrons tried to win a little time by charging the oncoming Allied masses. Once formed, the French squares tried to advance, but the horde of fugitives broke against them and forced them to retire. For a time the Emperor sheltered within one of the squares before leaving with his staff and escort for Genappe, where he again hoped to rally his men. At one moment he narrowly avoided capture by Prussian hussars as he left his coach to proceed on horseback.

Behind him, the Old Guard continued to cover the retreat,

RIGHT *General Pierre Jacques Cambronne, Count of the Empire* (1770–1842) The character of this tough die-hard soldier, who commanded the squares of the Old Guard in their last defiant stand, is well brought out in this portrait

BELOW *Napoleon at Waterloo* by G. Sigriste. Napoleon, riding Marengo, preceded by two *Chasseurs-à-cheval* of his personal escort and followed by his *petit quartier-général*, heads away from the battle-field

whilst over on the eastern flank, the Young Guard contrived to retain some hold over Plancenoit until 9 p.m. The fighting withdrawal of the Old Guard was a model of valour and cool determination. General Cambronne's reputed reply to a summons to surrender—'The Guard dies but never surrenders' —may be a myth, but it reflects the spirit of these last desperate hours. Large numbers of the *élite* of the French army gave their lives to cover the flight of their compatriots.

The pursuit was at first mainly a British affair. Vandeleur (who had succeeded to command of all the cavalry after Lord Uxbridge received a serious leg wound at the time of the final repulse of the Guard attack on the ridge) gratefully handed this onerous task over to Gneisenau, who led 4,000 Prussian cavalry after the French well into the night. Some time after 9 p.m., Wellington and Blücher met at either La Belle Alliance

or near the village of Genappe—the exact place and time is disputed although most commentators favour the former location. In later life Wellington described the meeting as follows: 'We were both on horseback; but he embraced me, exclaiming "*Mein lieber kamerad*" and then "*Quelle affaire!*" which was pretty much all he knew of French.' Blücher reputedly wished to name the victory 'La Belle Alliance'; Wellington, more prosaically if less symbolically, insisted on 'Waterloo' —the village two miles to the rear of Mont-St. Jean, which had been the site of his main headquarters.

In the gathering gloom of 18 June both commanders ordered the cease-fire to be sounded, as amidst the confusion of the pursuit Allied and Prussian formations were firing into one another. The Duke ordered his army to halt for the night no further south than Rossomme Farm. The fresher Prussians pressed considerably further. Blücher in person reached Genappe before his weariness and shaken condition forced him to rest, but Gneisenau passed Frasnes before mounting casualties caused him to call off the moonlight pursuit for what was left of the night. By that time he had captured all of 200 French guns and over 1,000 wagons and *caissons* of all sizes, besides large numbers of prisoners.

The French, meantime, poured away to the south. Napoleon's hopes of rallying them at Genappe proved illusory as the fleeing men crowded through the little town, fighting amongst themselves to pass the single bridge there. The Emperor himself took an hour to get through the town, but the Guard bypassed the town to ford the Dyle. Napoleon was now pinning his hopes on a reserve division (formerly commanded by General Girard) moving over from Ligny to present a rallying point near Quatre Bras. When he reached the town, though, there was no sign of this force, and the retreat went on into the early hours of the 19th. But this operation was more successful than some have supposed: Gneisenau's pursuit harried the stragglers, but the Guard cavalry performed sterling service in covering the retreat of the formed bodies, and on the 19th, as he continued his retreat through Charleroi to Philippeville, the Emperor could even write that 'All is not lost. . . . There is still time to retrieve the situation.' By 9 a.m. that morning all contact with the pursuers had been broken, and Napoleon ordered Soult to rest the survivors and re-form them whilst he continued on for Paris to prepare, he hoped, a defensive campaign.

Another part of the French army which was operating well at this juncture was Grouchy's command over by Wavre.

The Meeting of Wellington and Blücher by A. Tholey. As the evening of the 18th turned into dusk, Wellington and Blücher met near the farmstead of La Belle Alliance. Blücher wished the battle to be given the symbolic name of 'La Belle Alliance', but the prosaic Wellington insisted on 'Waterloo' because that was where he would write and sign the battle-despatch

OVERLEAF *The Evening of the Battle of Waterloo* by E. Crofts. The disorganization of the defeated *Armée du Nord* deteriorated into a full-scale rout. Napoleon was persuaded to leave the Old Guard square where he had first taken refuge, and mounted his coach. When it became clear that he could not force his way through the press, he transferred to his horse, and rode on through Genappe towards safety

Throughout the night of the 18th/19th, the fighting with Thielemann occasionally flared up, as IV Corps continued to hold and expand its bridgehead around Limale, aided by Pajol's cavalry. No word had yet reached the French of Napoleon's defeat, although the Prussians learned of it during the night. To Thielemann's surprise, therefore, dawn on the 19th brought a strong French response to his probing attack when he had expected them to retreat. Moreover Colonel Stengel had marched off without orders towards Chapelle-St. Lambert with his brigade in search of his parent I Corps, and this left the Prussians very thin on the ground to the west of the Dyle. Indeed overnight Grouchy had received General Teste's Division of VI Corps (serving on detachment), and his superiority became

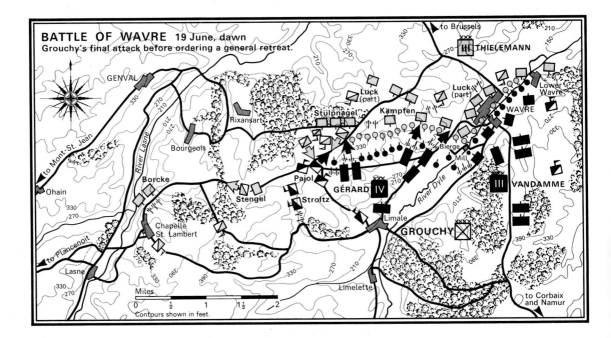

BATTLE OF WAVRE 19 June, dawn
Grouchy's final attack before ordering a general retreat.

paramount. In consequence, by 10 a.m. Grouchy was in a position to claim victory as Thielemann—his strength utterly exhausted—began to retreat, abandoning Wavre. It proved a hollow French success, for at 10.30 a.m. Grouchy at last learnt of Waterloo's outcome and ordered a withdrawal. The single Prussian corps had done very well to defy twice its own number for so long; at the very least it had tied down the full attention of the French right wing for forty-eight critical hours. But by the 21st Grouchy was able to pull back to France over 30,000 formed troops after having evaded Pirch's Corps, sent to intercept him.

The scene on the former fields of battle was appalling—heaps of dead and dying, thousands of wounded clamouring for attention or lying unconscious, ready to become victims of exposure and neglect as well as of their wounds. The Allies did what they could—and so did many of the local countryfolk, and long lines of straw-lined wagons ceaselessly passed towards Brussels crowded with the pitiful remnants of all nations, friend or foe. Many buildings, as for instance the great farm and barn at Mont-St. Jean, and the farm of Le Caillou, were pressed into service as hospitals, and many a local cottage also took in and cared for a victim or two. But the reverse side of the medal must also be mentioned. Human scavengers were at work at the stricken scene, and many a wounded soldier was robbed and stripped—and left to die—before the searching stretcher parties

The grim aftermath of battle: the dead are stripped and their bodies thrown into pits, whilst the wounded are carried away for some form of treatment. In the distance of this painting by D. Dighton is the height of Rossomme, near which stood a tall observatory tower constructed for hunting purposes

could find the unfortunates and bring some relief to them.

As Wellington himself remarked, nothing was more horrible than a battle won save one that had been lost. His own trusted aide, Colonel Gordon, died in the headquarters building at Waterloo that night; Picton, de Lancey, Ponsonby, du Plat and Ompteda were gone. Lord Uxbridge—wounded at the very end of the battle—lost his leg (a memorial can still be seen raised at the spot where it was buried); Lord Fitzroy Somerset, the Duke's military secretary, lay gravely wounded, but would live, as would Alten, Cooke, Kempt, Halkett, Adam and Pack.

Indeed, the cost of this culminating double-battle, and of the three days that had preceded it, made a grim tale. At Waterloo there fell 15,000 Allies and 7,000 Prussians, who also suffered another 2,500 casualties at Wavre. As for the French, the events of the 18th had cost them 25,000 killed and wounded at Waterloo besides a further 8,000 prisoners and as many more deserters over the following days. Grouchy had lost another 2,600 at Wavre. Thus total French losses (to include deserters) amounted to over 43,500 to the Allied 25,500. When we add the losses sustained by both sides since the 15th, the total casualties become more even—60,000 French to 55,000 Allies, but of course the former represented far more proportionately in terms of military strength in the strategic sense. The Allies and Prussians had started the campaign in Belgium with a considerable numerical superiority—and could thus absorb their grievous losses better; moreover, the vast Austrian and Russian forces were now on the march and in the former case already pressing against the French frontiers—with but token forces to face them.

Cold statistics mean little by themselves; they mean more if the sacrifices sustained by a small selection of British regiments are described. Of the 840 British infantry officers who served in the campaign, nearly half were killed or wounded before the 19th. The cavalry lost over a third of its strength. Thus the 12th Light Dragoons, as their memorial testifies in Waterloo church, lost three officers, two sergeant-majors, five sergeants, three corporals and thirty-eight dragoons killed at Waterloo itself. The 79th Highlanders, 16–18 June, had three captains, five lieutenants, nine NCOs and seventy-five privates killed, besides another twenty-four officers and 375 rank and file wounded— or 491 casualties in all. Over the same period, the First Foot Guards had no less than five lieutenant-colonels slain besides many guardsmen; the Royal Scots lost thirty-one out of thirty-seven officers; the 27th Foot sixteen out of nineteen officers present. In all, it is estimated the British contingents suffered over 10,000 casualties; the troops of Brunswick and Nassau some 1,300; those of the Belgians and Dutch lost over 4,000 in all. To include the French, over 47,000 men lay dead or wounded at Waterloo in an area little larger than three square miles.

Wellington was fully aware of the scale of the sacrifice that had been required to win the battle. In Brussels he wept when friends sought to congratulate him. 'Oh! Do not congratulate me. I have lost all my friends.' Late on the 18th he had declared to the wounded Lord Fitzroy-Somerset: 'I have never fought such a battle, and I trust I shall never fight such another.' That wish, at least, would be fulfilled, for although the campaign was not yet over the remaining phases would not hold another major action on the north-eastern front.

Early in the morning of Monday, 19 June, the weary Wellington completed his Waterloo Despatch, to Lord Bathurst—a succinct and simple account of what had transpired since the 15th, completely devoid of heroics—just the bare facts. On a later date he would admit that he '. . . should have given more praise'; only a few individual units found a place in his concise sentences, and many deserving names also went unmentioned.

The table and chair used by Wellington on the night of 18/19 June 1815, as he wrote the Waterloo Despatch. They are preserved in his headquarters at Waterloo village. While he was writing, his senior aide-de-camp, Colonel Gordon, was dying of his wound in the adjoining room

'It gives me the greatest satisfaction to assure your Lordship that the army never, upon any occasion, conducted itself better,' ran part of this historic document. 'The division of Guards, under Lieut.-General Cooke, who is severely wounded, Major General Maitland, and Major General Byng, set an example which was followed by all; and there is no officer nor description of troops that did not behave well.' He also paid a generous tribute to Blücher's Prussians. Some were offended by the way he engrossed almost the whole of his own army in the single phrase 'description of troops'. Others, including Sgt. Cotton, praised the despatch's 'noble simplicity, perfect calmness and exemplary modesty'. The wounded twenty-three-year-old Prince of Orange's note to his Royal parents was shorter but more effusive, full of the exuberance of youth and (perhaps) of shock from his injury. 'Victory! Victory! My dearest parents. We have had a magnificent affair against Napoleon today . . . it was my corps which principally gave battle and to which we owe the victory, but the affair was entirely decided by the attack which the Prussians made on the enemy's right. I am wounded by a ball in the left shoulder but only slightly. In life and death I am ever thine, William.'

Chapter Nine

Aftermath

Nathan Rothschild (1777–1836) A prominent member of the great banking family who financed, through its various branches, most of the European armies of the early nineteenth century, his excellent sources of information enabled him to make a killing on the London Stock Exchange before official news of the outcome of Waterloo reached the capital

OVERLEAF A ledger-page from the Rothschild's accounts, showing the sums the banking-house loaned the British government to finance the army in Belgium which fought and won the campaign and battle of Waterloo. It will be noticed that the loans were repayable, with interest, after a number of years

Wellington entrusted his despatch to his aide-de-camp, Major Percy, together with the eagles captured during the main battle. The evening of the 21st found him in London. Mrs. Boehm was entertaining the Prince Regent and the cream of society to a dinner and ball when Henry Percy made an abrupt appearance—'such a dusty figure!' she commented. Major Percy approached the Prince Regent, dropped on one knee, laid the two eagles at his feet, and exclaimed 'Victory, Sir! Victory.' After reading the despatches, the Prince left the house, and the ball broke up amidst the greatest excitement and confusion. Thus came the news of Waterloo to London—at least officially.

However, one gentleman appears to have had prior knowledge even ahead of the Government, which he did not hesitate to use to his own advantage. Nathan Rothschild, a member of the famous family of international bankers and responsible for the financing of the British Army in Flanders, seems to have received the earliest tidings on the 19th or 20th, possibly by carrier-pigeon. On those dates London was still absorbing the news of Quatre Bras—and when Nathan went to the Stock Exchange to sell his 'consols' everybody hastened to follow his example, convinced that the financial wizard had received news of the further defeat that many expected. Then, judging his moment with customary nicety, Nathan Rothschild proceeded to purchase a huge number of depreciated shares a few hours before news of Waterloo broke—and reputedly cleared a profit of a cool million pounds in the process. Most people, however, were consumed by conflicting emotions—relief and jubilation at the news, clashing with anxiety to see the lists of killed,

The Lords Commissioners of His Majesty's [Treasury]
for Money advanced for the payment, to the Duke of
the Army at the Battle of Waterloo.

Date of Account	Number of Exchequer Bills.	Date of Exchequer Bills	Principal	Interest			Total		
June 2	11,588 @ 11,634	30 May 1817	£47,000	14	13	9	47,014	13	
"	11,513@11,519 - 3,853.. 3,884	24 Do .	18,000	16	17	6	18,016	17	
3	11,561 @ 10,575	30 Do .	15,000	6	5	.	15,006	5	
5	15,635@15,659. 3,910@3,915. 2,431@2,435.. 5,861@5,870	2 June .	30,000	9	7	6	30,009	7	
6	10,692@10,733. 3,925@3,935. 5,090@5,094	5 Do .	48,000	5	.	.	48,005	.	
7	10,735@10,783	6 Do .	49,000	5	2	.	49,005	2	
9	10,917@11,016	" Do .	100,000	31	5	.	100,031	5	
"	11,027@11,044	" Do .	18,000	5	12	6	18,005	12	
13	3,796@3,827	10 Do .	32,000	10	.	.	32,010	.	
"	3,829 @ 3,896	12 Do .	68,000	7	1	8	68,007	1	
14	3,898@3,907.. 283@290	" Do .	14,000	2	18	4	14,002	18	
16	3,908@3,977.. 3,982@3,985	14 Do .	74,000	15	8	4	74,015	8	
17	3,015@3,019	10 April .	5,000	35	8	4	5,035	8	
"	4,329.. 4,356.. 5,154.. 4,210 5,560.. 4,257@4,260.. 5,150 @5,152.. 5,350@5,358.. 5,697.. 5,698.. 5,998	18 Do .	24,000	150	.	.	24,150	.	
"	6,599 @ 6,609.. 6,625@ 6,627.. 6,644.. 6,645..	22 Do .	15,000	87	10	.	15,087	10	
"	6,944.. 6,973	28 Do .	2,000	10	8	4	2,010	8	
"	7,303.. 7,313@7,322.. 7,283.. 7,284	2 May .	13,000	62	5	10	13,062	5	
"	7,916@7,905.. 8,116.. 7,951@ 7,953.. 7,944.. 9,527.	12 Do .	9,000	33	15	.	9,033	15	
"	10,392.. 10,393.. 10,399	22 Do .	3,000	8	2	6	3,008	2	
"	11,290.. 11,291	7 June .	2,000	2	1	8	2,002	1	
"	916@922.. 337@339.. 2,860 @2,864.. 136.. 137.. 2,114	9 Do .	18,000	15	.	.	18,015	.	
"	3,986 @ 4,032	14 Do .	47,000	14	13	9	47,014	13	
							651,548	17	

Premium at 10s. ⅌Ct. on the above Bills . . . . 3,255 .

Commission on the purchase of Do 325 10

Cash 42,306 10

697,435 17

Interest on the above, from the dates of the
respective Accounts to the 19 June 1817 . . 745 6

Discount on Bills for £500,000 dated 19 June, & due
the 11 August, in part payment of the above . 3,630 2

Discount on Bills for £203,393.14.5 dated 19 June, & due
the 21 August, in further payment of the above . 1,755 7

£ 703,566 14

By Bills on the Lords of the Treasury,
accepted the 19 June, and due the 11 August 1817   500,000 . ..

By Bills on the Lords of the Treasury,
accepted the 19 June, and due the 21 August 1817   203,398. 14. 5

By Cash { repaid to Mr. Rothschild, vide }   168 . .
         { Account with His Grace the }
         { Duke of Wellington }

£ 703,566. 14. 5

wounded and missing. Triumph and tears were mixed.

In Paris the mood was understandably very different. On the 18th itself the guns at the Invalides had fired to mark news of the victory at Ligny on the 16th. News of Waterloo only began to be widely appreciated on the 21st. 'Have you heard the news?' fellow-students asked Labretonnière. 'We are assured that the army has been destroyed and that the Emperor arrived in Paris this morning.' He hastened to the Elysée (Napoleon's summer residence), where he found intense activity taking place—confirmation that Napoleon was indeed back in the capital. 'Several cavalry soldiers of the Imperial Guard were sitting gloomily on a bench by the gate, while the tethered horses waited in the yard. One of the horsemen had his face bandaged with a black scarf. The whole scene betokened shame and grief.' Clearly, the news was all too correct.

Hopefully, Napoleon spoke of creating a new army. Rapp should be recalled from Strasbourg, the 15,000-strong Paris garrison mobilized, the National Guard and 17,000 volunteers sent to fill gaps in the ranks, and Soult was to reorganize the remnants of l'Armée du Nord, joined by Grouchy, around first Philippeville and thereafter Laon (eventually he gathered 55,000 men in all). But already the political situation was moving out of the Emperor's control. Both the Senate and the Chamber of Deputies were openly hostile, and to avert any danger of being dissolved they declared themselves permanently in session. Comte Lavallette revealed to the Emperor the mood of the politicians, '. . . that exasperation was at its height, and that the majority seemed determined to demand his abdication, or to proclaim it if he did not proffer it. "What!" he exclaimed. "And if they take no action, the enemy will be at our gates within a week. Alas," he went on, "I have made them used to such great victories that they cannot bear a single day of misfortune! What is to become of this poor France? I have done what I could for her.' And he sighed profoundly.'

Of course, now that the gamble the entire campaign represented had been lost, Napoleon had to face the reckoning. Davout, Carnot and his brother, Lucien, had advised him to dissolve the Chambers before they could act, but in his exhausted state the Emperor proved indecisive, and then it was too late. The use of force was considered, but even Davout opposed this, although the ordinary people of Paris seemed ready for a fight to the finish. However, Napoleon decided against this course. 'I have not come back from Elba to have Paris run with blood,' he declared. So, on 23 June, he issued a new document of

On the road from Waterloo to Paris by M. Stone. Napoleon broods over his defeat at the post-house of Mezières, where he paused for a few hours rest whilst his horses were changed on the night of 19 June

abdication, and retired to Malmaison. A temporary government was extemporized by Fouché, but spent most of its time debating constitutional niceties rather than taking steps to preserve the country and capital. Fouché was determined that no further resistance should be offered, and was already in secret touch with the Allies.

In fact the military situation was not quite as hopeless as has sometimes been represented. The garrison towns of the north-east frontier were strongly held, and Davout and Soult between them had a considerable force—perhaps 117,000 men; more-over some 150,000 conscripts were already in the depots. The

news from the frontiers was also far from discouraging. It is true that the Austrians were slow in closing up to the Rhine, that the Russians were still distant and that the Spaniards were proving slow in mobilizing beyond the Pyrenees, but whilst the last main acts of the drama of 1815 were taking place around Paris, the scratch French formations—euphemistically designated armies—holding the outer ring were to prove their mettle when put to the test. The much-wounded General Rapp, whose small *Armée du Rhin* contained a fair proportion of experienced troops, had advanced boldly on Germersheim in early June to challenge Schwarzenberg's expected advance. News of Waterloo caused Rapp to pull back behind thc River Lauter and thence to Strasbourg, but when General Wärttenberg's III Corps at last crossed the Rhine between 23 and 26 June, it sustained a sharp rebuff at La Suffel on the 28th. Thereafter, Rapp shut himself up in Strasbourg with a second detachment in Colmar, and proved in no hurry to make his submission to the Bourbons. However, General Wrede's IV Austrian Corps managed to penetrate the skeletal defences further north, and pressed ahead from Saarbrücken to Nancy despite a degree of popular resistance to the invaders.

The battle of La Suffel, 28 June 1815, was General Rapp's considerable success over the Austrians in the vicinity of Strasbourg. All too often the history of events on the minor fronts is entirely overlooked. In fact, the outnumbered sector commanders achieved a considerable amount both before and after Waterloo, before yielding to circumstances

Further south, the small *Armée du Jura*—mainly made up of National Guardsmen and other second-line troops—fought as staunchly under General Lecourbe. Four delaying actions were undertaken against General Colleredo's I Corps at Foussemague, Bourogne, Chévremont and Bavilliers between 30 June and 8 July, and only on the 11th did Lecourbe consent to the signature of a local armistice. Hohenzollern's and the Archduke Ferdinand's II and Reserve corps had already become deeply involved in the sieges of Huningen and Muhlhausen—and everywhere the invaders faced the inconvenience of pestering actions by bands of French irregulars, for memories of Allied occupation the previous year were still fresh in the local mind throughout Alsace and Lorraine.

Meanwhile, based upon Lyons, the experienced Marshal Suchet and his rag-bag *Armée des Alpes* (now barely 17,000 strong owing to detachments made in favour of Lecourbe) was proving more than a match for General Frimont's 40,000 Austrians. On 14 June Suchet had boldly taken the initiative and invaded Savoy, to the dismay of the Austrians. However on news of the disaster to *l'Armée du Nord*, the Marshal concluded an armistice on 30 June and fell back to Lyons, where on 12 July he signed a further convention, giving up the city to the Allies. Further south again on the Ligurian coast, Marshal Brune fell slowly back before General Onasco's Neapolitan forces, and then shut himself up in the fortress of Toulon, where he kept the *tricolor* flying until 31 July, when he at last surrendered the great naval arsenal to the Marquis de Rivière. As he set out to travel to Paris as ordered, he was waylaid at Avignon by a band of Royalist sympathizers, who not only shot him dead but then proceeded to stab his corpse 100 times before depositing it in the River Rhône, where it was used as a musketry target for another hour. Provence, of course, like much of Brittany, had long had a reputation for loyalty to the House of Bourbon. However, when the population of La Vendée had predictably risen in revolt against Napoleon's restoration in late March, taking Bressuire and Cholet, they had been rapidly contained by General Lamarque, and the rebels were finally crushed at the battle of Rocheservière near Lézé on 20 June—an event that led to the Treaty of Cholet signed five days later.

However, the news of Napoleon's reabdication and then departure from France took much of the heart out of the French forces on the frontiers, and desertion began to spread as the futility of offering further resistance to the Allies became apparent. The arrival of the first 150,000 Russian troops at

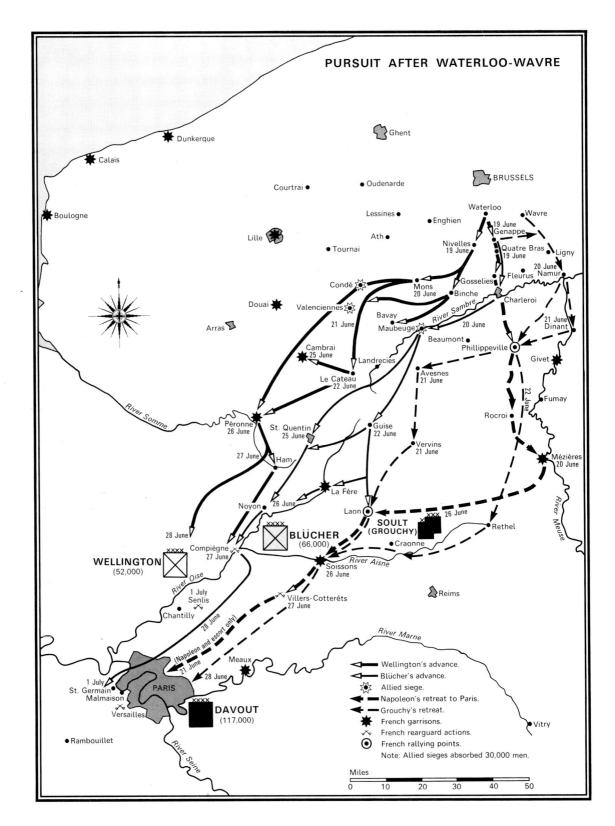

PURSUIT AFTER WATERLOO-WAVRE

Ghent

BRUSSELS

Courtrai

Oudenarde

Waterloo

Wavre

Lessines

Enghien

19 June
Genappe

Boulogne

Lille

Ath

Nivelles
19 June

Quatre Bras
19 June

Ligny

Tournai

20 June
Namur

Gosselies

Fleurus

Condé

Mons
20 June

Binche

Charleroi

Valenciennes

Bavay

Douai

Maubeuge

River Sambre

21 June
Dinant

Arras

Beaumont

Phillippeville

Givet

Cambrai
25 June

Landrecies

20 June

Le Cateau
22 June

Avesnes
21 June

Fumay

22 June

Rocroi

River Somme

Péronne
26 June

St. Quentin
25 June

Guise
22 June

Vervins
21 June

Mézières
20 June

27 June

Ham

La Fère

Noyon

26 June

Laon

26 June

Rethel

BLÜCHER
(66,000)

SOULT
(GROUCHY)

River Meuse

28 June

Compiègne
27 June

Craonne

WELLINGTON
(52,000)

River Aisne

Soissons
26 June

Reims

1 July
Senlis

Villers-Cotterêts
27 June

Chantilly

River Marne

28 June

(Napoleon and escort only)

27 June

Meaux

28 June

Vitry

1 July
St. Germain
Malmaison

PARIS

DAVOUT
(117,000)

Versailles

Rambouillet

River Seine

→ Wellington's advance.
→ Blücher's advance.
☼ Allied siege.
→ Napoleon's retreat to Paris.
→ Grouchy's retreat.
✹ French garrisons.
⚔ French rearguard actions.
◉ French rallying points.
Note: Allied sieges absorbed 30,000 men.

Miles
0   10   20   30   40   50

Mannerheim in late June caused a brief resurgence of popular resistance as they advanced on Landau—for the Cossacks in particular had left a bad memory behind them the previous year —but little by little the fighting died down, and then stopped. Once again, eastern France lay at the mercy of the invader.

Meanwhile, the victors of Waterloo had been marching into France from Belgium along two main routes. The Prussians marched faster than Wellington, and left a trail of devastation behind them: French excesses of 1806 were being avenged. Blücher moved through Charleroi to Avesnes, and thence marched on to Guise. Prussian cavalry reconnoitred towards Laon, where on 26 June Grouchy took over command of the French forces from a disgruntled Soult on the orders of the Provisional Government. Meanwhile the main Prussian columns hurried on to St. Quentin. Grouchy, hoping to bring his army back to Paris, fought a number of minor actions at Compiègne, Senlis and Villers-Cotterets against the Prussians, but nowhere made a determined stand. However, he reached Paris with some 50,000 men on 29 June.

Wellington's route was rather more to the north. Marching through Nivelles and Maubeuge, he was compelled to seize Cambrai and Péronne by assault, but both fortresses surrendered without offering too much resistance. The Allies used the French countryside more considerately than the Prussians, and one reason why Wellington prosecuted a slower march was his determination to keep his forces in a proper state of discipline. But as they marched ahead for Paris, both the Allied and the Prussian armies found it necessary to drop off sizeable detachments to observe enemy garrisons and in general protect their lines of communication, which inevitably became increasingly extensive and not wholly immune from attack by small parties of French troops backed by substantial numbers of peasantry. Over 30,000 troops—including the whole of Pirch's II Corps— were absorbed in these trying duties, and by the 29th, Blücher's effective strength, as he approached the north-eastern outskirts of Paris, was down to only 66,000 men, whilst that of Wellington, two days behind his Prussian colleague on the northern bank of the Oise, could call upon 52,000—and many of these were spread out over a considerable area.

Napoleon, pacing up and down the corridors of Malmaison like a frustrated lion, realized that a great opportunity for a telling counter-stroke was developing before his eyes. Davout had almost 120,000 troops of varying calibre in and around Paris, and given the growing Allied dispersal might well have

snatched a quick victory—or so the former Emperor believed. Vainly he implored the Provisional Government to give him the temporary position of commander of the army so that this chance to avenge Waterloo might not be missed. But Fouché had no intention of allowing Napoleon any such opportunity, and Davout was also determined to avoid further bloodshed, having become convinced that Louis XVIII would have to be recalled.

However, Davout was determined that his former master should not fall into Blücher's hands. The Prussian commander had sent out a cavalry force on the 29th with orders to take Napoleon dead or alive, but Davout got wind of this and thwarted their intention by having the Seine bridge nearest Malmaison blown up. When, on the 30th, the main Prussian forces began to enter the outskirts of Paris, it was Davout again who ordered Exelmans to take his cavalry and attack the Prussian Lieut.-Colonel Sohr, currently raiding Versailles. The Prussians received a drubbing. This gave Blücher food for

Napoleon going on Board the 'Bellerophon' at Rochefort by Jazet. Despairing of escaping to the United States, and warned that the provisional French government had issued a warrant for his arrest, on 15 July Napoleon gave himself up to Captain Maitland and boarded HMS *Bellerophon*. This was to prove the first step on his last journey into exile on the South Atlantic island of St. Helena. This time there would be no return

thought, and he paused in his operations, to give Wellington time to approach. At last, on 3 July, a Convention was signed at St. Cloud, by which the French army was to evacuate Paris and retire south of the Loire. The Provisional Government recognized Louis XVIII, and on 7 July, the Prussians at last entered the heart of Paris. The next day King Louis returned to the Tuileries Palace, just 110 days after quitting it.

Meanwhile, what of Napoleon? His thoughts for some time had been turning towards finding a place of refuge, and he

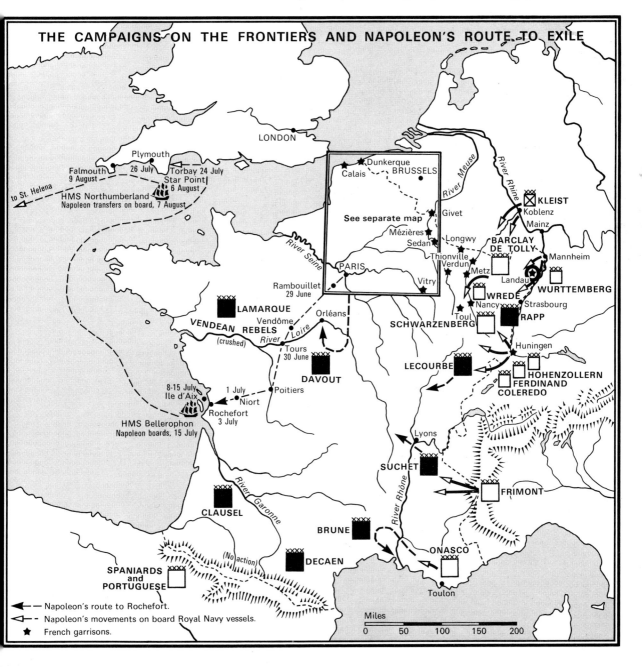

THE CAMPAIGNS ON THE FRONTIERS AND NAPOLEON'S ROUTE TO EXILE

requested Fouché several times for a frigate in which he could sail from Rochefort. Fouché temporized, but in due course agreed, and 29 June saw Napoleon's timely departure for the coast—just one move ahead of the vengeful Prussians. On reaching Rochefort, his first hope was to be allowed to travel to

For a time Napoleon deluded himself that the traditionally generous British people might permit him to live in Great Britain. To this end he wrote a solemn and touching letter couched in the classical style to the Prince Regent. He never received a reply. 'General Bonaparte' was considered far too great a security risk to be accorded a haven so close to France

America, and on 8 July he actually set sail and reached Aix, where he was forced to await a favourable wind. However, the Royal Navy was now fully alerted, and it soon became clear that Napoleon would not be permitted to sail across the Atlantic. Learning that the shifty Fouché was rumoured to have ordered his arrest, Napoleon decided to throw himself on the mercy of the Prince Regent, and on 15 July he went aboard HMS *Bellerophon* with a small staff and surrendered himself to Captain Frederick Maitland, RN. His hopes of finding sanctuary in England proved illusory, and he was soon on board HMS *Northumberland* on his way to the rocky South Atlantic island of St. Helena, where he would spend the remaining six years of his life.

The campaign of Waterloo was over.

Any attempt to analyse the outcome of the most critical four days of this celebrated campaign and battle must differentiate between psychological and physical factors; states of morale and quality of leadership come under the first category, numerical strength, weaponry, tactical doctrine and organization belong to the second. The ultimate result cannot be attributed to any one particular cause—it was the product of a combination of factors, both tangible and intangible, as is the result of any battle. To achieve a wholly just evaluation is practically impossible, as many facts remain unclear, and national bias— British and Prussian as well as French—has done much to cloud the issue.

It is fitting to consider the criticisms that can be levelled at Napoleon and his army as a starting point, for they seized the initiative from the outset and deliberately played a massive gamble. On St. Helena the former Emperor made great efforts to lay a major share of the blame on Marshals Grouchy and Ney. There can be no denying that such charges hold an element of plausibility. Had Grouchy marched on the sound of the guns on the morning, or even early afternoon of the 18th, Blücher's march to reinforce Wellington would have been intercepted and its effect at the very least impaired, and the effects this might have had on the fighting before Mont-St. Jean are almost incalculable. On the other hand, it can also be argued that Grouchy was more sinned against than sinning. The orders he received were vague and indecisive, some of them were inexcusably delayed in being sent, and in justice to Grouchy the most he can be really accused of is an unimaginative execution of what he deemed to be his duty. His unsuitability for command over a wing of the army has already been mentioned, but by the time he had adjusted to his new and unaccustomed situation the campaign was lost, and although he conducted his retreat ably enough it was far too late to salvage anything of strategic importance except (never to be discounted) some 30,000 French lives.

The case against Marshal Ney is somewhat stronger. Once again, he was an unsuitable appointment for a quasi-independent command, and his performance was very uneven. The fits of lethargy and undue caution that typified his actions on 15, 16, and 17 June gave way to the bursts of ill-considered energy on the climacteric battlefield. If the earlier hesitation may in part be attributed to the abruptness of his appointment, the later rashness proved even more fatal. He made a whole series of false deductions, and flung away attack after attack, any one of which, if properly planned and co-ordinated, might have achieved his objective—to make Mont-St. Jean untenable for Wellington. Brave to a fault, he did not fully measure up to the challenge of the chief battle command.

Marshal Soult's showing as chief-of-staff was also far below the standards of the great Berthier, whose precision and clarity he lacked; on several occasions his inability to express Napoleon's intentions clearly and concisely, or to manage the administrative tasks of his daunting position, led to failures and disappointments.

But all these three key commanders and staff officers owed their appointment to Napoleon's personal choice, and he alone therefore must inevitably bear the ultimate responsibility. If their shortcomings should have been predictable to so experienced a commander, it is even harder to understand why he failed to appoint the better men available. There is little to fault in the broad strategic scheme that Napoleon contrived in 1815— it stands amongst his best, and the opening of the campaign, despite the friction and hitches, was masterly. As Wellington described it in 1820, 'Bonaparte's march upon Belgium was the finest thing ever done—so rapid and so well-combined.' Despite blunders and oversights, the campaign could still have been won until the afternoon of the 17th, when the scales began to tilt inexorably the other way.

However, from the outset there were signs of deterioration in Napoleon's performance. Some commentators have attributed a great deal to declining health and mental powers. It is clear that he was rather ill on the night of the 16th/17th, and that lethargy gripped him at certain crucial moments—most particularly during the morning of the 17th, when he failed either to sanction an immediate pursuit of the Prussians or to order an immediate switch of attack against Wellington—but it would be wrong to read too much into his physical condition. The situation is rather different when certain of his mental attributes are examined more closely. At times he was strangely indecisive, as he once admitted to have been the case years later on St. Helena; at others, he was overbearing towards his subordinates—as during the morning hours of the 18th—and distinctly over-scornful regarding his opponents. He deprecated Wellington's staying power, discounted Blücher's loyalty to his ally and inveterate hatred towards himself. He delayed the opening of the battle for several critical hours, failed to recall Grouchy in time, and insisted upon the adoption of an unsubtle battle-plan. Perhaps he should not be blamed for the various tactical follies Ney and Prince Jérôme committed, but he can be criticized for not exercising at least a watching brief over their activities. Ney's brashness had been known to him for almost ten years; his own brother's incapacity had been graphic-ally demonstrated in Russia three years earlier. In consequence the attack on Hougoumont was allowed to get out of hand; the I Corps was not prevented from adopting an outdated forma-tion; the escalation of the virtually unsupported cavalry onslaughts went unchecked until it was too late to salvage much from the ruins of his mounted formations; the Prussian inter-vention towards Plancenoit was not effectively countered— merely contained (and this was a part of the battle the Emperor personally supervised); the critical reserve—the Imperial Guard —was dissipated so that it could not intervene at the truly critical moment; and its ultimate grand attack was mishandled and mistimed. In other words, the Emperor's battle control, once one of his finest attributes as a commander, was poorly exercised on this occasion, and the sum total of all these errors was defeat, renewed abdication and exile.

Perhaps the critical errors of the campaign were four in number: the failure to bring Lobau's VI Corps into action on the 16th; the confusions that led to the waste of d'Erlon's I Corps the same day; the oversights and confused intentions that allowed Grouchy to stray beyond recall during the 17th and early hours of the 18th, and, lastly, the barefaced deception of his men when Ziethen approached at 7 p.m. at the crisis of Waterloo.

It is true that the weather was unfortunate for the French for eighteen critical hours from the Saturday afternoon until the

Sunday morning, and this certainly increased the scope of the difficulties for the attacker at Waterloo, but this provides no excuse for the lethargy, indolence and even absent-mindedness that typified Napoleon's performance. Given these short-comings, it is amazing how near he came to achieving success at several moments. If Napoleon in decline was still so redoubtable an adversary, how awe-inspiring he must have been in the golden years of his prime.

What then of the victors? When Wellington's performance is examined, it is interesting to note that his revealed strengths and weaknesses were, in some measure, the antitheses of Napoleon's showing. The Duke proved a master of minor tactics, but showed up less well at the strategic level. His initial dispositions before the campaign were rather scattered, but if he was to cover his area of responsibility, and maintain his life-line to the Channel coast, it is difficult to see how he could have deployed to better effect. On the other hand, there is no denying that the timing of Napoleon's offensive took him by surprise, and that his first estimate of the direction of the main French attack was wholly wrong and led to a near-fatal movement by the Allied army away from the inner flank—the true scene of the impending crisis. Once his error was clear, however, he took every step to remedy it, but it is doubtful if the outcome of Quatre Bras would have been so generally satisfactory had not Ney com-mitted his mistakes in turn. Wellington's conduct of the retreat on the 17th, and his selection of a good battle-position at Mont-St. Jean, were both masterly. The latter was much criticized by Napoleon, it is true, whilst before his death General Picton also had some reservations about its suitability, but events proved how sure was the Duke's eye for ground. A past-master of the defensive battle, he made the utmost use of the advantages the terrain offered; even in the event of defeat, he was convinced that his army would have been able to retire through the Forest of Soignies to his rear, as it was not very dense but much intersected by tracks and clearings—as indeed it is still today.

Wellington made certain questionable decisions that might have gravely affected the issue on the 18th. The leaving of as many as 17,000 men away to the west near Hal was a sensible precaution to protect his links with the Channel and to guard against the possibility of a French attempt to envelop his outer flank, but it deprived him of a large number of potential battle reinforcements which he might well have needed had the Prussian intervention been any later. As we have seen, his

Wellington at Waterloo— The End by Lady Butler. 'Nothing save a battle lost is so terrible as a battle won.' Wellington, drained by the efforts of the day, rides thoughtfully away from Mont-St. Jean towards his headquarters in the village of Waterloo

Napoleon the Fugitive by
Lady Butler. 'To die is
nothing, but to live defeated
is to die a thousand times
every day.' Napoleon pauses
for one last backward glance
towards the stricken field of
Waterloo

centre and left flank were perilously weak by the time Ziethen's
Corps arrived—and its intervention at the correct sector was
almost a matter of chance, rather than careful design. But it is
also true that Wellington only decided to fight around Mont-St.
Jean on the clear understanding that Blücher would move to
his aid with at least one corps—and his faith in his colleague
was not misplaced.

No greater contrast can be painted between Napoleon's role
in the great battle and that of his opponent. The Duke, wrote an
observer, '. . . was everywhere . . . the eye could turn in no
direction that it did not perceive him either at hand or at a
distance; galloping to charge the enemy or darting across the
field to issue orders.' Throughout the day he was energy
personified—always at hand to raise morale, ever cool and
collected even in the closest proximity to mortal danger. Here
was the true personification of the leader in battle, all-seeing and
all-seen. His tactical flair is seen in the way he handled his
reserves, and somehow maintained the cohesion of his front
and of his forward posts, La Haie Sainte excepted, as he played
what was essentially his waiting-game—hanging on to his
positions grimly until the Prussians could come up to redress
the balance of the battle in his favour. Of course there were
blemishes of a sort. The gallantry and effectiveness of the charge
by the heavy brigades should not disguise the fact that they got
out of control and reaped a grim punishment thereby—effectively
depriving the Allied army of one-third of its mounted strength.
Similarly, the exposed position of Bylandt must have been an
oversight, and some Allied formations did indubitably leave the
firing line in the greatest disorder at one or two moments of the
hard-fought day. The loss of La Haie Sainte was mainly due to
its garrison running out of powder and shot—a rare example of a
breakdown in the Duke's administrative arrangements on
which he lavished so much care and attention.

Nevertheless, Wellington's grit and staying-power—together
with that of the men of many nations under his command,
particularly (although not exclusively) of his British infantry—
was a vital ingredient of victory. His personal contribution was
immense by any standard, and if he was rather aloof and
disapproving, a severe disciplinarian and chary of giving praise
even when deserved, his men knew they could rely on him and
his basic care for their welfare in times of crisis. 'If England
should require the service of her army again,' wrote Sergeant
Wheeler, 'and I should be with it, let me have "Old Nosey" to
command. Our interests would be sure to be looked into, we

should never have occasion to fear an enemy. There are two things we should be certain of. First, we should always be well supplied with rations. . . . The second is we should be sure to give the enemy a d--d good thrashing. What can a soldier desire more?' In sum, Wellington achieved wonders with the men at his disposal; in return, they gave him steady, loyal service, and proved capable of withstanding all that Napoleon and his far more experienced army could devise and throw against them. In the case of the Allied army, both the leader and the led were worthy of one another in the hour of action.

Chelsea Pensioners Reading the Waterloo Despatch by Sir David Wilkie. Nowhere was news of Waterloo greeted more appreciatively than at Chelsea Hospital. Here a group of Pensioners drink the health of the cavalry courier who has delivered them a news sheet describing the great events of 18 June, 1815

As must have emerged from the earlier chapters, the role of the Prussian army was equally important in achieving the ultimate decision. As the Duke wrote in his Waterloo Despatch, 'I should not do justice to my feelings, or to Marshal Blücher and the Prussian Army, if I did not attribute the success of this arduous day to the cordial and timely assistance I received from them.' This was no more than the truth. There can be little doubt that Waterloo would not have been won had not the Prussians arrived. This has sometimes been questioned by British historians, but the Prussian contribution was vital. At the same time, there is no foundation in the belief held in some German circles that Blücher's role was wholly the vital factor. The Prussians could no more have defeated Napoleon on their own than Wellington could have mastered the French with the Allied army alone. The element of co-operation—and of shared achievement—was the major cause of victory on 18 June.

Field-Marshal Blücher was not of the same intellectual calibre or professional standing as either Napoleon or Wellington. He was, however, a great fighter, a true 'soldier's general', and was moreover inspired with a hatred for the Emperor that amounted to a personal vendetta; he felt equally strongly about keeping his pledges to his ally. These factors in his make-up account for the immense drive and determination which ensured that Bülow, Pirch and Ziethen marched to Wellington's aid, and arrived in time to swing the fortunes of battle. This was a great feat for a septuagenarian, sick and battered though he was after his rough adventures at Ligny just two days before. Here was a man who was a born fighter.

The army he commanded was not *sans réproche* in either its efficiency or its conduct, whether on the field of battle or off it. Gneisenau, for all his cold, brilliant intellect, was no Anglophile, and late on the 16th would have headed for the Rhine from Wavre after the defeat at Ligny had not his superior reappeared in time to insist on the army drawing closer to Wellington. Further, the Prussian chief-of-staff could issue as vague and permissive orders as Marshal Soult on occasion—and the non-appearance of Bülow at Ligny was largely due to indecisive instructions from Gneisenau, who was his junior in the Prussian army and seems not to have wished to presume to issue strong orders to a senior general. There were further staff errors and confusions that bedevilled Prussian effectiveness. Their military intelligence proved very deficient in the days before the offensive opened—the corollary being the effectiveness of Napoleon's security measures—and the rather belated appearance of the

Prussian columns on the battlefield of Waterloo was in part due to staff errors resulting in intersecting lines of march which caused delays. Much credit must be paid to Baron Müffling for his vital aid in maintaining effective liaison between the two armies, and his critical intervention to redirect Ziethen's Corps onto its correct line of march was probably one of the most important individual contributions to the winning of the day at Waterloo.

We have noted the Prussian positioning of their troops in full view of the French artillery at Ligny, and their similar error in placing their second line too close to the front—mistakes that positively invited heavy casualties. The general inexperience of many of their battalions is indicated by the fluctuating fortunes which Bülow's men faced at Plancenoit—particularly their abrupt repulse by the two battalions of the Old Guard. But if these criticisms seem severe, it must be remembered that many of the troops were engaged in their first campaign, and due allowance should be made if inexperience led to disappointments. The same factor, together with a burning desire to avenge the slights and humiliations piled upon their Fatherland after 1806 by the French, explains, if it does not condone, the indiscipline that tended to typify the Prussian conduct of the advance on Paris in late June and early July. On the other hand, Thielemann's resolute stand about Wavre and Limale stands as testimony for the fighting skills of the men, and indeed Ligny and Waterloo hold many instances of Prussian valour and toughness. Their ability to recover from a set-back such as Ligny so quickly is also notable.

These then, are some of the conclusions that can be drawn from the conduct of this celebrated campaign and the four battles that the four critical days contained. The entire episode holds a special place in the traditions of at least five countries and armies of Western Europe, and forms the great climax of the long and significant Napoleonic Wars. Few campaigns in all military history, indeed, have been shorter in duration, more dramatic in conduct, more decisive in outcome, or more celebrated in fact and legend. Whilst mankind continues to read the history of his past, the campaign and battle of Waterloo will never be forgotten. In the words of Field-Marshal Blücher, *'Quelle Affaire!'*

Chapter Ten

The Legacy of Waterloo

'The great battle which ended the twenty-three years' war of the first French Revolution', wrote Sir Edward Creasy in 1852, 'and which quelled the man whose genius and ambition had so long disturbed and desolated the world, deserves to be regarded by us, not only with peculiar pride, as one of our greatest national victories, but with peculiar gratitude for the repose which it secured for us, and for the greater part of the human race.'

It is frequently asserted—and with some justice—that Waterloo marked the end of an important era in modern history. That it did inaugurate a considerable period of international peace cannot be denied: although there were numerous internal commotions—such as the Revolution of 1830 in France, the Spanish Carlist Wars (which included a French intervention at one point), intermittent troubles in Italy as patriots challenged Austrian rule, and in Poland as nationalists struggled against Tsarist hegemony, and above all in 1848, the 'year of Revolutions', which witnessed serious street-fighting in several European capitals—there were no major wars involving two or more of the great powers in Europe for about forty years. Outside its confines there were numerous colonial wars of various sizes. Some, as in South America, were struggles for independence against Spanish and Portuguese rule. Others, as in Algeria and Morocco, and far-off India, were wars of imperialist expansion and consolidation. But until the outbreak of the Crimean War in 1854 dragged Great Britain and France into a war with Tsarist Russia in support of Turkey, it seemed that the 'balance of power' that Metternich and other statesmen had striven to create and preserve at the resumed Congress of Vienna, and the subsequent international meetings, had brought at long last a certain measure of stability to international relations—hopefully demonstrating that the pen wielded at the conference table was stronger than the sword wielded in battle. This was to prove at best a pious hope—for from 1854 until 1871 the world would be torn by successive crises and no less than five major wars—but the almost 'Forty Years' Peace' that followed Waterloo had not been matched in European history for a number of centuries, and was welcome indeed.

The fortunes of the victors and the vanquished in this period of comparative international quiescence make for some interesting comparisons. In the case of Great Britain, the steady rise in national prosperity that had taken place from 1811 as Napoleon's continental blockade fell to pieces did not long survive the restoration of peace. A short post-war boom in manufactured articles led to a crash in 1819, and this had been preceded two years earlier by an agricultural slump—disappointing harvests leading to soaring grain prices, and good harvests to corresponding falls. Both phenomena aggravated unemployment—a problem immensely increased after 1815 with the demobilization of an estimated 300,000 soldiers and sailors, for whom, it has been calculated, there was the prospect of employment for barely one in three. The result was widespread misery and unrest, leading to repressive legislation, social discontent, political uncertainty fostered by radicals and popularist movements and even a plot (the Cato Street Conspiracy) to assassinate the Cabinet. Thus it can in no way be claimed that the achievement of victory ushered in an immediate period of contentment and progress for Great Britain. If anything the reverse was the case. As Sir John Clapham wrote in 1920 of the situation prevailing in 1816, 'Great Britain, though victorious, suffered acutely. Mismanagement was largely responsible for her sufferings—mismanagement of ... demobilisation; mismanagement of taxes . . .; mismanagement of food supplies . . .; and so on. But suffering due to international dislocation following war could not have been avoided by management, however good.' Such would indeed prove the case yet again on two not wholly dissimilar occasions in the twentieth century. Thus a great international reputation consolidated by Waterloo did not bring Britain immediate commensurate prosperity.

France, surprisingly, came through the immediate post-war period with greater economic success. Despite being restricted in the main by the terms of the Second Treaty of Paris to her pre-Revolutionary frontiers, and required to pay a heavy in-

An Episode of the 'White Terror', 1815 by Cordova. The aftermath of defeat often includes witch-hunts conducted at the expense of the vanquished. After Waterloo, and the restoration once again of Louis XVIII to the French throne, the Bourbonists set out to hunt down the fervent Bonapartists. Some 300 were killed during the 'White Terror'. Here, a former officer, surprised at table with his wife, prepares to offer resistance to a mob seeking him out

demnity as well as to support a sizeable army of occupation for five years, by 1818 France was well on the road to recovery. By the time of the Congress of Aix-la-Chapelle in late 1818 the indemnity had been paid—no small reflection of the innate strength of French finances stemming from the Napoleonic reforms—and the withdrawal of the Allied forces began ahead of schedule. Even more significantly, the same Congress saw France admitted to the Quintuple Alliance—implying full readmission to the centre of European affairs. In terms of internal politics, of course, France had some problems to face. The restored Bourbon government of Louis XVIII had to adjust itself to the concept of ruling through a constitutional system. The returned *émigrés* won a majority in the Chamber of Deputies, and some old scores were settled in the 'White Terror', during which some 300 'extremists' were killed. Purges in the French army and civil service were pressed by the *Ultras*, and perhaps one-quarter of Napoleon's former officers and public officials were sacked. Thus political divisions remained very much part of the scene in France, but there was no mass social agitation in the immediate post-war period of the sort that afflicted Great Britain during the same period.

For Prussia, events since 1806 had held massive humiliations matched by equally impressive achievements. Following the collapse of Jena-Auerstädt and the eventual pacification of Tilsit, Prussian mercantile interests had feared that the imposition of Napoleon's Continental System would spell irremediable ruin for the nation's economy. In fact there was no general drop in production levels—and some industries had actually shared in the stimulus of the wars (including iron and steel). Trade patterns on the other hand—particularly those with England—had been disrupted, causing some problems to individuals and enterprises, but this had led to more political agitation than economic, reinforcing the growing clamour for Prussia to throw off the French yoke in early 1813. Inevitably, after Waterloo some industries in Prussia regressed, and high tariffs were soon being raised against British goods. But as a nation Prussia emerged from the wars immensely strengthened. The shock of defeat had led to massive reforms from 1807. Serfdom had been abolished, public education introduced, more powers granted to the municipalities, and a wholly reformed military system introduced, whilst the organs of government had been centralized and modernized under the Councils of State and of Ministers. The final collapse of the Holy Roman Empire in 1806 would in the long run prove to Prussia's advantage, and above all the growth of nationalistic patriotism—directed towards the Prussian state and its monarch, Frederick William III—strengthened by the achievement of the nation in playing a major role in the final defeat of Napoleon between 1813 and 1815, would set in train the sequence of events that would ultimately lead to the creation of the German Empire a little over half a century later.

So much for the fortunes of the three major nations most intimately connected with the events of 1815. What were the destinies of the three great military commanders who had led their armies in Belgium and northern France during the hectic summer? For Napoleon there lay only the frustrations of life on the South Atlantic island of St. Helena, where the internal problems of this Longwood household, the vendetta with the Governor, Sir Hudson Lowe, and the dictation of his memoirs were the sole alleviations of the former Emperor's captivity. 'To die is nothing,' he had once remarked, 'but to live defeated is to die every day.' Such was the fate of one who as a schoolboy had written in his notebook on geographical subjects: '*Sainte Hélène—petite île.*' Death—whether from natural or other causes—came as a release on 5 May, 1821.

Blücher by Feder Dretz. Prosecuting his personal vendetta against Napoleon, Blücher encourages his men on towards the French capital after the victory of Waterloo–Wavre. The Prussians looted the towns and villages on their route, exacting revenge for their humiliations of 1806

Field-Marshal Blücher faced different frustrations. After occupying Paris on 4 July—'Paris is mine!', he wrote in a triumphant postscript to his wife—his avowed ambition to blow up the *Pont de Jéna* over the Seine was narrowly thwarted by the opportune arrival of the Allied monarchs and Louis XVIII in the capital. Even then it required all of Wellington's conciliatory skills to dissuade Blücher from exacting reprisals on the city. Further bitter recriminations with the French authorities continued, and the Prince of Wahlstädt passed his time in rash gambling and the occasional horse race. At last, in October, he received permission to return to Prussia. By this time the veteran's health was declining, and he was again suffering from delusions. For the next three years he spent his time between Berlin and his estates near Breslau, finding pleasure in farming but also great sadness over his son's developing mental illness. His restless energy remained unabated, and his taste for wild gambling earned him a royal rebuke, but he retained the favour of Frederick William III and also his popularity with the populace at large. In mid-1819 he was planning a visit to Prince Schwarzenberg, but returned to his estates feeling ill. In early September he took to his bed, and on the 12th of that month *Alte Vorwärts* died. Thus Blücher lived a little over four years after the battle, and died in his seventy-seventh year.

For Field-Marshal the Duke of Wellington, the future held a further thirty-seven years of eventful life. For him, the battle of Waterloo marked the ending of one career and the beginning of a second. His fervent post-Waterloo wish—'I hope to God that I've fought my last battle'—was granted. Although he remained *generalissimo* of the Allied occupation in France until 1818, and was later appointed commander-in-chief of the British Army from 1827 to 1828, and then again from 1842 until his death, he was destined never to see active service again. The battles he was now called upon to face belonged to the political and diplomatic arenas, not to the military. But first the hero of the Peninsular War and the Waterloo campaign had to face the adulation of his countrymen—and of much of the world. Honours, titles and awards were showered upon him, and in 1818 he was made Master-General of the Ordnance with a seat in Lord Liverpool's cabinet. From 1819 to 1826 he was Governor of Plymouth; he was made Constable of the Tower of London in 1826, Lord Warden of the Cinque Ports in 1829, and Chancellor of the University of Oxford in 1834, and held all three posts until his death. His town residence, Apsley House, became known as 'No. 1 London', and his seat at Stratfieldsaye in Hampshire was set amidst beautiful countryside. He was presented with further broad estates in Spain, Portugal and Belgium.

In domestic politics he championed the cause of aristocracy, and at first strongly opposed Catholic Emancipation proposals, but in the early post-war period his main work was in the diplomatic field. In 1818 he attended the international meeting at Aix-la-Chapelle, and a few years later the Congresses of Vienna and Verona. He failed in his attempts to avert French intervention in Spain, and his disapproval of British recognition of the newly independent former Spanish colonies in South America earned him the reputation of a diehard. He was sent on several missions to foreign capitals over problems in the Balkan region, and was personally much opposed to the forcing of Turkey to grant Greek independence in 1826. The following year he refused to take office under Canning, but next year reluctantly agreed to become Prime Minister. His ministry was not a great success, and was mainly noted for the passing of the Catholic Emancipation Act (in contravention to his earlier strongly expressed opinions) in 1829. Faced by mounting

For Wellington, although his wish to have experienced his last battle was granted, long years remained of public service in the diplomatic and political fields. In this painting by George Joy he is shown in extreme old age as Warden of the Cinque Ports, gazing out over the Channel near Dover

pressures for Parliamentary reform, in 1830 he resigned office. His unwavering opposition towards the Great Reform Bill earned him some unpopularity, and he earned his nickname 'the Iron Duke' at this period for fitting metal shutters to the windows of Apsley House to thwart the hostile stone-throwing attentions of the London mob.

The year 1834 saw him briefly both premier and Home Secretary, but later that same year he accepted office under Sir Robert Peel as Foreign Secretary. In Peel's second ministry (1841–46) he held the position of Minister-without-Portfolio, and in 1848 he was called in to advise the government during the climax of the Chartist troubles. A trusted adviser and friend of Queen Victoria and Prince Albert, he was a patron of the Great Exhibition of 1851. He died at Walmer Castle on 14 September, 1852, aged eighty-three years, and was accorded a full state funeral.

But if Waterloo led to varying fortunes for the combatant nations and their respective leaders, the military legacies of the great battle, and of the entire Napoleonic period of which it was the final climax, were destined to be protracted and, in many ways, stultifying. Almost forty years of international peace— however welcome from every humanitarian and civilized point of view—led to a period of military complacency and stagnation on a scale that Europe had not known for centuries. Throughout the continent, martial conservatism became the rule rather than the exception; there was scant incentive to experiment, to develop or to question. And when at length the Crimean conflict threw three great powers into direct confrontation, the military concepts of the commanders, the tactics and equipment of their armies, and the expectations of their governments, were still basically those of the Napoleonic Wars. So deeply engrained were the habits of four decades earlier, that the British commander-in-chief, Lord Raglan (who had fought in the Peninsula and at Waterloo), could not break himself of the distressing habit of referring to his French allies as 'the enemy'. Furthermore, the succession of major wars (the Austro–Sardinian War, the American Civil War, the Austro–Prussian and the Franco–Prussian Wars) that followed hard upon the heels of the Crimea were all fought according to concepts that in the main would have been instantly recognizable to the shade of Napoleon, despite such technological developments as the introduction of railways, the electric telegraph, breech-loading artillery and, latterly, the *mitrailleuse* and the Gatling gun.

It might be thought that France, vanquished at Leipzig and

then at Waterloo, would have experienced the greatest incentive to remodel its army. In fact this did not prove to be the case. The restored Bourbons and then the July Monarchy effectively left the Napoleonic army untouched. True, there was an initial purge of senior officers: Marshal Ney was shot after a trial before a court of his peers, a prominent victim of the 'White Terror'. Numerous other generals suffered lesser penalties, ranging from periods in prison to years without employment, but in the course of time the vast majority were reinstated. In terms of doctrine and organization, however, the post-1815 French army bore hardly a trace of change. The writings of Baron Jomini, chief-of-staff to Marshal Ney from 1805 to 1813, became required reading for aspiring soldiers in both France and the United States of America, and his careful analyses of the Napoleonic Wars conditioned the thought of generations of future generals. The belief steadily grew that the attack *à l'outrance* with cold steel, following an intensive artillery bombardment, was the standard formula for battlefield success. Although, for France, the requirements of colonial campaigning in Morocco and Algeria involved a degree of extemporization in tactical method, the main army in metropolitan France remained dominated by heady memories of *la gloire*—a process that was greatly encouraged by Napoleon's nephew as first Prince-President and later as Emperor.

If France's military men remained long in the grip of nostalgic inertia, the same was true of the other European powers to at least the mid-point of the nineteenth century. France, for so long the bully of Europe, was bound to exercise a dominant influence in the military sphere, her ultimate defeat notwithstanding. Prussia, so deeply humiliated in 1806, had rebuilt its armies under the inspiration of Scharnhorst and Gneisenau along broadly French lines, and then, with numerous setbacks to be sure, had proved its ability to play a major part in Napoleon's defeat from 1813 to 1815. Based upon a system of patriotically inspired universal conscription, the Prussian army had proved a match for the French, and its stolidly loyal and unshakeable citizen-soldiery drilled and exercised according to adapted Gallic concepts of training. For the rest, the Prussian generals of the 1830s and 1840s came to regard Napoleonic concepts of manoeuvre and organization—above all the columnar shock attack—with much the same unquestioning respect as their predecessors had accorded (with such fatal results) to the teachings of Frederick the Great. In one respect, however—that of staff organization—the Prussian army was already moving far ahead of the rest of Europe, thanks in large measure to the work of Carl von Clausewitz, who, besides writing his famous treatise *On War*, also laid down the foundations of what eventually became the Great General Staff, destined under the inspired control of the elder Moltke to be the basis of Prussian martial success in two important wars later in the century. In other respects, the Prussian Army remained as much in thrall to the Napoleonic period as did the French.

This pervasive influence was equally felt in Russia and Austria. The huge armies of the Tsars remained organized and trained along the lines laid down by Barclay de Tolly in the years following Tilsit. In the case of Austria, the influence of the Archduke Charles—a considerable tactical innovator in his own right, who in effect broke away from the 'column and line' fixations of his contemporaries and in their place substituted a more fluid form of infantry tactics—remained strong right up to his death in 1847, although the 'grand old man' of the Austrian army was the revered Field-Marshal Radetsky (chief-of-staff from 1809), whose last field success was at Novara in 1849 at the age of eighty-three years, and who continued in the highest command a further nine years beyond that. But once again the influences of the Napoleonic period—with a few adjustments—remained paramount.

The only European army not tied to Napoleonic practice was that of Great Britain, but far from being in the *avant-garde* of military thought and experiment, the British Army was in many ways more backward-looking than any of its contemporaries. The British answer to the challenge of the French system had not been to adopt its stronger features but rather to perfect the preceding eighteenth-century system of linear tactics to make infantry firepower more than a match for the cold-steel attack. The Duke of Wellington was in no way to be regarded as an innovator in matters military. The deadening hand of the victor of Waterloo proved a powerful reinforcement to the forces of economy and inertia that gripped the army for forty years after the battle, and most plans for reform were blighted until after his death. Most of the challenges faced by the military—with the exception, of course, of the Indian Mutiny—were in the course of generally small-scale colonial expeditions and punitive raids.

The short-sightedness with which the army's role was regarded in the post-Waterloo period is evident in the cut-backs which were imposed. In 1816 the army's strength was reduced to 225,000 men; by 1821 this figure had shrunk to 100,000 troops, half of whom were stationed overseas in India and other colonial possessions. The 50,000 men on the home establishment proved barely enough to permit the authorities to maintain law and order through years of grave social unrest. Nor were the conditions of life of the rank and file anything better than execrable. Pay was low, barracks were overcrowded and unhealthy, food was bad and welfare non-existent. Discipline was ferociously maintained by liberal use of the lash. The worst aspects of the purchase system blocked the chances of deserving but poor officers to promotion. The outcome of such neglect and so many outdated attitudes was the incompetence and suffering of the Crimean War, where only the valour and hard fighting of the troops maintained the reputation of the army and the honour of the nation.

Such, then, were some of the effects in the short and medium terms of the celebrated battle of Waterloo. The dramatic promise which it seemed to portend was not borne out in practice, or not in forms that might have been anticipated. Yet it has left a lasting imprint on the popular mind. Five towns in Great Britain, and one major railway terminus in the capital, are named after the battle, as are a further four places in North America. The battle site in Belgium soon became a popular place for sightseers, and it was not long before the entrepreneurs moved in. One enterprising Englishman bought the famous elm tree which marked the spot near the cross-roads on the ridge of Mont-St. Jean, where Wellington passed part of the battle, cut it down, and sent it back to England in a thousand pieces for resale as treasured souvenirs. Sergeant Cotton, at the end of his career, set up as an alehouse keeper near the battlefield, and created a small museum of relics of the battle for the edification of the curious. Today, the museum in the former posting-inn at Waterloo, which served as Wellington's headquarters before and after the battle, the assortment of panoramas, film-shows, museums and souvenir shops which cluster beneath the Lion Mound at Mont-St. Jean, and Napoleon's headquarters at Le Caillou, cater for the annual flood of visitors who find the lure of these haunted acres too strong to resist.

'It was', said Wellington on one occasion, 'the most desperate business I ever was in. I never took so much trouble about any battle, and never was so near being beat.' Waterloo is certainly the best-remembered battlefield in western Europe, and with its varied national associations and strongly romantic connotations it is likely long to remain so.

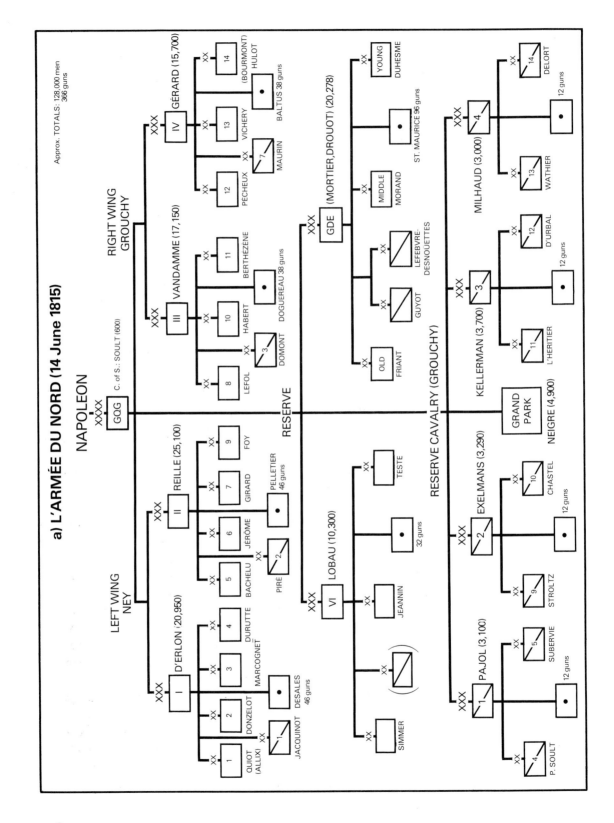

a) L'ARMÉE DU NORD (14 June 1815)

Approx. TOTALS: 128,000 men
366 guns

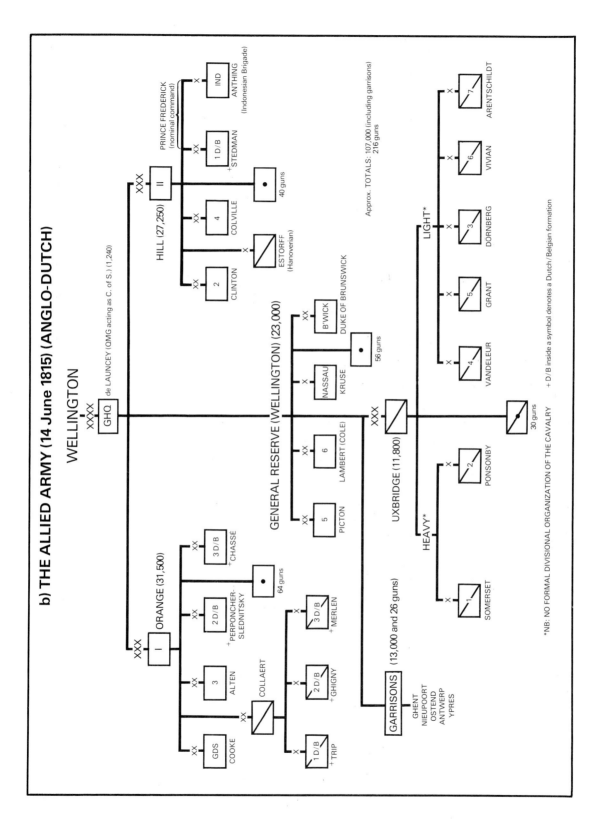

b) THE ALLIED ARMY (14 June 1815) (ANGLO-DUTCH)

WELLINGTON

XXXX
GHQ   de LAUNCEY (QMG acting as C. of S.) (1,240)

XXX — HILL (27,250) — II

PRINCE FREDERICK (nominal command)

1 D/B   STEDMAN
IND   ANTHING (Indonesian Brigade)

40 guns

2   CLINTON
ESTORFF (Hanoverian)
4   COLVILLE

XXX — ORANGE (31,500) — I

GDS   COOKE
3   ALTEN
COLLAERT
2 D/B   +PERPONCHER-SLEDNITSKY
64 guns
3 D/B   +CHASSE

1 D/B   +TRIP
2 D/B   +GHIGNY
3 D/B   +MERLEN

GENERAL RESERVE (WELLINGTON) (23,000)

5   PICTON
6   LAMBERT (COLE)
NASSAU   KRUSE
B'WICK   DUKE OF BRUNSWICK
56 guns

XXX — UXBRIDGE (11,800)

HEAVY*
1   SOMERSET
2   PONSONBY

LIGHT*
4   VANDELEUR
5   GRANT
3   DÖRNBERG
6   VIVIAN
7   ARENTSCHILDT

30 guns

GARRISONS   (13,000 and 26 guns)
GHENT
NIEUPOORT
OSTEND
ANTWERP
YPRES

Approx. TOTALS: 107,000 (including garrisons)
216 guns

+ D/B inside a symbol denotes a Dutch/Belgian formation

*NB: NO FORMAL DIVISIONAL ORGANIZATION OF THE CAVALRY

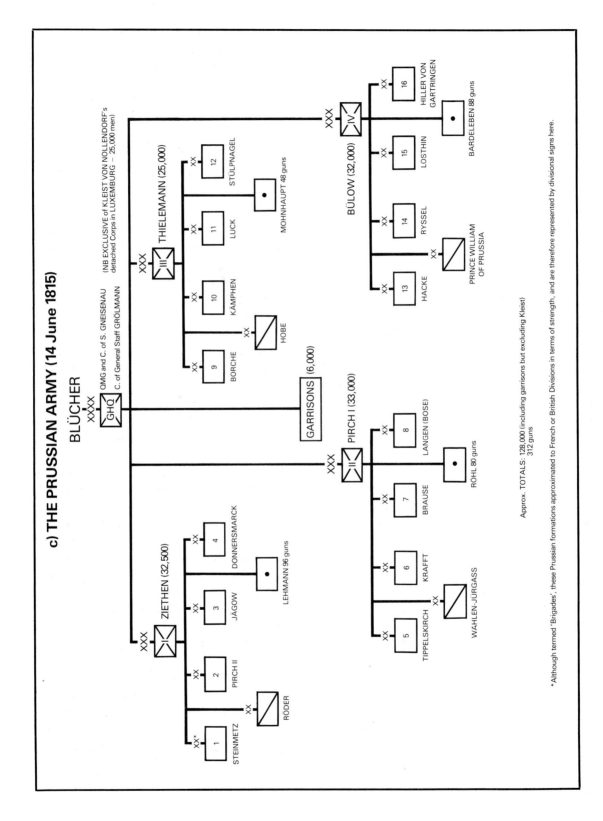

c) THE PRUSSIAN ARMY (14 June 1815)

BLÜCHER

OMG and C. of S. GNEISENAU
C. of General Staff GRÖLMANN

(NB EXCLUSIVE of KLEIST VON NOLLENDORF's
detached Corps in LUXEMBURG — 25,000 men)

GHQ

GARRISONS (6,000)

ZIETHEN (32,500)

1 STEINMETZ
2 PIRCH II
3 JÄGOW
4 DONNERSMARCK
RÖDER
LEHMANN 96 guns

PIRCH I (33,000)

5 TIPPELSKIRCH
6 KRAFFT
7 BRAUSE
8 LANGEN (BOSE)
WAHLEN-JÜRGASS
RÖHL 80 guns

THIELEMANN (25,000)

9 BORCHE
10 KÄMPHEN
11 LUCK
12 STÜLPNAGEL
HOBE
MOHNHAUPT 48 guns

BÜLOW (32,000)

13 HACKE
14 RYSSEL
15 LOSTHIN
16 HILLER VON GARTRINGEN
PRINCE WILLIAM OF PRUSSIA
BARDELEBEN 88 guns

Approx. TOTALS: 128,000 (including garrisons but excluding Kleist)
312 guns

*Although termed 'Brigades', these Prussian formations approximated to French or British Divisions in terms of strength, and are therefore represented by divisional signs here.

Appendix B:
The Campaign Area
and Battlefield Today

The compact area that forms the scene for the events of 15–18 June, 1815, can be visited and thoroughly explored in the course of two days. The suggested itinerary that follows has been employed by the author on a number of occasions in the course of directing battlefield tours for parties from NATO headquarters, from the Royal Military Academy Sandhurst, or from various historical societies and other interested groups.

The proximity of Brussels to the major scenes of action makes it a very convenient base. Leaving the capital along the Avenue de la Belle Alliance, follow signs for Waterloo along the N5. The latter part of the journey passes along the edge of the Forest of Soignies: a passing glance at the intervals between the large trees that form this feature will bear out Wellington's conviction that it would have been possible to evacuate his army, including gun-teams, through the forest had this proved necessary (*pace* Napoleon's belief that the Duke had committed a cardinal error in drawing up his army with the dense area of trees to its rear).

Leaving the car in the park in front of or behind the church of St. Joseph with its distinctive dome, the visitor crosses the road to the clearly marked *Quartier-Général de Wellington*, the hostelry (formerly the Hôtel Boderglieu) where the Duke spent the nights of 17 and 18 June, and where he wrote his victory despatch. The museum it contains is open from 10 a.m. to midday, and from 2 p.m. to 7 p.m. (but is closed all day on Mondays, and from October to April closes at 4 p.m. and is also closed on Tuesdays and Thursdays). This is the ideal place to orientate oneself for the battlefield tour. In the large coach-house to the rear of the main building, a new museum was opened in 1965, where displays trace the history of the campaign and large illuminated maps illustrate the successive stages of the battle. There are also many interesting weapons and other relics on show. The main house fronting the high road contains more weapons and relics, including a collection of Wellington's furniture and personal effects and a number of interesting prints and portraits.

Two other places merit a visit. A short way up the N5 (the *chaussée de Bruxelles*), in the garden of No. 214, is the tomb that originally contained Lord Uxbridge's leg. A small ivy-hung shrine holds various plaques, but the leg itself was exhumed in 1854 on the death of Lord Anglesey (as Uxbridge ultimately became) and reinterred in the family mausoleum. Secondly, the church of St. Joseph (used as a hospital during and after the battle) contains several monuments to individual officers and units involved in the campaign and battle, including one to the cavalry general, van Merlen, and a plaque commemorating the 33rd of Foot (later the Duke of Wellington's Regiment), which reveals that the unit lost 228 officers and men (or approximately one-third of its total strength) between 16 and 18 June, 1815.

If the intention is to study the complete campaign, it is in many ways most convenient to follow the unfolding of events from the French point of view, as Napoleon enjoyed the initiative in the operations. For this purpose, it is best to drive down the N5 Charleroi high road past Mont-St. Jean and Quatre Bras to a point a few kilometres south of Frasnes-les-Gosselies, where a transport café built around a mill tower stands to the west of the road. This is the site of Marshal Ney's quarters on the night of 15 June. Returning towards Brussels, the site of the first engagement between Ney's advance guard and that of Saxe-Weimar lies just south of the village of Frasnes. Continuing towards Quatre Bras, there is no longer any sign of the Bossu Wood which the French feared might conceal a substantial part of Wellington's army, and consequently decided not to press ahead to occupy the important cross-roads.

Quatre Bras can be usefully surveyed from the car park attached to the *estaminet* at the cross-roads. Looking south, the large farmstead of Gemioncourt stands 200 yards to the east of the Charleroi high road. West of the road at this point is the sunken meadow where the 69th Regiment was scattered by the French cavalry, who captured its King's Colour. To its east, the lines of trees in the distance lead down to the mere which marked the extreme flank of the battle area; and the first part of the N49 road leading to Sombreffe and Namur to the south-east formed the line along which Picton drew up his brigades on their arrival at Quatre Bras. In the opposite direction, towards Nivelles, stands a monument to the Belgians who died on 16 June, whilst half-way to Gemioncourt along the N5 is the granite memorial to the Duke of Brunswick, mortally wounded at the height of the battle of Quatre Bras near the Bossu Wood.

From Quatre Bras, take the N49 past Marbais towards Namur in order to visit the battlefield of Ligny. This road was the vital lateral link between the Allied and Prussian armies that Napoleon was so eager to sever and use for his own reinforcement purposes on both 16 and 17 June. Turning off to the right for Brye, close by the village to the south are the ruins of the Mill of Bussy, where Wellington conferred with Blücher in the early afternoon of the 16th. Slightly to the east is a country lane which passes over the railway line to a steep-banked cutting. From this point a good over-view of the battlefield of Ligny can be obtained—and the villages that played so important a part in the main fighting can be identified, together with Fleurus, where the tower of the windmill used by Napoleon as his observation post can just be picked out through binoculars on the eastern side of the town. Returning into Brye to drive down into Ligny itself, the course of the slow-moving stream can be traced as it meanders through the village, and the restored church—whose graveyard was the scene of much fighting on the 16th—is worth a brief visit. Continuing down the road, turn right on to N21 to Fleurus; to the right Napoleon's windmill (le Moulin de Naveau) bears a plaque, as does *la Ferme d'En Haut* in the centre of the town, where Napoleon spent an uneasy night after the battle. On the outskirts of the town is a modern memorial which recalls the three battles fought around the town—in 1690, 1794 and 1815. Elsewhere is a vast siege gun of the Napoleonic period.

From Fleurus return by the N21 towards Gembloux, turn left onto N49 (towards Nivelles) and (passing Sombreffe) after five kilometres turn right at Marbais for Tilly, Mellery and Mont-St. Guibert to Ottignies. This route is following the general line of the Prussian retreat after Ligny; the French pursuit, once it began at midday on the 17th, being more to the east, having started off towards Namur before swinging north through Gembloux to Sart-les-Walhain and Corbaix. The town of Wavre, set on both banks of the Dyle, is eight kilometres beyond Corbaix. The place has grown considerably since 1815, and the complexities of the Belgian motorway intersections in the area make a visit for the purposes of reconstructing the events of 18 and 19 June rather difficult, but it is useful to follow the road N168 along the banks of the Dyle as far as Limale, scene of much hard fighting on the evening of the 17th. Crossing the Dyle at Limale, the scene of the successful French outflanking attack and final efforts on the morning of the 19th lies to the north and east of the town, and the steep wooded ridges give a good idea of the terrain that obstructed the French deployment both in this area and nearer to Wavre. Depending on time, the driver may now either take the main road (N4) or motorway (E40) back to Brussels (some twenty-five kilometres distant), or follow the small winding roads north and west of Limale towards Chapelle-St. Lambert and Ohain, thus tracing the route of Blücher's march at the head of three corps (one in fact kept to a more northerly but parallel route via Rixensart and Genval) towards the distant battlefield of Waterloo. The twisting roads through broken wooded countryside and the many intersections with minor routes give a fair impression of the problems faced through the mud and dank undergrowth during that late Sunday morning and afternoon of 165 years ago. Moving on through the Wood of Paris, one reaches the point beyond Lasne where the leading formations of Bülow's IV Corps began to emerge from the trees shortly before 2 p.m. on 18 June. Lasne contains a monument to the Prussian General Schwerin, set amidst the fields west of Lasne church, marking the place where he was killed in command of a brigade of IV Corps cavalry. Bearing left along the local road for Plancenoit, you will reach the scene of the frantic fighting which began at 4.30 p.m. on the 18th. The village today is mostly modernized, but the Prussian memorial with its Gothic column recalls the fluctuating struggle for the place that raged on until after dusk before the Prussians at last asserted their mastery.

Leaving Plancenoit to rejoin the N5, turn right at La Belle Alliance and head for Brussels (twenty-two kilometres) past the farmstead of La Haie Sainte and the ridge of Mont-St. Jean. Ten hours are required for the above itinerary, or longer if the visitors wish to explore the ground at Quatre Bras or Ligny during the day's expedition.

On the second day drive from Brussels to Quatre Bras down the N5 (thirty-three kilometres), and then turn about to retrace the main stages of Wellington's withdrawal to Mont-St. Jean during the 17th. In 1815 the main Brussels road passed through Genappe, and this interesting village is today reached by a short byroad. Before visiting it, however, a stop is recommended to the east of the main road, where a side-road to Baisy-Thy leads past a very tall, distinctively shaped tree beside the small stone shrine of Saint Anne. From beneath its branches Napoleon paused to encourage his rain-sodden troops to hurry forward during the afternoon of the 17th in his thwarted bid to catch the Allied rearguard. Next, driving down to Genappe as described, the narrow streets of the town are much the same as they were in 1815. The *Auberge du Roi d'Espagne*, where Wellington took his luncheon and Prince Jérôme Bonaparte his supper on the 17th, is worth a pause. On its walls is a modern plaque, noting the fact that General Duhesme, commander of the Young Guard, died there on 20 June after being mortally wounded in the battle of Waterloo. His tomb is also to be found nearby, in the graveyard of the church of St. Martin de Ways. By following the line of the Dyle on foot, the original bridge can also be discovered—its narrowness explaining much of the panic and overcrowding that affected the fleeing French *Armée du Nord* late on the 18th at this bottleneck over the River Dyle. It was also near here that Napoleon almost fell into Prussian hands as he transferred from his jammed travelling-coach to his horse.

Returning to the N5, drive north to the intersection with the Chemin d'Ohain at the crest of the ridge of Mont-St. Jean, and park as near to the cross-roads as possible. The road running down to the Lion Mound (*Butte de Lion*) originally ran through steep banks, but these, together with neighbouring ridges, were much altered to find the earth for the famous 125-foot-high *butte*, erected to mark the spot where the Prince of Orange was wounded on the shoulder. Just beside the cross-roads in its south-west angle originally stood the single elm tree under which Wellington established his command post at various times in the battle. From the roadside, several monuments can be seen—including those to the Belgian and Hanoverian dead, and, down the N5 towards La Haie Sainte, the monument raised in 1817 to Colonel Sir Alexander Gordon, Wellington's personal aide-de-camp, who died in his headquarters in the adjoining room whilst the Duke was writing his Waterloo despatch. This monument is placed on top of a bank which gives an indication of the original level of the ground at this point. From this memorial walk down to La Haie Sainte in its hollow, past the site of the sandpit east of the road defended by the 95th Rifles. The farm has undergone considerable changes since 1815, but the great gate and the main house, together with the barn, are largely original—and from the farmyard some feeling of the stout defence conducted by Major Baring and his battalion of the King's German Legion can be obtained. A fine view from the exterior barn door towards the Lion Mound—over the area traversed first by Ney's massed squadrons and later by the Imperial Guard—is worth a photograph (with permission having been sought from the farm's present owners).

Returning to the cross-roads, pass over the road to the

eastern side, and from the enclosed area of a water-pump a good view can be gained of both the exposed forward slope which saw the decimation of Bylandt's Brigade and of the line held by Picton's 5th Division. The original roadway had a thick hedge-row on its southern sides, through which embrasures were cut for the cannon, but today this feature has disappeared. Next, preferably by car, go down the Chemin d'Ohain to the east as far as the farm of Papelotte—forming, with La Haie hamlet and the Château de Frischermont (or Fichermont) the extreme left of Wellington's position. Papelotte is open to visitors from 8.30 a.m. to 7.30 p.m. during the summer months, but closes earlier in winter and spring. The gatehouse tower was added in 1860, but the massive walls of the original set of buildings show how formidable these farmsteads must have been to attack. On 18 June the position was held by Saxe-Weimar's Nassauers, lost to the French at 2.30 p.m., but subsequently retaken in the early evening.

Two miles beyond Papelotte up a windy lane is the village of Lasne—scene of the arrival of Blücher's Prussians during the afternoon of the battle.

Next, returning to the N5, drive south as far as the farm of Le Caillou—site of Napoleon's quarters on the night of the 17th. This is now a museum devoted to relics of the Emperor and his army. Its collections are well worth studying and the museum is open from 9 a.m. to 7 p.m. most days of the year, but is closed on Tuesdays in winter. From Le Caillou, drive back to La Belle Alliance (now a restaurant), and turn right towards Plancenoit. On a bank 100 metres from the main road is '*l'Observatoire de Napoleon*' (marked by a board). From its summit a good view of the battlefield area—as seen by Napoleon and his staff at various moments on the 18th—can be obtained ranging from Plancenoit in its hollow to the right-rear, past Papelotte and the remains of the Wood of Paris (to the right-fore) and then westwards past La Haie Sainte in the centre towards Hougoumont to the north-west, although the Château is not visible from this point. Nearby—alongside the N5—are the 'stricken-eagle' memorial to the French casualties, and the column raised to commemorate Victor Hugo, whose celebrated (although rather inaccurate) description of the battle in *Les Misérables* was written nearby.

At this juncture some refreshment is indicated, and if a picnic has not been brought it may be as well to drive to the area surrounding the Lion Mound, where there are several restau-rants and other facilities. The lures of the souvenir shops, the waxworks and the two cinemas showing ancient (and highly deceptive) films on the battle having been resisted or succumbed to, visits to the Waterloo Panorama and (for the fit and enterprising) hikes up the Lion Mound are highly recommended. The former (open 8 a.m. to 8 p.m.) provides an excellent life-size portrayal through 360 degrees of this precise point of the battlefield, whilst Wellington's squares were resisting the charges of Ney's cavalry; the latter, after the 226 steps have been safely negotiated, provides an unforgettable view over the whole battlefield—and recorded descriptions of the main stages of the action are also provided in various languages. On a fine day, some good photographs can be obtained from this vantage-point.

Returning to ground-level, a walk to the area of ground some 200 metres to the west of the Mound brings you to the area where the attack of the Middle Guard's westernmost column was met and repulsed by Maitland's Guards. The lie of the land has again been considerably altered by the building of the Lion Mound (1823–26), but looking south the sweep of ground between La Haie Sainte to the left and the Château of Hougoumont to the right can be well appreciated from this point. Regaining your car, drive down the Chemin d'Ohain to the south-west as far as the Brussels to Nivelles road (N6), noticing to the right of the road the reverse slopes Wellington employed to conceal his men (although these are now crossed by the new sunken motorway, which only missed being routed over the centre of the battlefield by a hair's-breadth after frantic negotiations in the early 1970s). Turn left on to the N6, and 1,200 metres down it turn sharp left again up a small road signposted for the Château de Goumont (the alternative spelling of Hougoumont). Cars can be parked outside the north gate. This is one of the most famous sites, and despite considerable changes since 1815 (when most of the original Château was laid in smoking ruins by the end of the day's fighting) it well repays a leisurely visit. The old north wall and gatehouse have completely disappeared, as has the orchard, much of the formal garden, and all of the area of woodland that stood immediately south of the buildings. However, the main house today (formerly the gardener's house), the damaged chapel (now a memorial to the Guards Division with its charred crucifix bearing witness to the fire that devastated most of the buildings) and the south garden wall with its loopholes battered through the brickwork, together with memorials to the French fallen, to Captains Blackman and Craufurd and to Sergeant Cotton, are all highly evocative relics of the nine-hour struggle which Wellington considered the most vital feature of the whole battle of Waterloo.

A visit to Hougoumont is perhaps the ideal place to conclude a two-day itinerary to the campaign and battle areas—and a thoughtful evening stroll along the 'hollow way' to the north of the Château and forwards to La Haie Sainte over the broad acres which saw the major French attacks on this part of the battlefield, forms a fitting finale. Many more individual memorials to the Allied fallen will be found in the Evere Cemetery in Brussels.

Note on reading. The visitor wishing to gain the full flavour of the events on the ground would be well advised to carry with him copies of Siborne's *Campaign of Waterloo*, and A. Brett-James's *The Hundred Days* (which consists of eye-witness accounts in extract from all stages of this celebrated period and battle). For a well-illustrated but strongly French-flavoured account of the campaign, reference should be made to H. Lachouque's *Waterloo*, and those wishing to appreciate the realities of combat-experience during the battle should consult the relevant chapters of J. Keegan's *The Face of Battle*. Fuller details of these and other volumes will be found in the Select Bibliography below.

The continental habit of frequently renumbering roads may have caused some alterations to those cited above, but it is hoped that sufficient information has been provided to permit a satisfactory and reasonably comprehensive two-day tour to be undertaken. It is likely to be a memorable experience.

Select Bibliography

A. *Documentary Sources* (published)

*La Correspondance de l'Empereur Napoléon Ier*, vols. XXVIII
and XXXI (Paris, 1868 and 70)
The Dispatches of Field Marshal the Duke of Wellington,
vol. XII, ed. Lt.-Col. Gurwood (London, 1845)
Documents inédits du Duc d'Elchingen (Paris, 1833)
*Supplementary Dispatches and Memoranda of Field Marshal
Arthur Duke of Wellington KG*, vols IX and X, ed. by his
son (London, from 1858)
The Waterloo Letters, ed. H. T. Siborne (London, 1891)

B. *Published Works*—especially of recent date

Correlli Barnett, *Bonaparte* (London, 1978)
A. F. Becke, *Napoleon and Waterloo*, 2 vols (London, 1941);
1 vol. ed. (1936)
A. Brett-James, *The Hundred Days* (London, 1964)
A. Brett-James, *Wellington at War* (London, 1961)
D. G. Chandler, *The Campaigns of Napoleon* (New York,
1966)
D. G. Chandler, *A Dictionary of the Napoleonic Wars* (New
York and London, 1979)
T. Creevey, *The Creevey Papers* (London, 1904)
C. Dalton, *The Waterloo Roll-Call*, 2nd ed. (reissued as a
reprint, London, 1971)
S. Forshufvud and B. Weider, *Assassination at St. Helena*
(Vancouver, 1978)
J. W. Fortescue, *History of the British Army*, vol. X (London,
1901)
J. F. C. Fuller, *The Decisive Battles of the Western World*,
vol. II (London, 1957)
E. F. Henderson, *Blücher and the Uprising of Prussia against
Napoleon* (London, 1911)
H. Houssaye, *1815—Waterloo* (Paris, 1893)
D. Howarth, *A Near-Run Thing* (London, 1968)

J. D. P. Keegan, *The Face of Battle* (London, 1976)

H. Lachouque, *The Last Days of Napoleon's Empire* (London, 1967)

J. Lawford, *Napoleon: The Last Campaigns* (London, 1977)

E. Longford, *Wellington, the Years of the Sword* (London, 1969)

F. C. F. von Müffling, *History of the Campaign of 1815*, new ed. (Leeds, 1970)

J. Naylor, *Waterloo* (London, 1960)

R. Parkinson, *Hussar General—the life of Blücher—Man of Waterloo* (London, 1970)

W. Seymour, E. Kaulbach, J. Champagne, *Waterloo, Battle of Three Armies*, ed. Lord Chalfont (London, 1979)

W. Siborne, *The Waterloo Campaign, 1815*, 5th ed. (London, 1900)

J. Sutherland, *Men of Waterloo* (London, 1967)

P. Thornhill, *The Waterloo Campaign* (London, 1965)

J. Tulard, *Napoléon* (Paris, 1977)

Jac Weller, *Wellington at Waterloo* (London, 1967)

P. Young, *Blücher's Army 1812–15* (London, 1973)

P. Young, *Napoleon's Marshals* (London, 1973)

Several of these books contain extensive bibliographies—for instance the volumes by Brett-James and Weller, which, together with Becke's work, constitute the most useful surveys of the subject, studied from different view-points.

Picture Acknowledgements

The publishers have made every effort to contact the owners of all copyright material, and apologize for any omissions due to difficulties in tracing such sources. While many of the photographs are the author's own, these people and organizations very kindly supplied the following illustrations: Army Museums, Ogilby Trust, pp 144, 163; Duke of Wellington (photo: Courtauld Institute of Art), p 154; Establissement Cinématographique des Armées, p 58; H. Roger-Viollet, p 36/37; Mansell Collection, pp 28, 42, 48, 55, 64, 86, 96, 124/125, 130/131, 134, 146/147, 149, 150, 158/159, 165, 167, 168/169, 184, 191, 192, 201, 203; Mary Evans Picture Library, pp 16/17, 21, 33, 54, 91, 100/101, 105, 179; National Army Museum, pp 113, 116, 156; National Portrait Gallery, pp 61, 118, 119; N. M. Rothschild & Sons Ltd., pp 174, 176/177; The Royal Library (pictures reproduced by gracious permission of Her Majesty the Queen), pp 138, 171; Sotheby Parke Bernet & Co., p 89; The Wellcome Trustees, pp 22/23, 24, 40, 44, 114, 186; Victoria & Albert Museum, pp 3, 23, 50, 121, 194.

Index